YALE AGRARIAN STUDIES SERIES
JAMES C. SCOTT, SERIES EDITOR

The Agrarian Studies Series at Yale University Press seeks to publish out-standing and original interdisciplinary work on agriculture and rural society —for any period, in any location. Works of daring that question existing par-adigms and fill abstract categories with the lived experience of rural people are especially encouraged.
—James C. Scott, *Series Editor*

For a complete list of titles in the Yale Agrarian Studies Series, visit yalebooks.com/agrarian.

**LOKA ASHWOOD**

# For-Profit Democracy

## Why the Government Is Losing
## the Trust of Rural America

Yale UNIVERSITY PRESS
NEW HAVEN AND LONDON

Published with the assistance of the College of Agriculture at
Auburn University.

Yale University Press books may be purchased in quantity for
educational, business, or promotional use. For information, please
e-mail sales.press@yale.edu (U.S. office) or sales@yaleup.co.uk
(U.K. office).

Set in Janson type by Integrated Publishing Solutions.
Printed in the United States of America.

Library of Congress Control Number: 2017961557

ISBN 978-0-300-21535-9 (hardcover : alk. paper)

A catalogue record for this book is available from the British Library.
This paper meets the requirements of ANSI/NISO Z39.48-1992
(Permanence of Paper).

10 9 8 7 6 5 4 3 2 1

*For Jason Michael and Michael Lee—*
*today and tomorrow*

# CONTENTS

# PREFACE

"They call it progress," William Gresham said to me, talking about his government. "That's a word I've never really learned."

He described the "checks from the government" that pay for plantations of pine trees that edge out native plants. Then there is the river, "completely radiated" by the military's industrial-nuclear complex. And worst of all, the government's treatment of his rural Georgia homeland. He seethed about how they "throw something down there on the table" and take the land.

William, like his black and white Burke County neighbors, harbors a deep-seated distrust of the government. Scholars typically understand politics like William's as conservative, with complementary variants of social and fiscal. Some call such politics contradictory, resting on a moral code that violates rural economic interests. Others call such views dead set against progress, stymied in a culture of poverty that breeds complicity. I offer a counterexplanation by taking at face value the state's historical and still persistent exploitation of rural people and places in order to centralize profit. I combine insights from the writings of Barrington Moore, James Scott, E. P. Thompson, and Alexis de Tocqueville to identify the state's violence of gradualism practiced against rural people and their livelihoods through majority rule, as well as the ways in which rural people push back through their moral economy.

I make the case for rural antistatism by documenting the government's centralization of people and profit through the creation and elimination of certain types of markets and property rights, like the privatization of nuclear technology and corporate claims over local land rights. The democratic state governs by what I call the "rule of numbers," by which most is considered best, whether what is being measured is dollar bills, kilowatts of energy, or number of people.

The sanctity of human life and choice fades from view as profit gains preeminence, and rural places are labeled externalities and write-offs for dangerous and risky industrial projects. I detail how the courts came to value profit and industrialization as the ultimate purpose of property. The rights of those with different reasons for ownership—such as subsistence, family viability, and household economy—are left with little legal standing. I thus understand the state, with the help of Karl Polanyi, as complicit in the process of dispossessing the many in favor of the few.

The state's mantra of most equals best as the ultimate aim of market-based governance leaves those fewer in number with little legal recourse and few rights. Minorities in space, race, and capital thus turn to their own and otherworldly means for reform outside the law, informed by what I call their "moral economy of democracy." I describe these accounts through observations gathered while living in Burke County for eight months. (I conducted eighty-nine interviews, and the subjects as well as some place details are identified with pseudonyms to protect identities. See appendix 1 for the methodological details.) Burke County hosts a marvel of the state's progress—nuclear power—in a space often stereotyped as the opposite—the rural Deep South. Exploited yesterday, as the heart of slavery's old reign, and exploited today, as the playground of nuclear power's renaissance, Burke County is in one sense an extreme case of profit extraction.

Profit, though, increasingly demands that any person who makes less money than corporations be dispossessed. I see for-profit motives instigating a crisis in governance that impacts not only the rural people chronicled in this book, but also the nation more broadly. Under utilitarian rule, profit comes to cannibalize people that once enjoyed majority status. As tragic as the outcomes are today, profit's rendering of majorities into minorities offers a symmetry, perhaps even a unifying call: profit's reign must be ended for the betterment of all.

I have structured *For-Profit Democracy: Why the Government Is Losing the Trust of Rural America* around four nuclear metaphors: first, the reaction set off by profit's rule in Burke County, which introduces the place and identifies nuclear power as an outcome of for-profit democracy; next, the meltdown of state legitimacy as a result of forcible takings and the sacrifice of moral goods; third, the fallout that ensues under its unjust reign; and finally, the hope of recovery for those wronged. In doing so, this book seeks to come to terms with the flaws in a system of governance bent toward the centralization of profit, historically and today. It is there that the spiraling apathy toward the democratic state and those who run it can be more than lamented or condemned—it can be understood.

# ACKNOWLEDGMENTS

This book has been seven years in the making, a longer time than I dared to imagine when I first began. During that time, the people I have met and the support I have received from colleagues, family, and friends have made this book what it is.

The people of Burke County extended hospitality and welcome to a stranger, focusing on what we shared rather than where we differed. I thank the Burke County Archive Society and Shell Bluff Concerned Citizens for allowing me to listen and learn from their expertise. I thank the regulators, workers, and legislators who were willing to speak with me. Most of all, I thank the brave residents of Shell Bluff and the surrounding area who extended me enough trust to share and print their stories.

This work would not have been possible without the help of the Philanthropic Education Organization's Scholar Award. That funding paid for me to live in Burke County and travel there repeatedly. Additional funds that helped me complete this work came from the Rural Sociological Society Dissertation Award; the Mellon-Wisconsin Summer Fellowship; the Raymond J. Penn Scholarship for Research in Development, Resource Conservation, and Environmental Conservation; the University of Wisconsin Holtz Center for Science and Technology Research Travel Grant; the University of Wisconsin–Madison Center for Culture, History, and the Environment Research Award; Jane Collins's research support; and the Department of Agricultural Economics and Rural Sociology, along with the College of Agriculture, at Auburn University.

My colleagues and friends have extended advice at every turn, helping me navigate the most challenging of choices. First, my thanks to those who read and commented on prior drafts and presentations, helping me realize the weaknesses and build on the strengths of this work: Conner Bailey, Jane Collins, Madeleine Fairbairn, Myra Marx Ferree, Jess Gilbert, Zenia Kish, Daniel Kleinman, Katy-Anne Legun, Roy Livne, Anna-Maria Marshall, Pamela Oliver, James Scott, Mildred Warner, Wylin Wilson, Keith Woodward, and Ayca Zayim. The Wisconsin Archival Society provided a quiet haven to write as well as research support to find and compile agricultural census statistics. Rozalynn Klaas in the Applied Population Laboratory was patient and thorough in helping me acquire data, analyze it, and produce maps related to Burke County landownership and socio-demographics. Bill Nelson did a fabulous job of reworking those maps into book illustrations. I owe a wealth of gratitude to Yale University Press. Kip Keller deftly copyedited the text with a hard eye but a soft hand. I learned from his reading. Michael Deneen and Margaret Otzel provided thorough and speedy assistance. Jean Thomson Black steadfastly supported the delivery and content of the book, even when it required venturing away from the norm. I am especially indebted to the painstakingly close reads, conceptual insights, and moral support provided by Sarah Lessem, Jason Orne, Lisa Pruitt, and Steve Wing, whose passing in 2016 devastated communities and practitioners fighting rural environmental injustices. My steadfast friend Meg Collins brought compassion and artistry to this book, as her photographs attest to. My advisor at the University of Wisconsin, Michael M. Bell, talked me through the moments when the stigmatizing of rural people and labels of backwardness common in the academy pushed me early on to consider leaving it. He provided a model of creativity and craft that transcends the boundaries of tradition. He practiced the impossible as the possible and did it in good humor. I am thankful for it all, and (maybe most of all) the many warm meals Diane and he cooked for my family and me.

And my family. Thank you to my sister, Barbara, and mother, Janice, for reading, and sympathizing with this book. Thank you to my father, Steve, and my brother-in-law, Shane, for keeping the fires going when I was gone for months in Georgia and Madison. Most of all, thank you to Jason, who has believed in this project and my discipline when I faltered. Who cared for our newborn son so I could write, who smiled with strength when I hesitated to go for another research trip, and who worked long and hard hours to help me get my education.

And that concludes my brief, and undoubtedly incomplete, attempt to thank those who made this work possible.

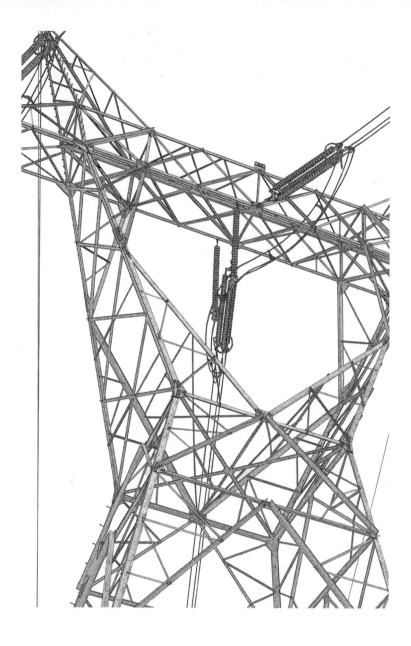

# Reaction

What reactors? I don't even know they're there.

—Jesse Whitehead

"I want you to know I'm legit," Jesse Whitehead told me.

Hundreds of workers were already on-site. Mounds of exposed red clay stained the skyline. The nuclear renaissance in Georgia had begun, some hopefully thought, after thirty years of no new construction. Jesse, like those who benefited from the boom when the first two reactors were constructed, in the 1970s, was looking to make some cash on a place considered unlivable in normal circumstances. Eager to establish his social capital with a stranger from afar looking to rent his Burke County trailer, he explained over the phone that he was close to the top level of authority at a reputable firm and encouraged me to check him out. I traced the Google hits to an article that named his firm's annual revenue in the triple-digit millions. We agreed to a rental contract shortly thereafter.

Jesse and I first met at the Burke County Byway Store, a bright bang of red and yellow along a primary route that attracted the thirsty throats and cars of plant workers, as well as regulars who wove their way from a nearby trailer park across a path etched into a grass field. An arrowed sign pointing toward the shop proclaimed "AMERICAN OWNED & OPERATED." Swinging underneath the overhang, green dry-erase ink stood out on a white board: "Welcome Hunters and Plant Vogtle." I pulled in and stepped outside into the sixty-degree breeze of a February day. As I waited, I leaned against my car, covered with salty dust that followed me from the frigid North into Georgia. Ladies watching from inside called Jesse to let him know of my arrival, and he soon pulled up in a pearly but aged Lexus SUV. An orange spattering of clay clung to the doors, and when Jesse put out a black leather shoe, it was soiled.

"I got called off for a cement run while I was waiting for you," he said, briskly walking toward me. He introduced himself with ease and warmth, holding out his hand. Two fine gold rings caught the light, one with a diamond larger than ones found in most engagement rings. Blue eyes stood out from his copper tan, which extended luxuriously and evenly from his face to the rest of his frame, ever so slightly bent with old age. His dark slacks and the black jacket sporting his firm's symbol were splattered with muck.

"I have been working to get a connection with the Plant Vogtle construction to get ahold of some of their cement," he said with a graceful Old South roll. "I've got plenty of places to put cement on 3,000 acres."

The cement that didn't make the nuclear grade had to go somewhere. Why not his property? Jesse knew how to navigate the web of private contractors completing the work. His own firm contracted for industrial and energy companies, including at one time Southern Company. Southern Company, ranked 145 in the Fortune 500, received an $8.33 billion federal loan guarantee and a potential tax credit of $125 million yearly to build the latest Vogtle reactors.[1] Without those funds and the $10 billion liability limitation provided by the Price-Anderson Act, finding the massive capital necessary to run and build a risky nuclear power plant would be a difficult, perhaps impossible, endeavor.

Since the government privatized fission technology in the 1950s, there has been money to be made from nuclear energy production. General Electric, ranked 13 on the Fortune 500, runs Hitachi, which describes itself as "a world-leading provider of advanced reactors and nuclear services."[2] There's also the UK Group 4 Securicor, the largest private security firm in the world, which purchased US-based Wackenhut, long a provider of "nuclear facility security."[3] Things, though, have gotten a bit tenuous of late, since the national government has lent substantial support to natural gas production. DuPont, ranked 113 on the Fortune 500 (and now merged with number 162,

Dow Chemical), recently got out of the business of managing nuclear weapon sites. Japan's Toshiba, ranked 169 on the Global 500, owns Westinghouse's nuclear division, once self-described as "the world's leading supplier of safe and innovative nuclear technology." Overwhelmed by a bad construction deal, the Fukushima nuclear disaster, and natural gas competition, Westinghouse went bankrupt in March 2017, leaving the future of nuclear power a bit uncertain.[4] Still, in addition to the two up-and-running Vogtle reactors, there remain 99 operating nuclear power plants at sixty-one sites across thirty states, accounting for 20 percent of US electricity production.[5] And all but one of those sites is privately owned.[6]

Private firms tied up in the nuclear endeavor protect nuclear plants from terrorist attacks, establish standards for nuclear-grade cement, and do myriad other jobs vital to the industry. That embeddedness points to an uncomfortable reality in American, and even global, public life: private profit firms often have governmental authority to act in the public interest, regardless of precisely who or what takes home the profit. Nuclear power is one of the most powerful of the government's corporate prodigies, but it is nonetheless one among many. Scholars reason that neoliberalism has much to do with privatization. Corporate profits have risen, and taxpayer money is redirected to the private purses of companies that provide public services.[7] And while much of this is true, nuclear power is simultaneously older than neoliberalism and newer than the very first corporations that received public rights to produce a product for private resale. Recent processes of neoliberalism are rooted in the structural organization of the state around the majority rule of money and product. In the "Reaction" section of the book, I propose the term "for-profit democracy" to help explain how profit has come to rule the purpose of the democratic state.

★  ★  ★

"Let's go take a look at the farm," Jesse said to me, using the casual name for his timber and pasture plots. He turned on his heel and headed back toward his SUV. I followed and climbed into his four-by-four. We had driven a mile from the Byway store when Jesse

turned off the paved road and onto a dusty path barred by an orange cattle gate with a "No Trespassing" sign.

"Your trailer's back here," Jesse said. He got out, removed the padlock, and then drove about a mile back along a sandy lane overarched by pines. By the time we reached the rusty old trailer at the end of the lane, the only other sign of human habitation was a deer stand. One way in and one way out. There was room for a view from a deck attached to the trailer's backside that had a few months of life left in it.

"Like I said, the trailer is fully furnished, and I can't think of anything you will need except some personal items," Jesse said, balancing on a rotting wooden step while he unlocked the thin metal door. Dishes, towels, furniture—it all was there under a layer of mice droppings and poison. Their littered treasures of nests, pellets, and poo rested between the layers of folded blankets, on pillows removed from cases, and tucked under the sink next to decade-old kitchen supplies. As soon as Jesse turned on the water, the toilet began perpetually running.

"I'll send my man to fix that," he said. He turned on the shower and the stream of water brought a cockroach out of the drain.

"If you make it through the night," Jesse said, as we walked back out the door, "and you still want to rent it, give me a call in the morning. If you decide you don't want to, it won't bother me one bit. We can forget you signed that lease. Do you know how to shoot a gun?"

"Not really," I said, surprised at the change in subject. "I shot a rifle a long time ago with my dad."

"If you are going to stay here, you are going to learn how to shoot," he said, looking squarely at me. "I won't rent to you unless you have a gun."

I returned his demand with a nod. Jesse's concern would turn into a habit. He regularly phoned and checked in to make sure I was okay.

"How far are the reactors from here?" I asked Jesse's back as he headed toward the SUV.

"What reactors?" he said, turning around with a slight smile as he continued walking. Holding my eye, he said, "I don't even know they're there."

I stared around me, pulling my mind from the quiet fog of trailer and timber. The reactors could not be heard. They could not be seen. But I knew they were there. And so did every other person that I would come to know who stood with some permanence in the plant evacuation zone.

Jesse's view, however unpalatable for locals, is sanctioned by the government. Gross domestic product, electricity sales, and high economic achievement are "vital to the health and welfare of the country," even "modern civilization," one federal approval document for a nuclear reactor claims.[8] Those outside the purview of electricity-for-profit are rendered out of sight and out of mind. A 1970s federal document required for approval of the construction of the first two Vogtle reactors states: "The Savannah River and Georgia State Highway 23 (approximately 5 miles distant) will be the locations from which the public will normally view the plant structures . . . Generally only the cooling towers will be visible, with the enclosure building below the line of sight."[9]

Countless roads for locals were closer, such as River Road, Hancock Landing Road, Ben Hatcher Road, Jack Delaigle Road, and Ebenezer Church Road. The line of sight that the regulators included, though, belonged to the larger number of people quickly driving by on the highway. Fewer in number, though paying more of the costs, locals were treated as incidental.

While the profit purview fails to see the people living around the plant, locals do not. Burke County is what the US Department of Agriculture calls a persistent-poverty county, meaning that for the past thirty years, over 20 percent of the population has lived in poverty. The designation isn't an easy one to get. Only 11.2 percent of counties nationally register as that poor, for that long. And most of such counties are rural.[10] Poverty has been even worse lately in Burke County: 33.5 percent of the county lives in poverty.[11] The region is part of what W. E. B. Du Bois called the Black Belt, for both its soil and people, where plantations once littered the landscape, providing the template for the later tenant-farm structure.[12] Both white and black poverty plagues such places. The legacy of the plantation system has left possession in the hands of the few, and dispossession the lot of the many, including white men like William Gresham and black women like Lela Roberts.

"No Trespassing. Hunting, Fishing or Trespassing for any Purpose Strictly Forbidden," Lela read out loud in a soft drawl as she guided me through my first tour of Burke County, a few years before I met Jesse and moved into his trailer.

"Violators will be Prosecuted. No trespassing," she continued reading, sign after sign as we drove slowly across what used to be her family's land. Now Georgia Power, a Southern Company subsidiary, owns it. Some of the signs were bright and new, others faded and covered with pinesap.

"The teacher would let us go home earlier so we could walk home through those woods," she said. "That's what you did. They let us out, and we come on home. Nobody stopped us from walking those woods. We'd walk to the river and fish. We didn't take no roads."

Lela guided me to a dock, now owned by Southern Company. The

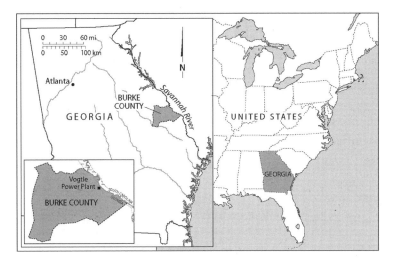

Burke County, Georgia, and the Vogtle Power Plant. Bill Nelson.

land was no longer open fields of peanuts and cotton, with patches of woods in between, so Lela could not meander to the river as she did as a child to catch dinner or cool off. That would be trespassing, so we took the graveled path.

"They tell us not to eat a lot of this fish," Lela said as we pulled up to the shore of the Savannah River. She pointed to a sign on the bank across its muddy waters: "No Trespassing. By Order of the United States Department of Energy." There, the largest nuclear waste repository in the country claimed 310 square miles of land at the Savannah River Site, now operated by Savannah River Nuclear Solutions, a limited liability corporation owned by another series of corporations: Fluor, Newport News Nuclear, and Honeywell.

We got out, and Lela walked to the edge of the water, standing next to a series of signs nailed to a tall post. A paled-to-pink bordered sign, with a small Georgia Power icon in the corner, warned: "Notice: If You hear The Emergency Warning Siren Turn On Your Radio Or T.V." Posted directly above on bright orange plastic was yet another decree: "Warning: Boat Launch Area, No Swimming."

Lela's shoulders curved under her lightweight burgundy T-shirt as she stared stoically into the distance. She was without makeup, her gray and white hair simply and shortly cut. She walked forward toward the lap of the Savannah's waters, slipped out of her flip-flops, and walked barefoot into the river. She stopped before the gentle current could reach the hem of her black capris, remaining silent. Her full figure stood apart from the quiet of the surrounding woods as she scanned north to south. Maybe Lela went back to a time when the Savannah River did not hold the third-highest amount of toxic pollution of any US river.[13] She turned around, and we wordlessly got back into the truck.

The democratic state has long enforced a utilitarian logic where those considered the least important, like Lela's slave kin, were sacrificed for those considered to be the most important, like propertied white people. The political theorist Alexis de Tocqueville captured the majority-minority problematic starkly: "[There are] no obstacles which can retard, much less halt, [the majority's] progress and give it time to hear the wails of those it crushes as it passes."[14] While the injustice of slavery has long been recognized, I offer an explanation for why such utilitarianism is not only alive and well, but also growing— and in unanticipated ways. Profit now subjects to utilitarian sacrifice those once immune to it. Lela stands side by side with white landowners who likewise count themselves as wrongfully dispossessed. In the section "Meltdown," I explain this process through terms such as "majority cannibalism" and "profit's majority," building on Tocqueville's concept of the tyranny of the majority. I describe how the enactment of majority rule violates the local moral economy of democracy common to black and white residents, which is centered on a landownership ethic. As the state violates the property contract between ruler and ruled, a meltdown of legitimacy ensues.

★ ★ ★

"How'd you like your first night in the trailer?" Jesse asked when I rang him the next morning.

"Went just fine," I lied. "Nice and quiet."

Now it was time to follow through on Jesse's demand that I get a gun. For the task, he called his close friend Vernon Davis and Vernon's wife, Debbie. A couple of days later, they arrived to pick me up and find an appropriate weapon. First I went with Vernon to Jesse's modest ranch-style weekend home to see whether any spare guns were available. At the entrance, a sign warned "Beware of Dog." Jesse had no dog and had refused to let me bring my own, adding that he would shoot any dog without a collar on his property.

The sign, though, served as a warning to poachers or thieves tempted to test their way onto his property. There certainly was plenty of crime. Over a six-year period, Burke County consistently ranked in the state's top five counties for the highest rate of aggravated assault, and in the top ten for the highest rate of violent crime.[15] When Vernon punched in the security code and we went inside the house, I saw dusty bobcats on the wall, hunted down near my trailer. A dead alligator with a bullet hole in its belly had already washed up on the shore of the pond a few dozen yards behind where I was staying. Arguably, only a fool would live out in the woods without a gun.

When Vernon couldn't find a handgun small enough to his liking in Jesse's collection, we headed up the road to his friend John Anderson's to find a more suitable weapon. Once we turned off the main drag, we twisted down a slight valley holding a still-watered pond, and then worked our way up the hill toward a picturesque, newly constructed two-story house. John, a muscled man who had moved with his wife, Mary, to the country for relief from the city, was delighted to welcome me and lend me a gun. He left us waiting at the kitchen table. Mary, taken aback by Vernon's introduction, said she would never stay out where I was living on her own. She feared for herself and her son while John was away on long business trips. Waiting defenselessly during the twenty minutes it would take for the nearest deputy to arrive after a telephone call would leave her and her son likely dead, she explained. That was why she had taught herself to shoot.

John returned to the kitchen with a Smith and Wesson handgun. I sat it down on the shiny finish of the new wood table and left the silver barrel facing Mary, who lurched up from her pine chair, leaving it clattering as she moved frantically away. Debbie took over the handling of the weapon after my amateur stunt.

Next were the bullets. We headed to a roadside shop. As we stepped out of the truck, Vernon fit in a lecture before we went inside. "You always leave your doors locked. Even if you're going into the shop. *Always* lock your doors," Vernon said sternly.

I followed Debbie through the glass door of the shop. Without pause, she strolled inside, dangling the .38 from the index finger of her immaculately manicured hand. She walked over to Vernon, who was leaning over a glass counter to find the right bullets. He pulled out a few boxes, checked the ammunition, and handed the correct box to Debbie. She grabbed it somehow with elegance, clenching .38 Special cartridges in her four- (or was it five?) carat diamond-studded clutch. None of the "welfare" customers, as Vernon described them, black or white, seemed to notice. They were busy grabbing drinks and snacks.

Back at Jesse's farmhouse, it was time for shooting practice. Vernon, in his jeans, green rubber boots, and a collared cotton shirt, seemed pretty harmless with a ball cap covering a head of white hair. He carefully instructed me on how to hold the weapon, guiding my hands around the wooden handle, smoothed with age. He stepped back.

I pulled the trigger, and the revolver reverberated as the bullet soared anonymously into the distance. Vernon said I was aiming high, and I steadied myself for my next shot.

"Lean in to it!" Debbie yelled. I looked back at her, with her perfectly tended pixie of blond hair, with a bit of awe. Her beauty was coldly classical: full lips, arched eyebrows, peachy skin, thin nose, and icy blue eyes. Vernon had said he wouldn't marry a woman who couldn't hunt and shoot. Even at a few decades younger than Vernon, Debbie could shoot nearly as well. He had been known to brag to locals during his hunting expeditions about her libidinousness.

I shot again, not terribly interested in my aim, and hoping it would satisfy my tutors. I felt removed from the power of the gun, detached

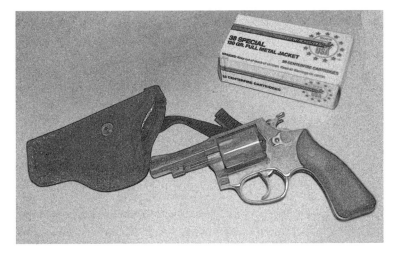

from its capacity to harm. Although that was exactly what I was supposed to keep it for, those unknown harms lurking, perhaps waiting for me. It was a lethal weapon, after all.

That night, I took the gun back to my trailer. I had promised Vernon I would shoot a little more on my own. I did, trying to find something that wouldn't mind a brass-cased bullet collapsing into a mushroom of lead as soon as it hit. I spotted a hollowed tree, aimed, shot, and followed the bullet as far as the hole it pierced through the bark on either side. I took the weapon back inside, unloaded it, and rested it in a holster. I slid it under the bed, and the dried-out carpet crackled under its weight. To practice, I had to hit something. And I didn't want to hit anything.

Hitting something, anything, in a place where the moral economy of democracy was violated by the majority's demands created an illusion of safety. Weapons provided a route to achieving what Isaiah Berlin identified as freedom from fear, in a place where injustice reigns under state targeting and neglect. People seek retribution amid the burden of profit's demands by taking back the land as what I call "rural rebels," and by turning to the church for ultimate liberation through transcendence. I explain these outcomes in the section "Reaction."

Matching his prophetic warning about a dangerous outcome, Tocqueville warned in his classic text that "if ever freedom is lost in America, that will be due to the omnipotence of the majority driving the minorities to desperation and forcing them to appeal to physical force. We may then see anarchy."[16] Burke County, in turning to guns and God, sought some outlet for justice and the retribution denied by what Karl Polanyi called the market society. These unorthodox politics of defense are crucial, as James Scott wrote, because they identify the "the creation of social dynamite rather than its detonation."[17] Understanding the dynamite helps us realize the mounting point of government intolerability for the minority.

Here, a reaction to for-profit democracy is under way. Welcome to Burke County.

This inventory consists of numbered statements. Read each
statement and decide whether it is true as applied to you or false as
applied to you . . . Remember to give your own opinion of yourself.

. . .

10. There seems to be a lump in my throat much of the time.

. . .

22. At times I have fits of laughing and crying that I cannot control.

. . .

48. When I am with people, I am
bothered by hearing very queer things.

. . .

50. My soul sometimes leaves my body.
True or false?

—Minnesota Multiphasic Personality Inventory (MMPI)

"So all this comes down to is, do I have enough regulatory authority?" Jeff Abbot said, repeating my question. He had been dancing
around an answer for five minutes. With his elite diplomas, military
training, industry experience, and high placement in the federal Nuclear Regulatory Commission, he was well positioned to provide an
answer.

"Umm," he said, leaving his Cobb salad untouched. "You know,"
he muttered, looking away from me into the restaurant. "Umm," he
said, filling the silence. "Some people will do the right thing," he
said, meeting my gaze. "Nuclear is a funny animal. The decisions
you make as a senior manager about resource allocation rarely have
an immediate impact. So if you decide you are going to compact the
budget, and not replace the components that are going to fail, they
are not going to fail tomorrow. They are going to fail five years from

now. You are no longer going to be in that position as a manager. So that decision does not come back to you. If you spend money to do something better, you are not typically going to see the fruits of that for a while. So there is a gap in time between the decision and the accountability, which I think causes problems."

In answer to a question about regulatory authority, Jeff cited private accountability to a balanced budget. Not quite the outside stick of governmental rule making and laying down the law that one might expect to hear from a Nuclear Regulatory Commission regulator.

Jeff again became silent, his green eyes leveling a long stare through his glasses. His gaze conveyed perhaps more than his words. "So the bottom line to answer your question is these plants are very safe," he said. "It is not about the technology, it is about the motives of the people who run the apparatus. Profit is a huge motive for them. Is safety not a motive? No, absolutely not. But it's tied back to the profit," he reminded me. "If you tank one of these plants, you are out a $4 billion asset."

Jeff earlier had described nuclear technology as "beautiful." It wasn't the problem. Risk, rather, came from profit, in his view. Catastrophe trailed bad management decisions aimed at short-term money-making. Safety was of concern, but only to the extent to which it preserved profit.

"You are potentially going to tank all the other ones, if you have a really bad disaster, right?" I asked in return. "So there is that fear."

"Yes. But if there was not that economic motive there, what would they do?" Jeff asked with a sly smile. "That's the question that nobody knows the answer to."

Jeff grew quiet again and the uncomfortable silence grew.

"Yeah," I said, drawing out the word, followed by a forced laughed. I quieted and let the silence hang on. Jeff was building up to put it more bluntly.

"That's my answer," he said, at last chewing a bit of his salad. "So, do I have enough authority? Yeah. The plants are safe. Can I effect change when I need to within our processes? Yes."

"Industry is *the* biggest stakeholder, with the most influence," he said with emphasis. "It is not the public. It is not Congress, because industry influences them. You have a couple of antinuclear folks that are kind of a pain in the ass. The industry is comprised of mostly the large, national utilities that have a very strong lobbying group. They pay a bunch of smart people to influence us," he said bluntly. "And that's what they do."

Laid out on our starched white tablecloth, there it was. Profit's undisputed reign—even over the Nuclear Regulatory Commission, which describes itself as created "by Congress in 1974 to ensure the safe use of radioactive materials for beneficial civilian purposes while protecting people and the environment."[1] Jeff felt the tension of the competing interests of profit and safety for those that "run the apparatus." Plants focused on profit, and his regulatory aims followed. When Jeff spoke of "influence," he understood the industry to be separate from the public, even though it was the "biggest stakeholder" in his agency's decision making. And his agency was an arm of the government. And the government is "of the people, by the people, for the people," or at least Abraham Lincoln contends as much in America's beloved Gettysburg Address. So his agency, according to a string of logic, should serve the public.

Somewhere, the wires of public and private had crossed and the whole setup imploded. The Nuclear Regulatory Commission was a *public* agency serving *private profit* while simultaneously treating the *public* as an outside actor of influence, not as one central to its very purpose.

58. Everything is turning out just like the
prophets of the Bible said it would.

. . .

63. I have had no difficulty in starting or holding my bowel movement.

. . .

68. I hardly ever feel pain in the back of the neck.

. . .

69. I am very strongly attracted by members of my own sex.

. . .

70. I used to like drop-the-handkerchief.
True or False?

—MMPI

Part of that somewhere began in the early 1800s, when the government decided that private firms could better achieve the nation's growing need for utilities as public necessities. Remarkably, providing public services justified the initial creation of the modern business corporation.

Corporations were originally devised as a rarely used tool of the state that conferred special legal rights to public-good projects. The oldest American corporation still in existence today, Harvard University, was chartered by the British Crown for such a reason in the mid-1600s.[2] With the formation of the United States, individual states took over the chartering of corporations, still mostly for public municipal and local governance purposes. By virtue of their public purpose and localization, charters remained subject to intense legislative debate and were rarely awarded.

But not for long. In the early years of the republic, the US government was short on cash and couldn't afford to fund public-works projects that it viewed as central to industrial development. Prosperous businessmen with ample capital offered a potential solution. They could bankroll such projects if they received exclusive benefits granted by the state. In exchange for their taking on risky projects, like rail building and canal digging, the government offered tax breaks and the use of eminent domain. The Supreme Court backed the process, finding in favor of the government's right to charter corporations as serving public need in an 1819 ruling, against objections that the government had no constitutional authority to do so.[3] The language of "incidental public need" gave business barons the legal justification they later needed to claim access to the corporate form. Even though they were not directly creating a public good and returning profit to the state, private interests could argue successfully in court that utilities like railroads and canals would eventually serve the public by enabling industrialization.[4]

Awarding the use of eminent domain to profit-seeking firms transformed the meaning of private property rights and the state's protection of them. Business corporations imposed industrialization by taking people's land, even when the owners didn't want to sell—a right formerly limited to the government itself. The threat of eminent domain was sometimes enough to push through a purchase if someone tried to hold out on a sale. But at the time, an important constitutional limitation slowed corporate use of eminent domain, one laid forth in the Bill of Rights. The Fifth Amendment stipulates, "Nor shall private property be taken for a public use without just compensation." If corporations wanted to claim someone else's land, they had to pay for it. And the price was often a handsome one. Some of those stripped of their property became indignant, sued, and often enough won. When courts got involved, juries regularly favored the person losing the land and awarded ample compensation. In some cases, the payment of just compensation accounted for half of corporate expenses. Particularly sticky was the idea of injurious consequences, meaning that corporations were not only taking property in the present, when people lost use of their houses and farms, but also claiming rights to the future—years of accumulated use, enjoyment, and income from property.[5] Neither the US government nor the corporation could afford to pay the consequences that the Fifth Amendment demanded of them.[6] The Bill of Rights was grinding industrial progress to a halt.[7]

To lessen the costs of using eminent domain, the state devised one of the most important elements of the corporation: limited liability.[8] Limited liability arose as courts gradually *limited* consequential damages from large-scale projects, like the long-term damage done to a farm split by a power line, and instead implemented one-time compensation. Second, courts separated the liability of the people funding a corporation from the liability of the corporation itself. Even today, if a corporation fails and owes a monumental amount of money, the corporation can simply fold, leaving the assets of those behind its veil intact.[9] At the time, corporate shares constituted a new, win-win organization of property, at least for those few privy to it. An owner could reap huge profits and simultaneously dodge bankruptcy in the case of losses. What was there to lose?

As Morton Horwitz describes, those people that corporations never paid back, and those people who never received full compensation for their property, in effect *unwillingly* underwrote America's economic development at a time when the country was "underdeveloped" and its state had "little surplus capital" to do so itself.[10]

Soon enough, corporations pocketing profit while acting with governmental authority were as powerful as the states that chartered them.[11] In wake of the 1839 depression, citizens took notice of corporate barons, and opposition to corporations developed across the nation. In the ensuing debate, "public" and "private" arose as terms to capture a government-versus-corporate distinction that did not actually exist. In practice, private and public captured different ends of the shared playground of the corporate-state quest for economic development. Private represented the idea of corporate shareholder, and public the process of legislative approval and oversight. Corporate proponents argued that the problem was not the corporation, but rather the legislature's control over who could incorporate. Debate shifted accordingly: why was the government (public) interfering in citizens' right to incorporate (private)?[12] At the end of the day, corporations and broader shareholder accessibility resonated with more than just business barons. The majority and their elected representatives viewed corporations as the next logical step to produce more profit at home and abroad.[13]

From then on, corporate accountability to the legislature decreased, and bureaucracy grew. Corporate utility providers successfully advocated the removal of limitations on charters, such as rate caps and generous public access at minimal costs, while keeping special rights of sovereignty, like eminent domain.[14] Laws shifted so that corporations could own interests in other corporations.[15] Legislatures across the country relaxed the size limitations on corporations as self-incorporation replaced special legislative approval.[16] The "de-

regulation" of the corporate form resulted in the creation of much more bureaucracy as corporations added layers of ownership and management to shield investors from paying their debts across state lines.

The railroad represents an egregious case of what I identify as a "private-public fallacy," whereby business corporations call themselves private agents of a free market while owing their very existence to a strong-armed government thick with bureaucracy. Railroads continued to take property at virtually no cost, blackmail localities, and provide little recourse for damages arising from, for example, nuisance and trespass suits. No individual property owner ever won a case seeking to halt the railroad's use of eminent domain.[17] Altogether, government bureaucracy mandating a suite of corporate rights dramatically expanded, while democratically distributed ownership took a hit.[18]

By the late 1800s, when Edison deployed the first electric power distribution system in New York, the corporate form dominated utilities.

Without access to eminent domain and the protection from risk provided by limited liability, centralized sources of electricity like coal and, later, nuclear likely would never have materialized.[19] Electricity corporations, regardless of whether profits from charges went back to a public or a private purse, took on the somewhat misleading title of public utility. Private in profit, but recognized as public by virtue of the good produced.

The corporation's private-public fallacy left the meaning of the Fifth Amendment in "shambles" and riddled with "hopeless confusion," according to the legal scholar Lawrence Berger.[20] The corporate form had already usurped the requirement of just compensation through limited liability. Still, some lower courts had argued, as the legal scholar and judge Richard Epstein does, that the constitutionally intended meaning of public use was "to capture without negotiation all the transaction surplus, but only for the benefit of the public at large," when eminent domain was used.[21] Those judges limited the ability of private utility corporations to forcibly acquire property when their profits went back into shareholder purses. To ensure that their claims on eminent domain prevailed, such companies needed the Supreme Court's validation that their purpose, as well as their profit, constituted public use. If not, their entitlements stood on a shaky foundation.

In *Fallbrook Irrigation District v. Bradley* (1896), the necessary legal authority arrived. The Supreme Court ruled in favor of an irrigation corporation's right to claim land from individual property owners based on the idea that "accomplishment" was synonymous with "industrialization": "A private company or corporation, without the power to acquire the land *in invitum* [against a person's will], would be of no real benefit . . . No one owner would find it possible to construct and maintain waterworks and canals any better than private corporations or companies, and unless they had the power of eminent domain, they could accomplish nothing."[22] Without eminent domain, the Court saw progress, or irrigation, as grinding to a halt. In this case, and in many more to follow, the property rights of those engaged in collective and industrial progress were deemed more valuable than those of persons engaged in agrarian or domestic endeavors. The latter offered less centralized profit than the former.

Perhaps it is of little surprise that an electric utility company struck the final blow to the strict interpretation of public use. In 1916, the Supreme Court ruled that the private company Alabama Power, today owned by Southern Company, rightfully acted on behalf of the public when it used eminent domain to take a body of water, produce electricity from it, and then sell that electricity back to the public for profit. Justice Holmes, delivering the opinion of the Court, reasoned: "But to gather the streams from waste and to draw from them energy, labor without brains, and so to save mankind from toil that it can be spared, is to supply what, next to intellect, is the very foundation of all our achievements and all our welfare. If that purpose is not public, we should be at a loss to say what is. The inadequacy of use by the general public as a universal test is established."[23] With environment treated as "waste," and energy its positive opposite, what became good for the public became what was good for production. And therein collapsed the strict legal protection of the public—the public of the people, for the people, and by the people that Lincoln talked about. A public of people who had direct rights to property forcibly taken in their name was replaced by a public of products like energy and the goods produced from its power. Since large firms had monopolized energy production, eminent domain became a default right for utility corporations.[24]

Once a product and profit became synonymous with public use, private energy firms seamlessly qualified as public servants. Regulators have often used such language to legitimize their approval of nuclear power reactors. One such 1970 approval document quotes the Federal Power Commission, which was formed in the 1920s to regulate utilities and is now called the Federal Energy Regulatory Commission:

> The electric utility industry has filled, and must continue to fill an important role in channeling the nation's productive resources into more efficient uses. As an auxiliary and, indeed, a breeder of economic

growth, the industry has furnished a rising proportion of the country's energy requirements as manual effort has been replaced by inanimate energy . . . The expanding use of energy-consuming capital equipment has been a principal source of improvement of national productivity and a stimulus to economic progress . . . Electrification has had an enormous and far reaching impact on other industries and on the living standard of people in every walk of life.[25]

Regulators thus merge energy as a necessary *good* with its status as necessity for *profit*. Without the private production of energy, people could scarcely live, nor could the nation maintain its economic productivity, so the logic goes. Nuclear, by virtue of such thinking, dominates any counterargument about risks or property costs, as does any other privately owned energy utility keeping the lights on.

Today, 68.4 percent of Americans get their energy from investor-owned utilities.[26] The United States has the most privatized nuclear power production regime in the world; the Tennessee Valley Authority constitutes the sole federally owned and operated nuclear power generating entity.[27] When it comes to a state-specific designation as a *public* utility, though, there is little or no difference between those that are traded on the New York Stock Exchange and those that are owned by cooperatives or the federal government. The State of Georgia defines public utilities as "any publicly, privately, or cooperatively owned line, facility or system" engaged in production that includes "power, electricity, light, heat, gas, oil products, water, steam, clay waste, storm water."[28] And Georgia is not alone. Across the country, states fail to distinguish utilities seeking a profit from those that don't.[29] Southern Company and its subsidiary Georgia Power receive the legal rights of public use, even though they are private, profit-seeking corporations—just like hundreds of corporations that preceded them.[30] Treating the public as more than just a source of profit—an ideal that persists today—had legally collapsed nearly a century before Jeff and I sat down for lunch together. I call this state of affairs "for-profit democracy," in which the utilitarian rule of the most people and the greatest profit defines the government's purpose.

In summary, for-profit democracy is enacted through the collective legal form of the corporation. In no universe would corporations exist without a legal system committed to economic development. Corporations enjoy liability protections not afforded to humans that go by their own name. When the Smith family can't pay their mortgage, they lose their house. But if a nuclear power plant defaults on a loan payment or experiences a core meltdown, layers of subsidiary corporations, limited liability, and special legislation protect shareholders from paying their debts. Further, private utilities have an absolute monopoly because the state (in addition to making them legally possible) allows them to buy up one another while also demanding that citizens fund them. And last, the irony of the corporate situation is that many of us are in part shareholders. Indeed, a portion of my wage mandatorily goes into a retirement fund that seeks profit and renders me a shareholder. Millions of other citizens speculate in the stock market. Nonetheless, we all have property that does not explicitly seek profit—perhaps a home, a car that gets you to work, something of your grandfather's, a favorite pair of jeans. Yet we live in a world of laws and markets deliberately designed to give the most protection to property that enables the centralization of revenue, at the expense of values that may matter more to us, like the love of family land or the security of a home.[31]

No wonder Jeff's use of private and public in understanding the Nuclear Regulatory Commission's purpose was markedly mixed. The democratic ideal of the public as "the people" still persists, and his agency's service to the nuclear energy product and its profit is legally backed as public service. It all makes for an ideologically confused, and quite charged, situation.

98. I believe in the second coming of Christ.

. . .

110. Someone has it in for me.

. . .

113. I believe in law enforcement.

. . .

115. I believe in a life hereafter.
True or False?

—MMPI

"It just never," Neill Hataway said, slowing down and releasing his breath, "ever," he pressed, "stops."

The Minnesota Multiphasic Personality Inventory (MMPI) is used to test the minds and resolve of the Vogtle Nuclear Power Plant's incoming employees. Some who begin the 566-question test never finish, as happened to the poor soul whose discarded copy was shared with me by a former examiner. Others, like Neill, endure the questions to become operators of one of the most powerful and dangerous technological marvels of the modern world.

Two days before I interviewed him, Neill had finished a training course to operate the cutting-edge Vogtle Reactor Units 3 and 4. As an operator, he will press the buttons or click the mouse at some of the newest reactors in the world if things go as planned. The stakes are high. One false move can trigger a shutdown of the plant, which costs Southern Company millions a day. In the worst case, failure to react correctly and quickly to a malfunction can trigger a meltdown. When that happens, the cooling system can't keep up, and the nuclear fuel elements inside the reactor pass beyond their melting point. Nuclear fuel leaches into the coolant, eventually breaking through layers of containment, and seeping into the environment. The infamous three—Chernobyl, Three Mile Island, and Fukushima—remind us of the havoc, fear, and radioactive fallout that can result in such a case. The endless training and protocols had Neill exhausted.

"Are you a military brat or anything?" Neill asked me, sizing up how much he could say about the armed forces. "Do you have any family in the military?"

"Well, my grandfather served during World War II," I answered. "That's as close as it gets."

"There are a lot of military families around here," he replied as he relaxed, leaning back and folding one leg over the other. His mahogany loafers were freshly shined, his shirt sharply pressed, and he rested with ease in his slightly shiny khaki slacks. His rosy cheeks stood out from his carefully gelled blond hair, unblemished by the harsh fluorescent lighting fixture buzzing over our heads. Neill, new to the area, had moved to nearby Augusta for love. We had met to talk at the Burke County library.

"I have never really been around the military, on bases and stuff, so maybe I am not used to this. But this place down here," Neill said, trailing off. "You've got to do this stuff somewhere. I am just not a huge fan of Burke County in general. It seems kind of like waste-land."

Even more so than other utilities, nuclear epitomizes for-profit de-mocracy by virtue of its military entanglements. The French scientists Frédéric Joliot and his wife, Irène Curie, relied on private funding. Irène, the daughter of the famous pair Marie and Pierre Curie, struck a deal with a Belgian radium mining company to fund experiments that led to the discovery of nuclear fission.[32] Without that technolog-ical foundation, the Manhattan Project would have been impossible, including its eventual creation of the atomic bomb. In the United States, though, the national security stakes of World War II were generally considered too high to risk trusting private corporations. The government limited its contracts to a few universities and re-search entities. Workers at nuclear arms plants and research stations wore secrecy like a badge of patriotism, although turnover limited the government's ability to keep operations airtight.[33] Those who op-posed the prevailing norm faced backlash from their neighbors and government.[34]

The incorporation of private firms into nuclear matters did not happen until the end of the war, when the US military outsourced some research labs and sites, including the Savannah River Site, to the corporation DuPont. Corporate profit met military protocols for accounting head on, and the corporate and military forms morphed to meet each other's demands.[35] To keep such sites lucrative, produc-tion shifted from nuclear weapons to nuclear reactors for civilian use and, later in the Cold War, nuclear-powered submarines.[36]

The full outsourcing of nuclear reactor technology from what is formally titled the government to what we often conceive of as private corporations began in 1954 when Congress permitted private firms using nuclear technology to seek shareholder profit.[37] When firms were slow to adopt, the government threatened in 1956 to construct and operate its own utilities. Still, the threat was not enough to motivate profit-seeking corporations to tinker with such an expensive, powerful, and dangerous technology. In response to worries about liability, a primary concern of the corporate form, Congress passed in 1957 the Price-Anderson Act, which today insures nuclear reactors for over $13 billion in case of a nuclear incident. If liabilities exceed the insured amount, the costs default to Congress, and consequently to the taxpayer purse.[38] President Dwight Eisenhower, caught in the midst of the substantial military outsourcing, issued in 1961 a prophetic warning to the public: "We must guard against the acquisition of unwarranted influence, whether sought or unsought, by the military-industrial complex. The potential for the disastrous rise of misplaced power exists and will persist."[39]

Today, the moving of military accounts from public oversight to private income sheets may be old news, but a curious culture has formed at the nexus of what is simultaneously military and corporate.[40] Nuclear energy embodies an awkward fusion of ideologies as part of a nuclear age of risk; the money and political clout invested in the security and safety of citizens has increased, and along with it the bureaucracy and military necessary to uphold such expansive goals.[41]

"I was out at Vogtle today for an interview," Neill said, beginning to explain why he was so irritated.

"How did it start off?" I asked.

"It was over webcam with a company called the Stress Center, that contracts for nearly all nuclear plants," he replied. "They pioneered the clinical evaluation over webcam for the nuclear industry."

"So anyway, the examiner started off saying, 'I need you to cooperate,'" Neill said, assuming a dry, sterile voice. He lost his southern welcome as his voice sharpened, imitating the inhumanity of his northern examiner. "'Ultimately, I will give a recommendation to the reviewing official from the utility. And it is ultimately up to them whether or not they want to give you clearance or not. But they will take into account my recommendation.'"

"He asked me if I gambled," Neill said, resuming his own voice. "He asked me if I think it is okay to smoke pot. How much I drink. When I drink. Where am I when I drink. If I ever had any mental health issue. Am I disgruntled with the government."

"Just boom, boom, boom for, like, thirty minutes," Neill said. "Then they ask you one question about drugs. Then they kind of trail off and tell you some story, or try to buddy up to you." Neill paused for a moment and pulled one finger slowly across his throat. "And bam!" he said, finishing an imaginary slash. "They ask you the same question again, five minutes later, to see if they can catch you in a lie. It is crazy. You'd think I was trying to be Secret Service or something. It's just nuts."

While not the same as being vetted to protect the president, the surveillance, gradings, and norms that Neill found himself subjected to share a common military lineage, as part of a democracy-military-surveillance triad. The military uses surveillance and associated bureaucracies to defend nation-states. And thanks in large part to nuclear technology, democracies are perpetually preparing for war.[42] This flourishing of the security state, at least for Neill, was daunting and unexpected when he thought he was going to be working for a private utility company.[43]

Neill found himself at the nexus of what I call "profit's tug-of-war," since the military needs nuclear power for dominance, nuclear power needs outsourcing for secrecy, and outsourcing needs profit. Militaries, like much of the rationalized world of democracies, use bureaucracy to regulate their operations, enforce laws, and keep order. The official secret, as Max Weber calls the creation of bureaucracy, provides some cover from the probing light of public accountability. But bureaucracies, even military ones, have a strange habit of breaking away from the authorities that create them, taking on a life of their own in order to ensure their survival and even expansion. Weber writes, "The 'secret,' as a means of power, is, after all, more safely hidden in the books of an enterpriser than it is in the files of the public authorities."[44] Nuclear, thus, outsources. There, it takes some shelter from the kinds of Freedom of Information Act requests required of public bureaucrats. And an iron triangle forms between the military, Congress, and contractors—the last of which maintain permanent offices in Washington, DC, to lobby Congress for what they want.[45] It is an absolute contradiction between structure and ideals for those, like Neill, living within for-profit democracy.

"They were asking questions I knew they didn't need to know the answers to," Neill said, continuing his complaint. "But they were asking them anyway, personal questions." Neill's voice took on a soft, condescending tone. "Like, 'What is your relationship with your wife like? Is your wife going to ever go to work, or is she just going to stay home with the kids?' And you want to say, 'That's none of your damn business.'"

"They ask you stuff like that?" I asked in surprise.

"Oh man," he said, leaning back in his chair, putting his arms behind his head. "It's crazy. But they want to see if you are going to say: 'You listen here,'" he said, shaking his finger at me and leaning forward again, "'this is none of your damn business.' I guess they want to see if you will snap."

"What did they tell you this was for—just a psychological review?" I asked him.

"Yeah," he said. "Probably seven or eight out of the twenty-four that have graduated [from training] have gotten called back to have clinical evaluations. And some were based on how they answer the MMPI."

"You already had to take that?" I asked.

"Yeah," he replied, tapping the table.

The former Vogtle worker who shared a copy of the MMPI with me initially read aloud some of the most offensive questions with laughter and disbelief. He told me at times he would give test takers a pass even when the results said they should receive a fail (he remained unaware of what actually constituted a right answer when I asked about a few misleading questions). For him, the exam lacked legitimacy, and he consequently deflated its power. For Neill, who was unaware of such practices, the MMPI was an unwelcome invasion of his privacy, one that he deeply resented.

"The application I filled out? That was forty pages long," he said, with building frustration as his list of bureaucratic appraisals lengthened. "I had to account for two days of my life, like four years ago, when I was between jobs. Like a weekend," he said, raising his eyebrows and nodding at me, as my face registered surprise. "I stopped this job on a Friday, and started out on Monday. They were like, 'Whoa, what were you doing those two days?'"

"What would they do with the millions of Americans that are out of work these last few years for months?" I asked.

"See, they want to know what you are doing in your spare time," he explained. "And they are calling everybody. They called a bunch of people I didn't even give them numbers to. They will call your references, and ask, 'Tell me three people we can call.' They won't even ask you. They know your references are going to say good things about you. They will just call the references and say, 'Do you have three other people that know him?'"

"Do you think when you have a job there it will have the same pressures?" I asked.

"Yeah," he said. "You have the pressure of the NRC breathing down your boss's back, and the pressure of the boss breathing down your neck, and safety safety safety safety safety."

"It is almost like being in the military," Neill said, after a long sigh. "You are just constantly being tested."

The nuclear power industry has plenty of company among outsourced former functions of the military. Perhaps most startling is the recent rise of the US government's use of mercenary armies. In 2010, 53 percent of those who died in combat and 54 percent of those deployed were contractors.[46] The most recent surge in surveillance was largely driven by the terrorist attacks of 9/11, which gave rise to the widespread use of increasingly detailed databases that trace citizens' everyday activities at alarming levels of detail, what the surveillance sociologist David Lyon calls "dataveillance."[47] As private firms take on public surveillance, the technology can end up any-

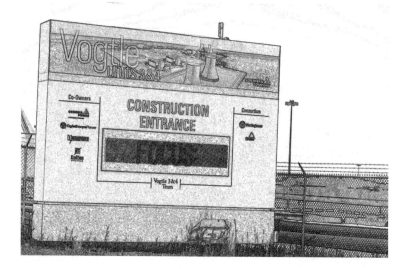

where, doing anything, moving from the Department of Homeland Security and ending up in consumer marketing.[48]

In part, it is futile, perhaps even unnecessary, to pinpoint the military or corporations as the perpetrators of for-profit democracy. What is important is that they are closely intertwined. Corporations reorganized themselves to best compete for massively profitable governmental contracts.[49] The revolution in military affairs—the outsourcing of military functions after the Cold War—restructured companies and the military as both scrambled to mix profit with military protocols.[50] Such efforts in part inspired "information age government," which reduced staff.[51] The intertwinement of military with corporations further reveals the constructed nature of the public-private dividing line as information is gathered, in the words of the surveillance sociologist Gary Marx, with "laser-like specificity and with sponge-like absorbency."[52] Public agency is so intertwined with private accountability that the two become next to impossible to disentangle. In any event, for-profit democracy reigns.

"Does it feel like Southern Company has the power at the plant, or does it feel like the government has the power?" I asked Neill.

"I have read a lot lately about solar power," he replied. "I think solar power is a lot more practical than people think. But I think the powers that be, they want the nuclear power because it keeps the people from being independent. With solar power, you can be independent. You might have to give a bit for an initial investment, and do maintenance on your panels. But your meter will run backwards when you are not running your meter. They will pay you! Look at the profits Southern Company is making. Their fourth quarter profits were like $270 million," he said with a smirk. "I mean, that is one quarter. And they are about to build two more reactors. It's just crazy. I think their revenue was like two and a half billion."

"It is hard to fathom," I said.

"All the powers that be, they are in this together. I don't think they are evil or anything," he said, trailing off. "The government is fully supporting this initiative," he began again. "That is obvious." We both knew the Obama administration had pushed through the $8.3 billion federal loan guarantee for Vogtle Units 3 and 4. "I think the Republicans were, too," he added. "Probably a lot of Republicans own in the company. I do not feel that the government is in control any more than the utilities are."

173. I liked school.
174. I have never had a fainting spell.
175. I seldom or never have dizzy spells.
176. I do not have a great fear of snakes.
177. My mother was a good woman.
178. My memory seems to be all right.
179. I am worried about sex matters.
True or False?

—MMPI

The outcome documented in this chapter—profit as the ruling motive in US governance—has not often been attributed to the inner workings of the democratic state. But some scholars have warned that democracy's treatment of people as numbers strips away the distinguishing characteristics that allow communities to resist despotism. Max Weber, a hundred years ago, warned that democracy creates bureaucracies like the military by treating people as an inarticulate mass subject to executive leaders who direct administrative activities. This structure readies people for bureaucratic control. Tocqueville, nearly a century before Weber, said as much when he talked about the delinking of the familial, community, and patrimonial chain that predominated before democracy. Unlike Weber, he did not anticipate privatization, but he did worry that administrative despotism could come to reign as local customs and control declined.

Most of all, Weber and Tocqueville feared that bureaucracy and administrative despotism could turn people into hapless followers, little aware of their own agency and readied like sheep for the slaughter. Isolated and caught up in their own endeavors, citizens would leave administrators to their own ends. Those self-serving ends, Tocqueville wrote, would whittle away at democratic liberties. Of all the types of power concentration that threaten democracy, he warned, this would be the worst; citizens would "fall below the level of humanity" and become mere tools of the state that rules them.[53] Weber ominously stated that someone caught within the control of the bureaucratic state is like "a single cog in an ever-moving mechanism which prescribes to him an essentially fixed route of march."[54] The democratic mass would become subservient to bureaucracy, he concluded. Michel Foucault says as much of modern politics, with its "mechanism of the perfect army, of the disciplined mass, of the docile, useful troop." That perfect army, he opines, self-regulates itself according to "an inspecting gaze, a gaze which each individual under its weight will end by interiorising to the point that he is his own overseer, each individual thus exercising the surveillance over, and against himself."[55]

What is missing from Weber's, Tocqueville's and Foucault's accounts is the transformative role of profit, and so they miss how people can (and do) resist bureaucratic despotism. The anthropologist David

Graeber aptly captures profit's role with the phrase "total bureaucratization," which he defines as "the gradual fusion of public and private power into a single entity, rife with rules and regulations whose ultimate purpose is to extract wealth in the form of profits."[56] Rather than pinning the problem on democracy, Graeber pins it on profit. Democracy, he counters, can be a solution if it is understood more as a movement and a means of consensus building rather than as a top-down apparatus. He blames much of the problem on electing very few legislators to represent the interests of millions, seeing such a structure as purposefully limiting the power of people. Rather than even vote—which should be a last-case scenario—he argues that democracy should rely on consensus building. Most of all, Graeber says that people do notice total bureaucratization and avidly resist it, as he explains in his firsthand account of the Occupy Wall Street protests.[57]

Thus, the rather abysmal conclusion that people will turn into mindless automata is perhaps overstated by classic theorists. This is likely because they, as well as many current scholars of bureaucracy and surveillance, overlooked the joined hands of profit and statism. What is important to distinguish here is the democratic state from democracy itself. The former can include aims targeted at an inarticulate mass, the dehumanization of value through bureaucracy, elected representatives in lieu of the people, and so on. But democracy often suggests much more—values that transcend profit, that center on communities and cultures, self-dignity, respect, and privacy, the kinds of things that Neill saw his work as violating. The dominance of for-profit over the many nuanced interests of democracy rests uneasily on those subject to its rule. Neill was painfully cognizant of the infinitesimally detailed observations he endured at the intertwined hands of the government and Southern Company, which were "in this together." The chummy relationship between his employer and the government elicited Neill's indignation. Together, they stagnated the "independence" of the American public while Southern Company reaped a "crazy" "$270 million" profit in a single quarter. Neill couldn't tease out specifically who had more control, but he recognized that his individual liberty, the liberty that democracy is entrusted with protection of, was experiencing the grip of constraint.

My point is this: for-profit democracy is a "contradictory state." The rule of profit is not reconcilable with the rule of the people. Forcing the centralization of profit upon the back of democracy is an absolute contradiction in meaning and purpose.

201. I wish I were not so shy.
True or False?

—MMPI

"When I first started at the plant, they called me and asked me about stress," Dale Fannigan, a retired operator of the Vogtle reactors, explained. Dale was one of the many who lived in the counties surrounding Vogtle whose farming operations collapsed during the 1980s farm crisis. After telling me with a crooked grin that his wife made him promise to try to be positive, he played with his cup of coffee as we spoke at a local breakfast spot.

"I told them, 'The only thing I can tell you is I have been farming for the last seven years at a loss, and that is driving me to this job,'" Dale recounted. His suntan stopped at the sleeves of his plaid shirt, tucked into jeans. He looked out at me through old-fashioned wire-rimmed glasses. "They said, 'Well, we can understand that.' I was a nobody. I didn't count. I didn't have all of the credentials. I wasn't out of the nuclear navy. Or I didn't have a mechanical engineering degree from Tech [Georgia Tech University]."

Military and technical dominance at the plant left Dale, like Neill, sensing that he was on the periphery of operations. Despite performing one of the most important and technically difficult jobs at the

*"There's no power like Georgia Power.
That was the biggest grind."*

Vogtle Plant—operating it—neither Neill nor Dale felt as if he belonged.

"The equipment, fantastic," Dale said. "The construction, like you've never seen before. I could only hope to see things built as well. But the way they manage people, primitive at best. That was the thing. It was all this power. The old saying about how power corrupts. We used to have a motto: 'There's no power like Georgia Power.' That was the biggest grind."

"You *knew* . . . ," he said, slowing his words and stretching them out. "You *knew* beyond the shadow of a doubt that if you made a mistake, you were the only one that was going to be there to help you. Right after I got my license initially, I flunked an exam. I said, 'Do you want a three-day notice? Do you want three weeks? I am leaving.' They said, 'You can't do that!' I said, 'Why can't I?' I said, 'I'd rather swallow a bullet than put up with this stuff.'"

I was stunned, and concerned that maybe Dale meant it. It seemed Georgia Power was concerned, too.

"So they sent me to a shrink," he said. "And this lady, she never let her cigarette go out. She named off the number of people at Vogtle that she had talked to, and she said, 'You guys are in a pressure cooker out there. You have no advocates.' And that's where we are. It was just one of those things, one of those challenges that you had to make up your mind whether you were going to endure. I think the whole idea is we are going to push these people, we are going to see how badly they want this job. You know?"

Exams like the MMPI, sometimes trickily phrased to promote failure in Dale's and Neill's experience, served as a mechanism to make prospective and current employees obedient. Foucault goes so far as to claim that psychiatry and the government, particularly the justice system, are mutually dependent, using one another to exert power by defining what it means to be crazy. In his discussion of madness, Foucault writes that the hierarchical examination makes it possible for psychiatry to claim legitimacy.[58]

By demanding answers to invasive and offensive questions, the plant tested Dale's and Neill's submission to its authority. MMPI questions like "My mother was a good woman" are intended to make workers amenable to institutional methods of control. Such psychological tests, as Foucault puts it, were designed for the individual who has to be "trained or corrected, classified, normalized, excluded, etc."[59] Personal accounts of their lives and their own personal histories, valued in their own individual ways, were recalibrated into a tool to define good and bad behavior.

"And once we determine that they want it bad enough, and we put them in that position, we will push them a little harder. How bad do they want to keep it?" Dale asked rhetorically.

"Are they always pushing you to see how bad you want to keep it?" I asked.

"To me, because I am kind of simpleminded, if you train me, if you tell me this is how something works, I operate under that assumption for two or three years," he said, beginning his answer. "Then you come back and you say, 'Oh, oh, oh, wait. We taught you this about this system here. It really don't work like that.' And then the next exam, guess what? They are going to load it up with questions that go both ways. You know, they try to trick you. I call it wordsmithing. They change the way they ask the questions, with 'maybes,' 'if then.' That kind of stuff, I didn't like it. I felt like either you didn't know what you were doing when you put this stuff out, or you are trying to trick me, or a little bit of both."

Incessant surveillance in modern society has irrevocably transformed power relationships from confrontation and combat to unending evaluations and perpetual exposition to standards, visible in the ceaseless use of grades and the consequent anticipation of failure or success that comes with those markings. Foucault writes of the "meticulousness of the regulations" driven by "economic or technical rationality," which results in no zone of shade and constantly supervises the very individuals who are entrusted with the task of supervising.[60] All these methods of control aim at more profit rather than more innovation, Graeber writes: "There appears to have been a profound shift, beginning in the 1970s, from investment in technologies associated with the possibility of alternative futures to investment technologies that furthered labor discipline and social control."[61] The "pressure cooker" that Dale was stuck in left him disgruntled with those who demanded control. Control just for the sake of it.

"The thing that troubled me, all of these alpha personalities. We had a general manager at the time, Bob, he was a horse's rear," Dale said. "He got mad at me because he wanted my oldest son, a Tech graduate, to come to work at the plant. He came to me one night and he said, 'Dale.' I said, 'Yeah.' 'Did you tell your son that he needs to come to work out here?' I said, 'No.' He said, 'Why? Come back here.'"

"You know, if you go into the control room, there is carpet," Dale told me, explaining the environment of the room where he worked running the plant. The carpet distinguished the spaces where operators had to stay while on shift. Otherwise, they could be out of reach in the event of a problem that required their immediate attention. "The reactor operator has to stay on that carpet," he said. "You can sit down at the desk, but you have to be able to get up and react to anything that happens. So you can't leave that for more than forty-five minutes in a twelve-hour shift, without doing a formal turnover, like if they call you for a drug test. Anyway, he said to me, 'Come back here and talk to me for a minute.' I went on back. He said, 'You mean to say that you are not going to tell your son to go to work out here.' I said, 'That is exactly what I am telling you.' I said, 'He is a grown man, he is married, he's got a wife. They are expecting a baby. If I tell him to come to work out here and you do not give him that engineering spot, do you think he is going to look at you or is he going to look at me? It is for him to make up his mind.'"

"Oh, he got *all* puffed up," Dale said. "You cannot control me, just because you've got the money." By you, Dale meant Georgia Power. He would tolerate so much, but his kids were off the table. "It is a good paying job," he said. "But I am *not* going to give you my soul."

Standardization, regulation, bureaucratization, and privatization combined in an assault on Dale's dignity—the offensive probes into Dale's and Neill's families, the unsavory triumph of profit over safety that Jeff experienced. The for-profit orientation of the corporate-state nuclear project, and countless other modern privatization schemes, jeopardizes the ideals of democracy that speak to the soul. That speak to humans, rather than to cogs in a machine. Foucault was right about the standardization and regulation of the panoptic state, perhaps even people's complicity in it—but not their hapless satisfaction. Rather than feeling docile and robbed of their agency, regulators and workers resent the authority shared between private corporations and the government. They are well aware that their roles make them troops servicing corporate-state interests. But they perform their roles with ceaseless unease in a condition of what I call "corporate-state reaction," in which people still believe in a public-private distinction—public as human decency, and private as profit—even though that line increasingly does not exist within the state, and perhaps never fully has. They react to the irreconcilability of the contradictory state accordingly.

"[Bob] come out there again to the control room one time, the same guy. He said, 'How are you doing, Dale? How's everything?'" Dale continued. "He leaves and then goes and gets my supervisor and tells him I was not being attentive to my board. And then my supervisor comes back and gets all down my case."

"So later again, he comes to the control room, and Bob says, 'Dale, I have got some real complimentary stuff in the mail on your son,'" Dale said, recounting the story. "I didn't look at him. I just looked at the board. He came and tugged on my shirtsleeve. He said, 'Dale, I am *talking* to you.' I said, 'I know. I am working on this turbine right now. When this is done, I'll see you later.' And he marched out of the building. I saw him a couple of afternoons later on the walkway between the turbine building and the control building. I said, 'How are you doing, Bob? Do you have that paperwork?' He said, 'You know, I lost it.'"

"So you think he was just trying to set you up?" I asked.

Dale nodded. The waitress stopped and poured us both more coffee. I was on my fourth cup, with the evidence of plastic creamers strewn in front of me.

"My shift supervisor, he said to me, 'You know, Dale, I think he was after you. I never saw him do like that.'"

"Why?" I asked.

"Control," he said, as pounded the table with his fist and laughed.

Jeff had explained to me further what that control meant based on his experience as both regulator and operator. "You think your job is safety when you come out of training," Jeff said. "They have been talking all about safety. But what they really want is for you to facilitate work and not make mistakes doing it. Rarely does someone recognize the mistake that wasn't made because you held up work. But they will recognize that the work is held up. At the end of the day, what is this about? It's about a commodity business that sells based on costs. You are not marketing tennis shoes because people like the color of the shoelaces. It's 'what is the lowest cost I can do this for?' And so, what do you look at? You look at expenses, you look at people, how many people am I putting at it. And you are there to meet business objectives."

All those ceaseless exams and safety protocols fit the bureaucratic bill; they suited the administrative apparatus. Safety in service of profit.

"There is a life before and after Vogtle, believe me. Agriculture taught me that disappointment is not a fatal condition," Dale said, bringing up his farm. "You have got to do what you've got to do."

Those at the front lines of the corporate-state nuclear endeavor sense something more important than profit demands of them. Something that rests in human lives, safety, and humility—values that the primacy of most money and majority rule increasingly fails to capture. And from that something springs a growing corporate-state reaction across the ranks of for-profit democracy.

435. Usually I would prefer to work with women.

. . .

441. I like tall women.
True or False?

—MMPI

Profit's accountants know no loyalty. Their appetite for addition comes full circle to exploit its own onetime benefactors. In February 2013, Burke County gossip channels were rife with the news that Southern Company had pushed through the state legislature a code change in the tax laws that meant it was exempt from paying sales and use tax on 90–95 percent of the construction costs for the new Vogtle reactors. Local administrators and politicians had been counting on the funds. Voters had just passed a public referendum that approved pricy updates to the Burke County courthouse and the construction of a new jail. But Southern Company had failed to inform county and municipal officials of the tax change. Instead of the $56 million that the county expected, it would receive only $3 million to $6.5 million. To add insult to injury, county officials learned that they might even owe the company $1 million in back taxes.[62] The county administrator hosted a special meeting of mayors, county board members, and other officials to discuss the startling discovery and the drastically reduced budget.

"They all knew what this money from the sales tax would be going to, Georgia Power and the others," one mayor said to the crowded room with irritation. "Nobody bothered to inform us."

"That's just business," a politician added sarcastically.

"That's just politics," a county board member said, followed by a half laugh as comments erupted around room.

Tempers flared, impossible to cool. In the innermost ranks of democracy, politicians reacted to the rule of profit, undermining even their own coffers.

"Of course they didn't do it on purpose," another mayor said with feigned understanding as the room quieted. "It just slipped their mind. And the General Assembly's, too."

A Georgia Power official, sitting stoically at my right side, didn't budge. The seven nongovernmental observers that showed up to the meeting, me included, were lined up, sitting with our backs against the wall, just feet away from the long table where the discussion was taking place. Before the meeting, that Georgia Power official had shaken the hands of the men and women, of many shades, now swapping sarcasms about his company. And not a person at that table turned their eyes toward him as their banter progressed. It was a moment of uncontrollable reaction. And when the meeting ended, the Georgia Power official slipped out the door, waiting patiently for a county board member to exit, to try to cool him down, one-on-one.

A meltdown was underway.

456. A person shouldn't be punished for breaking a law that he thinks is unreasonable.

True or False?

—MMPI

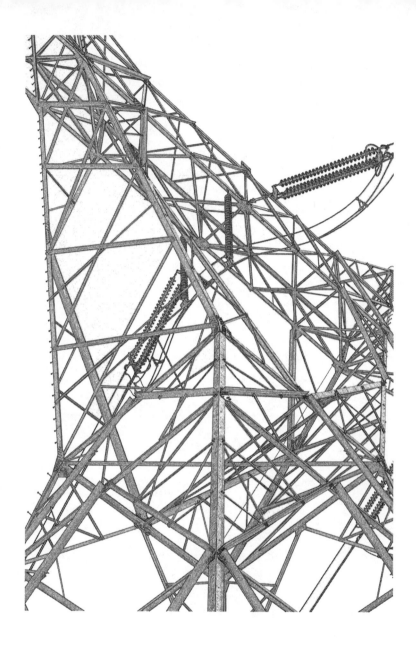

# Meltdown

The spirit of God is in this land. It is in the people.

—Sydney Jackson

"How would it make you feel," Patty Sutton thundered at me, "if they came and took over *your* land?"

"Terrible," I said. Patty knew my family owned land in Illinois. And she rightly assumed her question would rattle me into paying sharp attention.

"They got easements to run those lines all the way back through our property," she said, explaining how Georgia Power took her family land. On their way to the grid, Vogtle power lines split her property in two. "The easement does not give them access to go anywhere across the property. But they go on across my land any time they like, without permission," Patty complained, her hands slightly shaking with age. "[Georgia Power] will even go across the field rows. When my daddy was living, they stopped by and told him."

"But we don't count," she said, referring to herself and her siblings. Her bare, wrinkled fingers restlessly tapped on the desk. Her humming, so familiar when she found herself contentedly at work, stopped as soon as the name "Georgia Power" passed her lips. She was ready to nail the firm to the wall.

"Georgia Power hires in subcontractors to supposedly keep the lines maintained. Well, they sent two drunks down here from Madison [Georgia] to cut a two-foot wide pine tree by the line. You could smell the whiskey on them," she said with disgust. "They had a little rope about the size of your pinky that they tied around that pine tree to a six-inch oak tree. Now, that was supposed to hold up that pine tree," Patty said in a tone brimming with irony. Her eyes narrowed as her frown deepened. "The rope snapped and fell on the line. Now, the

whole power line went down. And it was burning on both sides into the trees."

Patty immediately called Georgia Power, but help was slow to turn up. When workers finally arrived, they attempted to put out the fire that was spreading rapidly, devouring the crunchy pine needles and leaping up the narrow trees. It was too late for hundreds of Patty's young pine trees. She lost fifty acres of her timber crop, and with it thousands of dollars.

"I had learned long ago that you check on the fires all through the night because they can spark up any time," she said, brushing back some white bangs. "Well, I went out there and checked after they left. When the fire hit the cross fence, I discovered that it had ignited another fire in the woods. Then they had to come back out and fight the fire again. That tells you how well they checked," she finished with a wry smile.

A few years later, another fallen line lit up Patty's property. Despite ample evidence to the contrary, she said that the county's forestry unit told her it was caused by "a single strike of lightning on a perfectly blue sky day."

"Did you try to get any money back from Georgia Power?" I asked.

"Yes," she said sharply. "My mother and I sent a letter. I didn't hear a thing back. They have the luxury of not caring about what they do wrong. They think they are invincible, that they can do anything."

One of Patty's local admirers once told me: "Patty? She's not afraid of anything." More than once after I got to know Patty, I overheard men swapping stories about her. The local favorite recounted how she caught a neighbor driving a four-wheeler on her property. She left her kids at home and charged after him in her truck, chasing him through the wilderness. He stopped when he reached his farm, and Patty screeched to a halt, jumped out of her truck, and said: "Keep that *damn con-trap-tion* off my property!" The best storytellers would enunciate every syllable in Patty's legendary style: "Sparks from that *ex-haust* could light up the whole place."

Another time, she held two burglars at gunpoint for forty-five minutes while waiting for the police. The thieves had broken into a house on her sprawling farm. Jesse had told me the story the first time I heard it. There were various renditions, of course, but Patty verified the accuracy of forty-five minutes.

But guns couldn't fend off the corporate trespassers in the climate of for-profit democracy. Neither could Patty's rage. She couldn't get into her truck and chase Georgia Power back where it came from. Even as a subsidiary of Southern Company, its operating revenue in 2016 was $8.38 billion, and its net income $1.33 billion.[1] Those figures seem modest compared with Southern Company's $49.3 billion value, $19.9 billion in operating revenue, and $2.4 billion in consolidated net income.[2] Those making use of eminent domain had such pervasive power that an attack with a gun or a lashing of the tongue could hardly phase them. The company had cut through her property and, in Patty's view, her inalienable rights as a landowner.

★ ★ ★

Patty's vigilant protection of her property and her indignant response to Georgia Power come with a good deal of democratic backing. The collapse of the aristocracy and the rise of democracy as the new organizing principle of the state pivoted on the treatment of private property as an individual person's right. A triumphant logic reigned: private property ought to reflect one's hard work.[3] In the seventeenth century, English yeoman farmers protested that the peasant-and-lord system based on commonage disabled their individual, productive capacities. Ringing supportively was the voice of fellow Englishman and theorist John Locke, who proposed that private property was a presocial right, like the outcome of the individual's relationship with the creator.[4] In the face of royal absolutism, what Locke proposed was revolutionary: "The labour of [a man's] body, and the work of his hands, we may say, are properly his. Whatsoever then he removes out of the state that nature hath provided and left it in, he hath mixed his labour with, and joined to it something that is his own, and thereby makes it his property."[5] And there arose the now widespread and continuously popular ideology that the government should protect and uphold the individual's right to private property—a notion that makes much sense to Patty.

The survival of such an understanding over the course of centuries required ample amounts of property that had not yet been legally claimed by a state. Burke County and the American colonies were what Locke's approach needed in order to flourish. Europe's land already had layers upon layers of aristocratic and merchant and yeoman claims. To justify taking land from indigenous populations, Locke's logic was applied seamlessly. Locke viewed indigenous populations as wasting land that was ripe for improvement: "There still are great tracts of ground to be found, which (the inhabitants thereof not having joined with the rest of mankind, in the consent of the use of their common money) lie waste, and are more than the people who dwell on it do, or can make use of, and so still lie in common." He asked "whether in the wild woods and uncultivated waste of America, left to nature, without any improvement, tillage, or husbandry, a thousand acres yield the needy and wretched inhabitants as many conveniences of life, as ten acres equally fertile land do in Devonshire, where they are well cultivated."[6] The lack of cultivation, in Locke's view, was a blow against virtue, although his logic excluded the many indigenous people who farmed.[7] Such a moral framework gave colonizers social justification for the violence practiced against indigenous people in order to dispossess them—an irony, since many of the settlers had left their native lands to escape persecution and the rigid class structures of a society of haves and have-nots.

Patty's family was among the droves of settlers who ten generations ago came to America seeking their independence and rewards on the basis of landownership. According to reports at the time, Burke County was a fine place to immigrate to. Patty's family settled nearby the aptly named Shell Bluff, where a spring poured from a bluff studded with gigantic oyster shells and landed in the current of the Savannah River. The picturesque spot, providing freshwater on the way up the Savannah River, caught travelers' attention. John Bartram, a Pennsylvania botanist working his way up the river in the 1760s, marveled that the shores of Shell Bluff held the "loveliest spring of clear water" he had seen during his entire journey throughout America. Bartram drank from it and wrote to King George III: "[It tastes] very sweet and just cold enough to drink heartily off."[8] A pamphlet issued by the English Crown to entice settlers boasted: "The soil will produce any thing with very little culture." The pamphlet continued, "The husbandry is so slight, that they can only be said to scratch the earth and cover the seed." Fine images of grandeur included American Indians, who would supply easy game at a cheap price: "They bring many a mile the whole of a deer's flesh, which they sell to the people who live in the country."[9]

The first Burke County pioneers flocked to the freshly founded colony in 1732. They came with the hope of a land-based future, but suffered a much starker reality. Those who made the initial inroads from Augusta found sandy and clay soils covered with trees. Alligators and wildcats lurked in the rich forests bordering the Savannah River. Rattlesnakes thickly populated the woodland. Piecing together a living from the land required the backbreaking work of clearing trees, and even then the soil did not yield a strong crop. Scottish Highlander, Northern Irish, German, and English Uplander settlers could hardly bear the steamy climate.[10] The swamps bred disease and dissatisfaction. Cherokee, Creek, and Uchee Indians waged war with the locals to defend their land and to fulfill political allegiances to the Spanish, French, and, later, British.[11] The murder and pillaging between those staking a claim to the land switched with the political whims of state authority. The land was lawless.[12] The historian Nancy Isenberg writes that it was "not a land of equal opportunity, but a much less appealing terrain where death and harsh labor conditions awaited most migrants."[13] The state was not doing what Locke proposed it should—defending the property of those settlers who were risking their lives to, in his conception, improve its productive capacity.

Locke's world of unclaimed virgin land, though, had never existed. Indigenous people had populated North America for thousands of years, and European nobility exerted militarized control over land access and production.[14] The colonies paid tribute to their royal rulers, and the largest land grants were bestowed on those with royal ties and others who did the Crown's bidding. Rulers with interests in the colonies wanted profit from them, in the form of resource extraction and the production of staple crops such as cotton and tobacco. When potential immigrants who heard of the rough conditions stopped coming in droves, some in the ruling state began to advocate the introduction of slavery. Elites labeled as idle those immigrants who resisted becoming landless laborers.[15] Without slavery, advocates reasoned, could the land provide products to fuel the Industrial Revolution at home?

Thus, two new types of property were introduced in America to fuel industrialization: that of landownership and that of human bodies. The state's privatization of America's land and of African people brought controversy and war. Conflict simmered between the gentleman elites who supported the introduction of slavery, and settlers, who, like the yeomen of England, favored tying property ownership to self-labor. Those in positions of power used royal authority to legalize slavery, disenfranchising small landowners and giving large landowners ample property to extract enormous profits from their plantations. In the words of two nineteenth-century historians: "Evil counsels prevailed. The idlers far outnumbered those who worked, and although the trustees stood out for a long time, slaves were eventually admitted, and the energies of the industrious whites correspondingly paralyzed."[16] By legalizing slavery in 1751, Georgia improved the positions of those who had too much land to tend themselves, but deflated the positions of those making a living off small plots through their own labor.

For those who believed property should belong to those who worked for and on it, the introduction of slavery was a severe blow to the land-centric idealism surrounding privatization. On the eve of the Revolutionary War, self-sufficient but poor white cattle drivers, derogatorily known as crackers for the whips they cracked at the backs of the cattle they drove, pushed against the unwelcome infiltration of slaves and their owners. Strained relations in the backcountry led, in one historian's charged view, to "gangs of outlaws . . . on both sides of the river, murdering and pillaging as they pleased," adding, "The gentlemen of the low country, for their part, were inclined to look upon these Crackers as no great improvement on the savage Indians they replaced."[17] When finally defeated, the indigenous people who had fought the commodification of their land and its subjection to a marketized agricultural system were forcibly removed. The American Indian cessions of 1763, 1773, and 1783 finalized their dispossession.[18] Privatization of flesh and of soil solidified.

Vigilante justice became the norm as the moral authority of the state's ruling class stood in question. Patriotism, amid lawlessness, ran low in Georgia, which at the time was what Louis Hartz called "the most radical state of the South."[19] As land rights further shifted to the rich, the state's political stability was tenuous. One estimate shows that during the Revolutionary War, only about 30 percent of Burke County men available to fight joined either the British or the Patriot cause in the area.[20] Some fled, never to return to their homesteads, rendering Burke County increasingly deserted and dangerous. According to an archivist, "[The county was] controlled by neither side but was a no man's land between the two belligerent camps. Not only were the people being harassed by the Patriots and Tories but also by bandits of neither side who took advantage of there being no legal authorities to apprehend them."[21] A British officer, marching along River Road in Burke County, noted: "Most of the Settlements (along both the roads) from Ebenezer to Augusta are in a ruinous, neglected state, two thirds of them deserted, some of the owners following the King's troops, others with the Rebels, and both revengefully destroying the property of each other."[22] Appeals to the ruling Patriots offered no recourse, even as Georgia became a state in 1777.[23]

Locke's moral heralding of private property, although stymied by the injustice of slavery and indigenous genocide, heavily influenced the Patriots' ideology. For European settlers escaping the clutches of the aristocracy and nobility, the privatization of land appeared to be the main way to prevent the rise of hereditary ownership and rulers. As the most coveted form of property, land inspired political support for private property without reference to the people whom the American property regime held in chains. Thomas Jefferson, a slave owner and Patriot whom Tocqueville distinguishes as "the most powerful apostle of democracy there has ever been," viewed white male ownership of property and self-earned rewards from labor as crucial to a successful democracy.[24] Proponents of this policy, which was known broadly as Jeffersonian agrarian democracy, urged that to have equality and sustainable democracy, landownership had to remain widely distributed, with emphasis on the implicitly white family farm.[25] The agricultural historian David Danbom writes that strident agrarianism proclaimed rural superiority, with the view that "owning farms made people self-sufficient and independent, responsible and mature, conservative and jealous of their liberties."[26] This agrarian view of ownership reflected the rural nature of much of the populace at the time. In his characterization of the United States, Tocqueville wrote: "In no other country in the world is the love of property keener or more alert than in the United States, and nowhere else does the majority display less inclination toward doctrines which in any way threaten the way property is owned."[27]

Thus, despite its revolutionary premises and centerpiece status in the democratic state, the just possession of land was nonetheless disjoined from just possession of self, denied to millions of slaves. The Statement on Rights adopted in 1774 by the First Continental Congress paired "property" with "life and liberty."[28] After some debate, the Declaration of Independence later replaced "property" with "pursuit of happiness." Still, private property remained listed as a natural right in most of the thirteen states' constitutions.[29] Private property was a weapon against tyranny, one to be closely protected by the judiciary, but only for white men.[30] Not others, like women or slaves.

The agrarian idealism of land privatization holds a tragic irony, particularly in the South. As soon as land was privatized, ownership of it became subject to the market demands of industrialization. Like any other commodity, land could be bought by and sold to the highest bidder. In a private property regime that also commodified human lives, slave owners, as central agents of international cotton and tobacco production, quickly amassed the most land and money. Between 1775 and 1790 in Burke County, the estimates show that the white population (7,064) increased by about 5 percent, while the number of those in slavery nearly doubled, to 2,403. As the wealth of the few increased, and the misery of those in bondage was compounded, a mass exodus of white settlers followed. Between 1790 and 1820, the number of whites declined by 20 percent, to 5,673, while the number of slaves increased by 59 percent, to 5,904.[31] Those that could left in droves to find plots of richer land and fairer economies where one's labor was tied more directly to one's property.

All this comes down to a key piece of historical evidence that largely has been forgotten in the reconstruction of American markets and private property rights to suit corporations and financial firms: just and fair access to land was a key motivator of democracy, one that undergirded popular support for privatization. Settlers believed that a democratic framework of private property rights could provide the golden ticket to land access, which their ancestors had long been denied. Later, freed slaves would believe the same. This dynamic is a key example of what might be called the "interdependence of the democratic state and property rights," justly distributed. Popular support of the democratic state ebbed and flowed with its capacity to defend land access, a sentiment that continues to linger prominently in rural America.

When the democratic state fails to uphold just distribution of property ownership, rural resentment, even rebellion, flourishes. Some of the wealthiest men in the world lived in Burke County in the 1800s, and they rose to the top of the political elite. Herschel Vespasian Johnson, born in the county, was the forty-first governor of Georgia, and ran as Stephen Douglas's vice presidential candidate in 1860. John James Jones, whose family was one of the largest owners of slaves in Burke County, served in the House of Representatives, and Lott Warren, born in Burke County, served in the Georgia House and Senate. Emily Burke, a northern schoolteacher who chronicled antebellum Georgia on her visit to the forty-nine-square-mile Birdsville Plantation, owned by one of the wealthiest men in Burke County, wrote that Burke County "has more wealth, larger plantations, and richer soil than any other in Georgia."[32] Plantations enveloped Burke County farmsteads, which were composed of small-scale wooded lots for grazing cattle, hogs, and sheep, and diversified plots of rice, cotton, corn, sugarcane, wheat, and tobacco. The private property regime in Burke County had achieved what a good portion of its supporters had sought to avoid: the concentration of power and money in the hands of a favored few.[33] Left were many casualties: dispossessed and dead American Indians, enslaved African Americans, a second-status tier of poor whites, and land pillaged to fuel industrialism.

★ ★ ★

Around 1854, Sydney Jackson's grandfather was born, still in bondage, the first of his family members to appear by the family name on a census. His son, Sydney's father, was one of the few men able to overcome substantial adversity to achieve landownership before the arrival of Vogtle. In fact, his father was among the 7.15 percent of Burke County farmers classified as colored in the 1930s who owned the ground they tended.[34]

I had known Sydney for a while before we had our first serious sit-down together. He would bravely break into a hymn on Sunday mornings, and the rest of the congregation would follow. His off-pitch singing didn't quite resonate with his deep and clear ebony skin, set off by elegantly high cheekbones, or his softly leveled attention, delivered by blue-rimmed pupils. His nobility stayed intact. The congregation was perfectly happy to have him break out the first few notes as he moved forward with a touch of rhythm in his pew, out of tune and all. Then all would join in together and the harmony would take over.

That particular morning, Sydney had organized a Walk for Christ, and a thin crowd had gathered at the church to dutifully work their way up and down the hills. I waited for Sydney on the sidelines as the walk began. He walked over to me and invited me to sit down in a lawn chair. We had been sitting for only a moment when he said quite bluntly what was on his mind.

"Do you know about racism here?" Sydney asked.

"Well, yes," I said.

"Blacks and whites," he said with a long, heavy stare, "don't mix much."

I answered his statement with a stare.

"Do you understand that?" he said forcefully.

"Yes," I answered, a bit surprised. Maybe as a grandfather of seven children, he often spoke with such reproach. My regular attendance at his Baptist church, the warm smiles and hugs, had somehow lulled me into thinking my color had worn off a bit.

"A lot of what has happened here with the plant, it's racism," he said, softening his tone. About then, a group of white men went roaring by in a big diesel Ford truck tailed by an extended cab Chevy. His eyes moved away from me and shifted to the road.

"Those trucks that just passed," he said. "They were over there running their dogs on the land over there. They thought my land was part of that land across the road."

"You told them to get off your land?" I asked.

"Yes," he replied.

"Were they okay with it?" I asked. Hunters had guns. Maybe it wasn't just my white skin that was agitating Sydney that morning. Next door to his land was the Hickory Plantation, an expansive parcel dedicated to bird dogs and hunting.

"They said, 'Yes, we thought this was a part of the plantation,'" Sydney said, retelling what happened. "I said, 'No, this is the Jackson estate.'"

"You cannot be fearful," he then said to me. "Fear is not of God, it is of the devil. And so when you come to be fearful, you deny God is power in your life. So you either live or die. You stand for what is right, or fall for what is wrong."

Ownership of land afforded power to Sydney, but a power that could slip away without his vigilant defense. Since the days of Sydney's grandfather, southern land idealism had wrapped itself in a plantation culture rooted in white ownership and access. On the eve of the Civil War in 1860, the Burke County black population outpaced the white population: 2.4 slaves to every white person.[35] But a minority within the white minority, the 26 percent of white men who owned slaves, ruled. They frequently took their families on summer retreats from their Greek Revival–style mansions situated in the "Grave Yard of Georgia," a nickname for the county because of its wet landscape, thick with disease-carrying mosquitoes.[36] White farmers without slaves were dependent on plantation owners for access to cotton gins and to markets where they could sell their crops. Slave owners' economic dominance increased their political control and simultaneously convinced or coerced poor white farmers into taking the war-trodden path of civil war.[37] Georgia governor Joseph Brown warned that if slavery declined, "The wealthy would soon buy all the lands of the South worth cultivating [and] . . . the poor would all become tenants . . . as in all old countries where slavery does not exist."[38] The land rhetoric worked. At the Secession Convention in 1861, three planters and slave owners representing Burke County voted to secede from the Union.

The binding of wealthy planter interests to those of yeoman farmers and whites fell apart as the war progressed. Plantation owners dodged the draft through slave-owner exemption laws, and often planted cotton rather than staple crops to feed the Confederate ranks. In southwestern Georgia, one man wrote to the governor, warning that "among the common people" there was "a strong union feeling."[39] In Macon, Georgia, another reported that the area was "full of deserters and almost every man in the community will feed them and keep them from being arrested."[40] In 1863, a slaveholder's wife complained to the governor that Burke County desperately needed a police force to "see to it, that [the planter] class of citizens are protected, & not left to meet a fate worse than death."[41] The Civil War laid bare the animosity between the rich planting elite and the society that it ruled.[42]

The Civil War cost Georgia dearly: countless dead, and $275 million lost in damaged property and cropland, a burden squarely placed on the backs of non-slaveholders. Those most apt to be Union supporters in Georgia—the independent small farmers that remained—bore the brunt of General Sherman's march, and the haunting aftermath of a landscape ravaged by war.[43] Looting Union troops took at will "corn, beef, mutton, sweet potatoes, poultry, molasses, and honey."[44] Drought and depressed commodity prices worsened the status of smallholders who could not afford to pay back their land mortgages. As for those with the most money, President Andrew Johnson restored the land to the slaveholding class, which had led the charge for war. The historian Steven Hahn writes, "Although the abolition of slavery struck the planting elite a telling blow, in a rural society control of land as much as control of labor defined the boundaries of social relations."[45] Slaveholders had lost their grip on their human pieces of property, but not their property in land.

For Sydney's family, the tenant farming structure rendered it nearly impossible to acquire land in the years following the Civil War. Widespread starvation and death threatened former slaves, who had little access to land or cultivation tools. Former slave owners and merchants moved swiftly to take advantage of freed slaves' vulnerability and to maintain their workforces.[46] Slaves became tenants. One labor contract signed between a Burke County planter and two women and a man ordered the former slaves "not to leave the place without permission, and to work six days a week—lost time deducted for sickness if protracted over one week." In return for their labor, they would receive a third of the cotton crop and a fourth of the corn and other grains, three pounds of bacon or its equivalent in syrup, and "one full peck of meal per week." Whipping, as in slave days, continued in Burke County.[47] Restless ranks of landless black and white tenant farmers led some plantation owners to fear a political union across races. One wealthy planter warned that a revolution was imminent: "Seven tenths of the people of the South would vote for ... confiscation of Southern property. Every negro would vote for such a proposition and a vast number of the whites."[48] Racial divides kept such a populist movement from gaining widespread political traction.

Acquiring property from white landowners required what Sydney called the "decency" of "good whites" willing to sell. "When Big Papa bought this land back in 1919 and 1928, he wanted his family to stand on their own," Sydney explained to me as we moved into the basement of the church, away from the traffic roaring past. In the cool relief, Sydney pulled out a clattering metal chair for me to sit in and respectfully removed his hat.

Sydney's parents were the exceptions. Although Burke County in 1910 had the largest percentage of black residents farming in Georgia, a full 94 percent of such operators were tenants who did not own the land that they farmed.[49] And they lived in dire poverty. Largely disadvantaged by policies that limited or prevented landownership, and a reign of terror that persisted through the Jim Crow era, black rural tenants moved away in pursuit of factory work in the North. In 1900, 82.4 percent of Burke County's population was black, the second-largest percentage in any Georgia county. Between 1900 and 1910, 8.9 percent of the black population left Burke County, signaling a sea change from the 150 years of black population growth. Despite this exodus, Burke County's population in 1930 was 77.7 percent black, the twelfth-largest concentration of African Americans in the Black Belt region of the South.[50]

Only later did landownership among black farmers follow the path

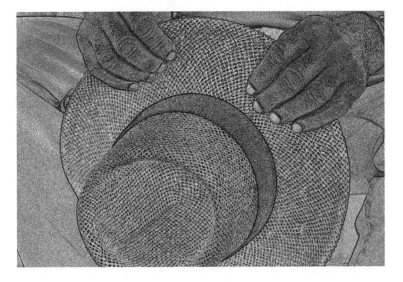

taken by Sydney's family. The first percentage increase in partial or full landownership for black farmers came between 1935 and 1940, when it jumped from 9 percent to 13 percent. In the same time period, the number of black tenants decreased by 27 percent as the Great Migration continued to alter the southern rural and northern industrial landscapes.[51] By 1964, nearly a third of black Burke County farmers owned their land.[52] Managers, who formerly oversaw large plots of ground for absentee landowners and planters, largely disappeared.[53] Whether black or white, more Burke County residents became landowning farmers and enjoyed the fruits of their own labor on their own land, although the numbers were small relative to the massive farming populations of the past.

While most black tenants left after being denied rights to land and the ownership of the fruits of their hard labor, those that remained and achieved landownership saw their private property rights as sacred. Violations of such rights were treated as sacrilegious.

"So this is our heritage," Sydney said of his land. "Our heritage is the spirit that Big Papa taught his children. But also, you've got to have the physical side in order to be able to maintain some place to live. That was his desire for his family and that has gone down through the generations."

Regardless of the political tides of control—Uchee, Spanish, French, Patriot, or Confederate—a moral value undergirds the interdependence of democracy and private property rights, what I call the "landownership ethic." Across gender and racial differences, persisting across the folding landscape of power is the belief that the possession of land is a sacrosanct right achieved through self-toil or heritage to ensure independence and sustenance in the face of scarcity. While I identify the landownership ethic as critical in the context of purchases and takings for nuclear power production, its relevancy is part of the context of any development, including hydraulic fracturing and pipeline construction.[54]

About three decades ago, Sydney and his family lost 300 of the 700 acres that Big Papa and Mama purchased. Big Papa and Big Mama could not write or read, and when they died, they verbally left the land to their children. This practice, often referred to as "heir property," is widespread among rural African Americans. The legal scholar Thomas Mitchell and the rural sociologists Conner Bailey and Jess Gilbert have thoroughly documented how this tradition is stigmatized by the current legal system.[55] Since Sydney's parents kept with the heir tradition, they did not appoint an executor for the property, but assumed that their word would suffice. Shortly after the children took control of the property, Georgia Power approached the family to acquire land for a railroad necessary for construction of the first two reactors of the Vogtle Power Plant. Most of the family refused to give them the right of way, although a few were ready to sell.

"Then, through the court system, they ran it through," said Sydney. Sydney described how the court appointed an executor for the property in 1973. Most of the nineteen children who inherited the land refused to sign a document that allowed the court to appoint an administrator. But some of them agreed. "Some of my aunts. They were from the old school that the white man is right," Bianca Weathersby, Sydney's cousin, later told me, explaining her aunts' trust in the judge's appointment of a black administrator. "The white man knows, la-de-da-de-da. So, they signed it."

Despite the family conflict over the appointment, Janard Kimbrel became the executor of the property in part because, as Bianca put it, "[He] was a black man! We thought that meant somethin'." Kimbrel informed the family shortly after he became administrator that to resolve alleged family infighting, he would sell 300 acres of the land to a corporation offering $450 an acre. When Bianca's brother tried to step in and buy the land at the same price, Sydney and Bianca said the administrator refused. Despite the wishes of the family, the administrator approved the selling of the land to a corporation called Eagle Mountain Resort. The same day, Eagle Mountain sold the land to Georgia Power and promptly dissolved, according to Bianca and Sydney. The original inheritors of the land never agreed to the sale, but the administrator did. Sydney and his family have been fighting to get the land back ever since.

To try to bring attention to the wrongful taking of his family's land, Sydney wrote a letter to county officials that powerfully articulated the morality he saw wrapped up in landownership. He described the origin of that morality during his grandfather's time: "Blacks knew the power of prayer and the power of owning a piece of property. They made the word of God their foundation. We look at land as provision through which our Lord and Savior (Jesus Christ) provides food, clothing, and shelter for our family." Sydney went on to state in the letter that most importantly, Big Papa "wanted his family to stand on their own." As with the Israelites in Abraham's Promised Land, holding ownership over the ground brought with it the capacity to survive, literally, to eat—a concern not too far from home for Sydney's father, born to freed slaves. Reclaiming that power, that land, was foremost on Sydney's mind.

"Within the framework, when you are in Satan's domain, the only light that you have is Christ," Sydney said, explaining to me his sustained effort to reclaim the land. "And Christ has already defeated the devil in everything that he do. The only thing that we can be is patient. And keep on workin' and doin' what we need to do, in order to do our part. And that's what we've been doin' ever since 1986 when Georgia Power obtained that land. We have been fightin' it ever since."

The framework that Sydney spoke of saturated its legally coded routes for justice with impossibility. The framework was evil to Sydney, a part of Satan's domain. The fight continued, but outside the law and the government, both part of the framework's realm. There, God offered defense of the landownership ethic. "There seems no way that we can get into them," he said, going on. "Everything that we do, they close it up or shut it down. So we lay aside our trust in God. That's what we have. And we are not goin' to stop. As long as we are alive, we'll stand our ground."

For Sydney, God provided perhaps the ultimate venue for justice in the face of a compromised state. He saw his landownership rights as closely tied to democratic legitimacy, and the government had failed him. To understand the point of intolerability for the exploited, E. P. Thompson coined the term "moral economy" to identify how "outrage to these moral assumptions" results when "a popular consensus as to what were legitimate and were illegitimate practices" is violated.[56] In such cases, even though markets and the ruling class may demand that a higher price be paid for a certain good, such as bread, revolt ensues because the populace agrees that it is simply intolerably high. You can exploit a person only so far, the logic goes. Similarly, the landownership ethic identifies a baseline of the moral economy. Sydney understood the $450 an acre given for his family land as unacceptable because the sale was never agreed upon—in short, it violated his moral economy of land. Further, his access to and ownership of land provided moral goods hard to translate into a simple price tag. Land provided him power and authority and security against outside encroachment. His landownership was undergirded by an ethic that profit couldn't speak to.

Sydney's land rights, democratically backed by the moral righteousness of John Locke and his liberal companions, ceased to exist against corporate claims to profit. Rather than a willing player in a market exchange, Sydney was unwilling. Rather than a right to property practiced in a "free market," Sydney's use of his property was dictated by markets that privileged profit over all other motives. Rather than a willing market exchange, his was a forced one. With those changes, a key component of liberal democratic rights ceased to exist: one's capacity to use private property however one chooses. The right to private property became perpetually subject to profit's rule.

★ ★ ★

Profit's authority over private property alters the notion of a right in two main ways: First, it allows corporations to force a sale by threatening or using eminent domain; second, it imposes pecuniary gain as the ruling justification for claiming private property rights.

The problem with profit's authority is that people often own property for a variety of reasons that have nothing to do with making money. Like Sydney, they keep a family farm for sustenance or even sentimental reasons. They own a car to get somewhere. They keep a tiller in the garage so they can annually sow a garden. They own books to access knowledge. They buy a round of drinks to reciprocate with friends at a bar. They hoard gold or guns in the case of the apocalypse. The state enforcement of profit as the preeminent value undergirding property rights can violate other norms and reasons for owning various forms of property.

The gap between people's moral backing of property rights and the state's imposition of moneymaking as property's ultimate purpose bodes poorly for democratic and economic legitimacy. The economy bases itself on a web of social relations that inform the buying, selling, trading, and keeping of property. A person's right to property depends on a sometimes unspoken moral code to legitimize ownership. There is simply too much property for the legal apparatus to protect itself, even in the age of the police state. The functioning of markets based on property rights consequently depends on the moral agreement by people at large that such a legal apparatus is legitimate.[57] Milton Friedman explicitly notes that property rights are the very foundation of capitalism, as does Hernando de Soto in his critique of dead capital.[58] Capitalism can work, de Soto argues, only in a legal regime of private property that enables types of economic activity to be legible to the market.[59] But since not everything can be coded and enforced by a state that upholds private property regimes, morality is a must. When property is forcibly taken or a sale imposed, thanks to the legal favoring of profit, that moral legitimacy falters.

Property as a subjective right underscores the authority of both an economy and a democracy, and this legitimacy informs the moral economy of democracy. By the "moral economy of democracy," I mean the baseline of morality that shapes the interdependence of economy and democracy. James Scott, in his rich work on acts of resistance and antistatism, captures the moral economy of those ruled as the on-the-ground view of "economic justice and their working definition of exploitation."[60] By bringing democracy into dialogue with the moral economy, I aim to capture the mutually constitutive role of the state and the economy in shaping private property, and consequently the morality that ultimately upholds market and state survival.

In part, the role of the government in creating and upholding markets is old news. Karl Polanyi notes that for the last five hundred years, the "deliberate action of the state" created international trade, enforced the mercantile system, and "freed" trade.[61] The current market economy is driven by "the expectation that human beings behave in such a way as to achieve maximum money gains,"[62] a state-market apparatus that often requires rescuing when the "satanic mill" of profit threatens the sustenance of the society it rules. What isn't discussed so much is democracy as a state form that upholds private property as an individual's right undergirded by the people's moral backing. Private property is not just a thing. As a right, it connects with humanity—the human right, or will, to use private property as a person pleases, what lawyers call the capacity to assert a right. If people decide that the state's defense of property rights is immoral, capitalism stands on shaky grounds.[63] Morality backs the legal system defining property rights. And democracy's legally coded

66

morality underscores the capitalist economy and the markets familiar from everyday life.

My term "moral economy of democracy" helps determine the point of exploitation, the place where the state's imposition of economic and democratic injustice intertwine to form a level of intolerability for the oppressed. The landownership ethic is a case in point. Treating property as only about profit transgresses on the morality of the economy and the very morality of democracy. In doing so, short-term profits come at the expense of long-term democratic legitimacy, especially in rural America, which is regularly subjected to corporate land claims.

★ ★ ★

Today, Southern Company and the state of Georgia own 42.6 percent of the land within a five-mile radius of the Vogtle nuclear reactors. Of the sixty-nine residents and local landowners I interviewed, sixty-three mentioned land loss as a local injustice. Of the six exceptions, four had moved into the area in the last decade and were unaware of the takings; one, a private contractor for Georgia Power, approved of the takings; and the last was a former politician who saw the takings as legitimate.

The landownership ethic plays a central role in the moral economy of democracy, drawing the idealism of Locke into modern values. Elijah Bennett, a white landowner who lives in the Shell Bluff area, drove me back over a steep, rugged dirt road to his family's prized property: twenty-seven acres situated around two ponds filled by a natural spring. Every descendant of his great-grandfather, now five or six hundred people, owns part of the property, a site for family reunions and community gatherings. Elijah explained, "If you can keep your land in your family, it doesn't matter how poor you are, you are not poor as long as you have land, even if it's worthless. It's not worthless to you." Such an understanding cuts through a polarized view, popular in academic circles, of private property as either preserved commonage or land doomed to privatization. In support of the latter logic, Polanyi stressed that "land is only another name for nature," a "fictitious" part of the market, and that to include it in the mar-

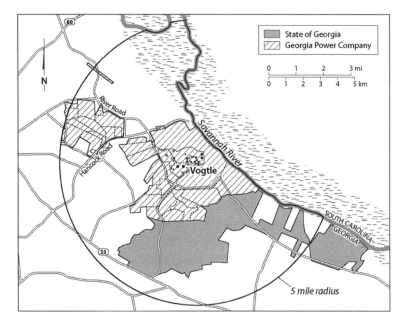

According to 2014 parcel data, in the five-mile radius around the plant,
the State of Georgia owns 6,192 acres (9.675 square miles) and Georgia
Power owns 8,500 acres (13.37 square miles). Together, Georgia Power and
the State of Georgia own 42.6 percent of the approximately 34,488 acres.
Bill Nelson.

ket is to "subordinate the substance of society itself to the laws of
the market.[64] And in part, he was right—privatization enabled many
deleterious social and ecological consequences. Yet simultaneously,
private property can serve any purpose, depending on its capacity
to be an expression of a person's right. If rights of ownership favor
intergenerational transfer, a vibrant ecology, and justice, then profit's
perpetual accumulation and dispossession falter. What becomes important is the larger legal apparatus that shapes what kinds of rights
are privileged, rather than privatization alone as the important point.
Privatization for profit is the problem.

Corporations have markedly changed the ability to use property
for much other than profit. They can take property and then ac-

cumulate it, backed by a legal system that favors profit as progress. Those living in Burke County see profit's rule as immoral. Dean Sawyer, a white man whose land rests within five miles of the plant, said: "They'll take whatever they want. Greed, it's a nasty thing. They'll never have enough." Dave Ray, a black man in his forties, explained: "For Vogtle, it's about the dollar. That's all it is." After a boat ride up the Savannah River, Beau Turner, an affluent white man, took me to view his cabin, a community gathering spot for annual parties; it is surrounded by land acquired by Georgia Power. Beau had pictures of his property dating back a hundred years as well as photos of recent community parties, and he regularly offered the cabin as a place for friends and neighbors to fish. From the river, Beau pointed to the Vogtle reactors peeking over the corner of his property. He said that he didn't know how he was "lucky enough that they didn't take this." The threat, though, was always there, making his treasured spot a tenuous one. "I am thankful every day I still have this. I don't know what I'd do if they came this far," he finished tearfully. Beau mentioned that he had put various rights, including mineral rights, into the hands of different owners, trying to complicate the taking of his property if it were threatened. The preparations consumed him, as did his distrust of the "corrupt politicians," which informed his view that the government was "bloated."

The moral economy of democracy demands more than the rule of profit. Beliefs in beauty and sentiments that locals privilege can prevail over bottom lines and profit potential. Private property as a right is morally just, but private property as a mechanism of profit (or only a market mechanism) is not necessarily just. Dave explained, "I am looking at a portion of the beautiful countryside. That if you wake up in the early morning, and you ride, and the sun is coming up, there are some spectacular views. When the sun goes down, and all during the day." He paused for a moment and said, "We are talking about people's lives and their homes." As Thompson writes in his description of the moral economy, Dave was informed by the "belief" that landownership represented "traditional rights or customs."[65] In her study of a Philadelphia community, the sociologist Debbie Becher finds that residential outcry against the use of eminent domain opposes neoliberal ideology by drawing on values associated with home and neighborhood to defend personal private property rights.[66] Family, home, and beauty exist in the moral economy. They offer a type of rationality that affronts profit.

Like the sentiment of beauty, the place-based sentiment of heredity lies outside the emotional grasp of the corporation's legal form.[67] Sara Tully, who traces her family back to the white founders of Burke County, recalled a Georgia Power official who approached her to buy land for the latest power lines. She prefaced the story by describing that he was part of the "dirty dozen" and appeared "shyster like." Sara saw her independent success as affording her insight into the situation, as well as the ability to see through corporate bullying. Her private property access was about more than profit—it was a right connected with moral values that she sensed to be superior to monetary value.

"I have been around a lot," Sara said. "I have owned my own business. I have been in retail management. Sales management. I had him pegged from the get-go. He was, like, 'Oh, well, all we need is a couple acres,'" Sara described. "I said, 'That's gonna ruin the property.' He was very vague. 'Two acres,' he says. He continued to play his little game. The more I got out of him, it started to sound like five acres. He was like, 'Well, why don't you just sell the whole property to me? 'Cause that land ain't worth anything.' He said the wrong thing. I looked at him and I said, 'That land was worth everything to my father. Therefore, it is worth everything to me.'"

The land's worth to the acquisition agent was minimal: sandy pine tree soil that would serve the single purpose of carrying a power line. Sara opposed his approach to her understanding of the land as a timeless connection with her father, now dead. She later called it "sentimental value," attached to her childhood memories and, most of all, to her father, who grew up a "farm boy." The land sustained her connection with that history. In Sara's view, the acquisition agent lacked ethics, playing "his little game" to try to take what symbolized her heritage and history. Her landownership, in contrast, was underscored by an ethic that Sara opposed to the tunnel view of market value that the land agent and his corporation represented. She had a moral code. And in her view, Southern Company, a profit-seeking corporation, did not.

★ ★ ★

The private-public corporate combo has created a fundamental challenge to people exerting their rights to private property according to their moral economy. As explained in chapter 2, the government's privileging of economic development and industrialization facilitated the rise of corporations as governmental authorities but nonetheless ones that failed to return profit to the public purse. To accommodate this process, the meaning of public use and public purpose changed dramatically.

If the corporate expansion over public purpose and private profit stopped there, profit-seeking corporations might not be such a substantial affront to the moral economy of democracy. Perhaps the legal creation of what I see as "for-profit property," like shares, derivatives, and securities, could stay in a sphere of corporate trade and not overpower the right to own property for other reasons. Perhaps limited liability could apply only when corporations squared up against other corporations, without dispossessing humans, who still bore liability for their own actions.

But corporate powers have not stopped there. On top of awarding them public and profit rights, the judiciary recognizes corporations as people.

Profit yet again played a key role in gaining corporations additional democratic rights. Profit made it seem as if the pursuit of more money wasn't only a human right, but *the preeminent* human right. With it came the value-laden notion of economic rationality, according to which the pursuit of profit was "natural." The germinal Supreme Court ruling on the matter goes back to 1886, when the Southern Pacific Railroad took Santa Clara County and neighboring California counties to court. At stake was whether the county could tax corporate shareholders more than it taxed the property that a person directly owned. Southern Pacific Railroad, powerfully endowed with public rights of eminent domain, argued that corporate individualism enabled human individualism, drawing on Thomas Hobbes's theory of liberalism. Shareholders had as much right to profit from their corporate interests, lawyers argued, as ordinary persons did from their property. Moreover, Southern Pacific's lawyers argued that the market should be left to determine that value, even though the markets they referred to had been constructed by their corporate client. Why, then, should corporations not have the same rights or legal status as people do if the businesses are simply motivated by monetary gain? Morton Horwitz remarks that when the Supreme Court heard the case, its awarding to corporations the status of people was "disquietingly brief":[68] "The court does not wish to hear argument on the question whether the provision in the Fourteenth Amendment to the Constitution, which forbids a State to deny to any person within its jurisdiction the equal protection of the laws, applies to these corporations. We are all of the opinion that it does."[69] Capitalizing on the very amendment that had made Sydney's grandfather a citizen, the corporation made the first gain in individual rights that would later enable it to dispossess his family. Theoretically and legally, the marketized version of corporate liberalism continued to overtake a private property regime that allowed for values more nuanced than simply monetary gain.[70]

From that point forward, the preeminence of the individual as a subjective person retreated in American jurisprudence and legislation. The corporation made its ascent as the individual best suited to achieve profit, which became the ultimate motive of a market society. The Supreme Court ruling in *Hale v. Henkel* (1906) noted "a clear distinction between an individual and a corporation, and the latter, being a creature of the State, has not the constitutional right to refuse to submit its books and papers for an examination at the suit of the State." Nonetheless, the Court proceeded to give the corporation Fourth Amendment rights.[71] The Court, though, did not go so far as to rule that corporations or their officers could exercise the Fifth Amendment right against self-incrimination. Still, a corporation could claim protection against unreasonable search or seizure. In practice, by gaining such rights, the corporation could better shield its private records from the public eye. Four years later, the US Supreme Court collapsed state-level limitations that constrained corporate rights.[72] In *Ludwig v. Western Union Telegraph Co.*, the Supreme Court ruled Arkansas's higher tax on out-of-state corporations unconstitutional. Justice Harlan reasoned such law "would deny it the equal protection of the laws and deprive it of its property without due process of law."[73] Corporations, public in their initial form, had rights increasingly equal to those belonging to humans.

That initial awarding of corporate personhood continues to be expanded. Economic development and making money are so confused with the ultimate ends of society that fictitious legal creations pursuing profit are treated as everyday people. In 2014, the Supreme Court ruled that corporations have religious rights and can use their beliefs to justify not hiring a person who does not share them.[74] In the *Citizens United* (2010) ruling, the Supreme Court again built on centuries of jurisprudence treating corporations as individuals to argue that they have the free-speech right to donate to political campaigns.[75] Deft lawyers cleverly press the extension of human rights to the corporate form through narrow legal jurisprudence, making profit's rule ever more pervasive in ever more corners of democratic and everyday life. Meanwhile, the scales of justice that favor corporations bring democracy ever closer to a breaking point—a breaking point for the moral economy familiar to Sydney, Sara, Dave, Dean, Beau, and Patty, who find themselves unable to compromise on their most deeply held principles for the sake of a profit-seeking legal apparatus.

★ ★ ★

Faced with what I see as the "four dimensions of corporate power"— preeminence in the pursuit of profit, preeminence in property rights, preeminence over the public, and preeminence in its status as person —the prospects of Sydney keeping his land did not seem good.

"Why haven't you just given up and sold the rest of the land?" I asked Sydney.

Sydney smiled in return, his teeth pearly white and perfectly even.

"Why haven't we just given up?" he said, repeating my question. "Heritage. You can go through struggles in life," he said, as he balanced his hands on his knees under the table and leaned toward me. "God can bring you to the point where just because you don't see no daylight at the moment, you don't have to give it up. You need to continue to stand, because for me I understand that this is not my home. I am just a steward of it while I am here. I am going to do my best to keep it going, because this is our family," he said. "And you have got to have some place to stay. Being under the foot of the man? We don't need to be under the foot of the man."

"Are you ever scared?" I asked him, thinking of the monstrous dominion he attributed to Georgia Power.

"No," he said. Despite the life-shattering repercussions of his story, peace reverberated around him. "Fear is of the devil, but reverence is of God," Sydney said again, stressing the moral of the lesson he was trying to teach me. "When we first went in Vietnam, we had to land on the runway, but we couldn't see the runway for the smell of gunpowder and smoke. We landed where we had no idea where we were goin'. You couldn't see no ground or nothin'. I was over there a few days, we were out there in the shed, and they started shellin' all around us. That brought me to the point where either I stand for God, or I be afraid and kill myself. What I mean by afraid is that fear gettin' inside of you. It will kill you. So I prayed and asked God not to let it get on the inside."

"So if I die, I die," he said, letting the silence hang for a moment. "If I live, I live," he finished.

I shifted my eyes to the pink silk flower arrangements scattered on the metal tables in the church basement. The ladies thoughtfully rotated the types and colors with the season.

"I try not to be afraid. But do it cross my mind?" he said. "Yeah, it crosses everybody's mind. It's the fool who'd say not to be scared sometimes. You don't let it stay down. If you let it stay down, it takes advantage of you. I pray to God to remove it. I am his child. He will take me back to where I need to be at. The devil will try to get inside of you. But Christ is love."

Sydney was ready to wage a moral battle to defend what he most firmly believed in, with or without the backing of his compromised state. The moral economy of democracy had been irreparably violated. The deal of defense, in exchange for deference, between the ruler and the ruled was broken. Burke County was turning away—away from a state no longer protecting the rights it held dear.

"In this area, you got poor whites and poor blacks," Sydney said as I pulled my eyes back toward him. Those living a stone's throw away from him were white. "And who cares about them? The poor?" Sydney asked. "God cares about them," he answered. "And they are his children. But when men begin to progress in society, they forget about those people. But the meek shall inherit the earth." He calmly explained, "We are fightin' spiritual warfare. The spirit of God is in this land. It is in the people."

You know how the government do. You know how the system is.

—Moses Dixon

"Mr. Bailey," Sydney said with welcome, leaning his tall frame against Mr. Bailey's rusty maroon Oldsmobile.

"Yes, sir," Mr. Bailey replied with a gold-toothed smile.

"How you doin'?" Sydney asked,

"I'm doin' all right. How you doin'?" he asked as he began a steady and prolonged look at me, leveled from beneath the tattered rim of a red baseball cap.

"I'm all right. This is Loka," Sydney said, with a casual nod in my direction.

"Hello, I'm Loka," I said, moving forward and extending my hand. I had been standing on the side of the road in the brittle grass, waiting for an invitation. "It's nice to meet you."

"You too," he said, reaching up from low in his seat, hunched over a bit with age. His plaid printed golf shirt bagged over his shoulders.

"She's lookin' around this area right here," Sydney explained, "lookin' at what's going on right here. And I was tellin' her that your land started right here," he said, gesturing at the piney tree line. "Is that right?"

"You wantin' to buy it?" Mr. Bailey said, keeping his eyes locked on me.

Sydney chuckled, clearly amused. The whole purpose of our winter walk was for me to see the land takings. We had wandered up the road that split his family's original plot in two. Rye fields edged against Sydney's lovely home, forming a thin blanket of green before we hit the creek and then worked our way up the valley to the top of the hill. That was when Mr. Bailey spotted us.

"No, I'm writing about Georgia Power," I answered, deliberately limiting the kind of information about myself that might put Sydney crosswise with a neighbor or spread unwelcome stories.

"So you wantin' to buy some land for Georgia Power?" he asked without restraint.

I laughed lightly in response, shaking my head no and waiting for Sydney to take over.

"No. Basically, she's just lookin,' seeing what's goin' on," Sydney said aloofly. He often talked in riddles, carefully avoiding but other times piercing with incredible veracity what troubled him the most.

"These plots are for sale," Mr. Bailey said, gesturing up the road and throwing me off the scent of his own land. He pointed in the direction of a house with the roof about to fall in.

"Two plots for sale?" Sydney asked to clarify.

"No, just the one. Split by the road," Mr. Bailey replied.

"What they askin' for it?" Sydney asked.

"$55,000 for 33 acres," he replied.

"We only got $450 an acre for this right here," Sydney said, barely tilting his head. Mr. Bailey knew good and well where the family's former land began and stopped. "That's all they gave for ours."

"They took that from you," Mr. Bailey said, with full attention on Sydney.

"They took it," Sydney said. He turned away from Mr. Bailey and me, facing the hill we had just come up. The car sputtered, waiting.

"Yeah, they took it. They took all this, so . . ." Sydney said quietly, trailing off.

"I wanted to stop and speak to you, man," Sydney said, regaining himself and bringing the conversation to a close.

"It was nice to meet you," I said.

"Take care now," Sydney said, patting the roof of the car, as Mr. Bailey pulled away.

Thirty years hadn't dampened the blow. Not for Sydney. And Mr. Bailey knew it.

★ ★ ★

There is something uncomfortable about democracy as we live in it today. We talk of the majority (often used interchangeably with the holistic notion of "the people") as the righteous ruler. If the majority wants electricity, and if providing that service requires a few people to give up their land or health, then the few should sacrifice for the whole. Under the judgment of the majority, perhaps Sydney is selfish. Further, perhaps a generous soul (unlike Sydney) would give freely to serve "the people." Sydney lamenting, contesting, and condemning his land loss is just another tired case of a "not in my back yard" (NIMBY) activist, the majority might contend.[1] One who loves electricity until the costs of it come home to roost in more than the form of a power bill.

How did American democracy get to the point where standing up for one's personal rights became understood as an affront to the broader collective good?

The short answer is that the democratic state's rendering of most things and people into numbers has created such a state of affairs. I call this the "rule of numbers." People, ecology, or really anything can be added or subtracted, and all that matters in the end is what comes out of the equation—more or less. The long answer requires a closer look at why the rule of numbers at first glance seems to be a perfectly reasonable way for a state to uphold law and order.

At the heart of the rule of numbers lies cynicism about people's motives. Four centuries ago, the English theorist Thomas Hobbes wrote that there is no natural, moral entitlement to human rights. People aren't born decent. People, rather, are akin to beasts. The horrors of the English Civil War had taught him as much. Without the state's presence and its capacity to limit the less savory proclivities of humanity, life is a long, brutal battle for survival.[2] That is why the state exists: to govern people's selfish tendencies. Through the state, chaos and anarchy are controlled, and civilization can reign.[3] A favored few may come to acquire better habits than the beasts' through the arts of civilization. But for the most part, the mass of democracy's denizens could easily threaten those enlightened few if left to its own ends.[4]

If one begins with the premise that people are basically bad, the state then exists to rule over the innately selfish rather than to rule for the well intentioned. From this premise, Hobbes pondered how the state could manage bad intentions, and he came up with the idea of the contract. Every human, it seemed to Hobbes, was "in the market for power."[5] Even the very worst people could agree that their selfish tendencies led inevitably to violence and war. And that was not good for anyone. So Hobbes proposed that people form a contract with the state to regulate and manage their selfish tendencies. That agreement, he argued, would be the basis for citizenship and the marketplace. The state exists to regulate the bad intentions of people, and people behave according to the rules it enforces.

Ironically, something seemed blatantly immoral about this proposition, even to those who adhered to its tenets at the time, like Jeremy Bentham, a philosopher and economist who wrote in the late eighteenth and early nineteenth centuries. The very admission that a state needed some sort of moral purpose in order to exist defeated the Hobbesian premise that people care about nothing more than themselves. But instead of reworking the basis of the state so that it would serve the good intentions of people rather than impose its rule, Bentham worsened the situation. Bentham attempted to make the Hobbesian state moral by arguing that if it served the greatest interests of the greatest number, it was morally sound. Bentham said as much in his definition of community:

> The interest of the community is one of the most general expressions that can occur in the phraseology of morals: no wonder that the meaning of it is often lost. When it has a meaning, it is this. The community is a fictitious body, composed of the individual persons who are considered as constituting as it were its members. The interest of the community then is, what?—the sum of the interests of the several members who compose it . . . An action then may be said to be conformable to the principle of utility, or for shortness sake, to utility, (meaning with respect to the community at large) when the tendency it has to augment the happiness of the community is greater than any it has to diminish it.[6]

Under Bentham's theory, people were reduced to numbers with interests that had no actual moral worth (that was fiction), but were relative to a person's selfish pursuits. Community denoted the greatest sum of those pursuits. Utility became the moral good that captured the most interests of the most individuals. And thus Bentham laid the foundation for utilitarianism.

This kind of ruling apparatus was and remains incredibly convenient for elites. Bentham had already devised a way for his utilitarian formula to include nonhumans as individuals. He proposed the joint-stock company as a means to achieve his own utilitarian goal: make himself more money.[7] With individuals as shareholders and most money as community interest, the state's pursuit of profit suddenly seemed like a fairly legitimate purpose. Altogether, the rule of numbers leaves the public good, and even private good, relative to how much they add up to, casting the nuances of humanity and morality aside.

Even for utilitarianism's adherents, the moral superiority of the rule of numbers has been somewhat hazy. Bentham's "sum of the interests" created a banal formula that left the outcome vulnerable to ill intentions. Openly admitting that the production of profit was the purpose of the state did not sit well with the ruled. Just before the US Civil War, the English economist and theorist John Stuart Mill came up with the greatest happiness principle. He merged the idea of happiness with utility, transforming utility from an open-ended formula and into a feel-good equation. He clarified that everyone had a right to happiness (synonymous with an absence of pain) except in the case of social expediency. Then, individual rights to happiness would have to submit to the right "of the majority among them."[8] He argued that utility, or the plain capacity to get things done, would be severely constrained if an individual's happiness could stop the train of society's development. Stalemate didn't suit the engines of industrial progress. Sacrificing a few people along the way would inevitably be good for everyone in the long run, utilitarians contended. Further, utilitarianism suggested that what was greatest in number was the most efficient. But it has ended up meaning that what is aggregated into the highest sum is the most efficient. These are not the same thing. Efficiency can happen in situations with a small number of features, but the rule of numbers has enforced the idea that the most-in-one-place is the best-in-one-place. My use of the phrase "rule of numbers" helps capture how for-profit goals are privileged, without the misleading claim of "utility" that accompanies utilitarianism.

The mistaken conjoining of utility with most-is-best makes a further error, what I call the "faulty opposition between private and public rights." The greater-good principle implicitly pits the good of everyone against some individual's happiness. This is where Hobbesian pessimism sneaks in, from right- and left-leaning thinkers, even today. Left-leaning planners and lawyers look to curtail private rights in order to achieve more public goods.[9] This is the latest form of what was at one time called American republicanism, which advocates for the "people's welfare" and the "public good" in the face of the "private greed of small ruling groups."[10] The assumption is that to control the worst of society, the central state—an overarching apparatus—must lead the way with an iron hand of enforcement.[11] Samuel Adams said as much when he saw the state as "a moral person, having an interest and will of its own," that could stand up to those less well intended.[12] Today's right-leaning thinkers conversely argue that public rights must be curtailed in order to sustain private ingenuity and self-ownership. In doing so, they draw on the classic tenets of liberalism, arguing that the purpose of the state is to defend individual rights. In either case, both lines of logic assume bad intentions, either the public menacingly taking from a hardworking citizen or a greedy citizen holding out on the public. Landowners just want to make money. The public just wants to gain on the back of the individual. In either case, such a way of thinking operates on a utilitarian logic: we are ruled by numbers, public or private.

In essence, this faulty opposition raises a fundamental question: why can't private rights—even rights to property—serve the public good? Private property can serve the public if the state chooses to facilitate markets that enable wealth distribution instead of wealth consolidation. Then, the basic ideals that inform why people stand behind democracy, ideals that usually are fairly esoteric, have a chance to flourish through property, not in spite of or against it. Ideals such as freedom, equality, liberty, happiness, and bounty are the kinds of notions that leave Jeff, Neill, and Dale in a state of bureaucratic discontent, the kinds of norms that come with the moral economy of democracy, the kind of faith that makes the taking of Sydney's land, even after generations of persecution, still sting. These people hold democracy accountable to a higher standard that informs their own interests. Their private rights are consequently very much part of the public good, and vice versa.

From this vantage, it becomes clear that the utilitarian justification of the state is not only wrong, but has also regularly incorporated the worst of intentions into our guiding framework, rather than the best of intentions from a public and a private perspective. And in the process, billions of lives and goods and ecologies and rights have been sacrificed, all under the mistaken assumption that these sacrifices were necessary.

The damaging rule of numbers largely plays out in two ways. First, the state enforces profit's rule by passing laws and building markets that ultimately serve to make money. In essence, the state stipulates which kinds of property rights are important. Currently, property rights that produce profit are valued as the ultimate aim of society, often against other important ends like health, sustenance, family, and security. Take the case of slavery. Lives were privatized for this reason: to produce private profit. Instead of rooting property rights in positive moral goods, the state favored rights that served profit, setting the basis for slavery historically and modern dispossession, too.

Second, the rule of numbers demands that a lesser people (again, confusing morality with numbers) be put in a subservient place. This is perhaps the most basic contradiction of utilitarianism. The system of numbers is based on the assumption that people are bad, but then argues that the majority will righteously figure out what is best for all. At the nexus of this faulty reasoning lies a group of people regularly demonized as the bad ones and punished accordingly.

Slavery yet again serves as a key historical example of such cruel reasoning. John James Jones, the wealthiest slave holder in Burke County on the eve of the Civil War, vehemently defended slavery to the House of Representatives in an 1860 speech: "The southern States, with one voice, say [slavery] is right; that it is the proper condition of the negro . . . It is necessary that the supremacy of the white man should be acknowledged, to evolve the greatest good and happiness to both races."[13] The rule of numbers uses social Darwinism, a teleological least-to-most argument, to justify its rule. While the particular group designated as lesser can vary in utilitarianism, a group of people treated as second class remains a consistent feature. Utilitarianism justified the slavery, bondage, murder, rape, and pillaging of a people by arguing that the resulting "good" was for the greatest number of the public and the private benefit of property holders.

In short, what does the rule of numbers, private or public, do? By assuming the worst, it creates a system that enables the worst, feeding itself from its own false premises.

★  ★  ★

While plantation slavery no longer exists, the rule of numbers still operates through what Tocqueville identified as the tyranny of the majority, the state-imposed rule of the most over the least, which continues to shape institutions and society.[14] That rule profoundly affects the life trajectories of those who, like Sydney, bear the intergenerational burden of minority status. After Sydney and I spoke to Mr. Bailey, we decided to follow his car back toward where we came from.

"They say about how this land is so poor and so bad, how would anybody want to live on it," Sydney said, his tone even and his pace steady as we walked on. "How could anybody want to farm on it? That's what they say when they want it," he said. "Well, why do they want it?"

He looked at me pointedly, and I nodded in return. He didn't need to further explain. Call land desolate, vacant, unfertile. They were all convenient adjectives that served the user's purpose of taking the land.

"We still own those four acres," Sydney said as we passed by a strangely vacant lot surrounded by pine trees. A mesh-wire fence stood about four feet high around a lonely pile of cinder blocks and tin resting near a few spidery trees. I had seen the house when I drove by it two and a half years ago. It was in sad shape then, but still standing.

"A house was there, my uncle lived here, in the home house I grew up in. We tore it down about two years ago because of the taxes. See the signs down here," he said, pointing to a string of flimsy white signs across from the acreage they managed to hold onto: "POSTED: NO TESSPASSING: Georgia Power Company."

A tired looking "Beware of Dog" sign tied to the front of a locked gate barked back at the orders. But the tiny space's "No Trespassing" sign lay belly up in the grass.

"That was all open land," Sydney said, pointing to the tall pines looming over the short grass inside the fence, dormant and dried up in the winter months. "They planted those pine trees, and those pine trees, and those pine trees right around the house here, to keep him in there," he said as he swung his walking stick around. "And he had no way out."

The fence appeared to close in whoever was inside of it as much as it kept Georgia Power at bay. "And all those years, he had farmed this land," Sydney said, gesturing again to the lanky trees. "Farmed that land, and farmed that land there."

"That must have been a terrible loss for him," I said, trying to imagine the clay exposed and Sydney and his family tending the land.

"He took it to his grave."

"What does Georgia Power use this land for?" I asked.

"Nothing."

"Do they hunt on it?"

"They be huntin' on it."

"Who do they let hunt on it?"

"The good old boys that are in the clique."

"Are they mostly white?"

"As far as I know."

"I think you thought that was a stupid question," I said, responding to what I viewed as a smirk.

"The only stupid question is the one you don't ask," he said kindly in return. We continued to walk down the clay road in silence, him knocking the smooth stick gently against his tan corduroys.

While slavery had ended, the majority's oppressive reign over the minority continues via the state and its imposition of the rule of numbers. That rule comes not only through top-down enforcement, but also through a majoritarian belief structure that operates on the idea that what is best for most is best for all. There, the minority has little breathing room to oppose the oppressive rule of the majority, which stifles dissenting opinions. Tocqueville called it the fencing of the mind that "leaves the body alone and goes straight for the soul."[15] Majority tyranny claims ideological superiority.

The racial and cultural rankings imposed by colonialism and later by the developmental state exemplify majority rule ideologically and institutionally. States used the teleological system of ranking ways of living and cultures to legitimize colonization in the so-called New World, to legalize slavery, and to lay the groundwork for the developmental project, which relied on big markets and transnational corporations.[16] For such a project to reign, people must believe that "developed" countries like the United States, which operate under the rule of numbers, are superior to those that do not. At the end of the day, those who don't look like the cultures associated with the rule of numbers become affronts to it. Majority thinking can then terrorize anything that does not live like or look like what the rule of numbers demands.

"I need to keep a stick on me like you do for snakes," I said to Sydney as we continued our walk.

"There are snakes and things around here," he said. "But the only thing you really need to worry about are two-legged snakes. That's the main ones to be concerned about, snakes. A snake is a snake. If you catch him when he is cold when he is out there, and he needs to be warm or something, you take him and bring him back to life. Once he gets warm again, he is going to bite you. It is the same thing with those people. There is no difference. You have blacks and whites the same way, in all different races. God says everybody who smiles in your face is not your friend. Judas betrayed Jesus Christ. We have people here that it is all about their position of power and who I am. It doesn't matter about who I hurt and how I sin. If you cannot be true to yourself, how can you be true to others?"

Sydney's biblical reference put an ecological and human face on majority rule and anyone who dared question it. His nephew had laid it down for me in starker terms. "You better be careful," he said, "because they might run you out of town. And I am just being real with you. I'd hate for something to happen to you down there. 'Cause it does happen. People down here . . . accidents happen to people when they feel they are trying to change their way of life. When they are trying to interfere with what they got." Those veering from majority rule, even those like me, embraced by the white majority for my color, could become vulnerable by questioning its rule. And as Sydney's nephew clarified, the majority drew on not only the power of whiteness, but also the power of money: both outcomes of the rule of numbers. The legal scholar Cheryl Harris says as much when she details how property functions as whiteness through reputation, status, use, and, perhaps most of all—exclusion.[17]

"There used to be black farmers here everywhere. They owned the land. They didn't have no way to fight the system," Sydney said, as we continued to walk down the hill.

"When you say the system, what do you mean?" I asked him, and our eyes caught.

"The one that has control," he said. "The one that's in my pocket."

"So the government is one," I said, trying to throw something specific after he grew quiet to see whether I was correctly understanding his reference to the dollar bill.

"Who are the government?" he asked me.

"White men," I said, taking a stab. That was who was printed on the currency, literally.

He nodded in return.

In 1966, the final year that tax parcel data in Burke County was divided according to race, 41 percent of the landowners in the Shell Bluff area where Sydney lives were black. And those owners claimed 26.4 percent of the acreage. Yet my analysis of tax parcel records revealed that assessors valued this property at a higher share of the overall market value: 36.8 percent.[18] The land in the region does not vary substantially in quality, and by most local accounts, the least fertile land was owned by black families. But black-owned land was taxed at 39 percent more than it actually accounted for, an example of the tyranny of the majority through the rule of numbers.

The perpetual rule of numbers creates a system of oppression, as Sydney calls it. The system delivers majoritarian rule over thought, law, and action, culminating in interpersonal and institutional oppression. The system at one time rendered Sydney's family chattel property. When his family gained freedom, it still took a generation for them to attain landownership. And even when they did, the land that they owned was taxed at a higher rate. Elijah Anderson and his coauthors write that the racial caste system, first identified by one of sociology's founders, W. E. B. Du Bois, continues to shape everyday relations between blacks and whites, "perhaps with unusual clarity in the South."[19] In the words of the sociologist of race Eduardo Bonilla-Silva, racism describes the "racial ideology of a radicalized social system."[20] C. Eric Lincoln describes the interaction between the state and culture aptly: "That Blacks in America may perceive differently is in no small part because they are differently perceived."[21] As critical race scholars, including Angela Harris and Richard Delgado, write, the persistence of racism is more than an individual problem relative to the uneducated or the exceptional. The legal institutions of America, part of a broader hegemony, can reinforce racism.[22] The "system," as Sydney calls it, captures the rule of numbers: the perpetual demand for minority sacrifice ideologically, institutionally, and culturally.

Moses Dixon, a black man who lives in the Shell Bluff region, used the same language of a "system" to describe land loss. "They bought some of my cousin's land. The Joneses," Moses said of Georgia Power. "They bought all the Joneses' land. They moved up the road right up from there," he said, pointing out the window of his double-wide.

"Did they pay a good price?" I asked.

"No, they didn't pay no good price," Moses replied.

"They just really took it," Veeona, Moses's wife said, jumping in.

"They took it because, like I said, for that plant to move there on that land, what the land is worth now, see how much they pay Burke County for the taxes on it," Moses said, referring to a $19 million property tax check paid by Georgia Power to Burke County. A photo of the giant check had just been proudly featured in the local paper.[23] "Now, that land, if they wanted it that bad, none of them guys down there shouldn't have to work nowhere, in their *lives*. You are talkin' Plant Vogtle. You talkin' billions, trillions of dollars."

"They probably paid that Jones man maybe $500 an acre or somethin'," Veeona added.

"Like I said, if they didn't sell the land, they were going to take it regardless," Moses said. "You know how the government do. You know how the system is."

Moses, too, understood the system as encompassing the government, which was compromised as much as any other authority, even Plant Vogtle, with its billions of dollars.

"You see, if they were white and they took the land, they'd get sued. For real," Moses's son Jamal said, explaining further what the system signified.

"But if they are black, they don't worry about it," Veeona explained to me. "They just take what they want. If you die here, they just take what they want and it's a hush-hush thing. I don't think they paid him what was rightfully his for that land. 'Cause he had a lot of land."

Majority rule fosters a fencing of the mind that leaves such unjust practices nonetheless justified, at least for many of those comforted by majority status, like Raleigh Langston, a white man and local politician. After we had Sunday dinner with his family, Raleigh took me out to his shed to show me a map of the land that his family once owned.

"The land finally just got away," he said, staring down at the map. "I wish I owned it all. All of that is poor land. The only thing it is fit for is pine trees. We had a many good times down in those woods before there was anything there. If I still owned it, I'd have it in pines," he said. "Pines, and do a little huntin' on it. Those times are passed. One generation is gone since then, and another generation will take over. Time keeps rolling. And real fast too."

"Did they pay you well for the land?" I asked.

He looked up as my question broke through the fog of the past. "Oh yes," he answered. "We were ready for them. We did real well. We got it up to $600 an acre. Now the blacks, they didn't get much. They threw whatever they wanted down on the table, and the blacks had to take it."

Raleigh did not suggest that black families receiving less for their land was wrong. In fact, although he in the end regretted selling his land, he still had what Cheryl Harris calls a consolation prize: because he was white, he could rationalize that someone else was below him. In doing so, Raleigh fell into the majority thought collective even as he suffered a loss. Majority rule prospers on the faulty opposition between minority and majority rights, by making what seems good for oneself require a sacrifice from someone else. In Raleigh's case, black families receiving less money seemed fine, as did his own receipt of more money. This temporary benefit conceals a long-term loss, even for those in the majority.

The "most"—in this case, the white majority—remains perpetually vulnerable to what I call "majority cannibalism," in which majority status can never be assured, but always shifts to fulfill the rule of numbers's latest need to feed. Raleigh, as a white middle-class man, stood with some majority affluence over Sydney, but he still had to sell his land and capitulate to the for-profit state. He knew the company could use eminent domain if he refused. Although he received $150 more an acre, he now regrets selling his property.

Sydney captured this irony of majority cannibalism through a story about hurricanes. "Those big storms that came through. First it came through the blacks down in New Orleans. Then it came through to the whites in the North," Sydney told me, contrasting Hurricane Katrina with Hurricane Sandy, and the system's response to the events. "Then it's the storm of the century. It's the amazing thing about life," he said, shaking his head as he looked down at the red dust around his feet. "Hatred will kill you," he told me. "You know that," he said, almost questioningly, as he looked up at me.

I nodded at him as we approached his home. The storm hit the black folks first, and then it hit the white folks. Weather didn't respond to utilitarian motives, but infrastructure certainly did. If only the white majority had paid attention the first time, they could have been better prepared for the cannibalism of majority rule. In failing to realize humanity's shared vulnerability, what could have been prevented was instead left to fester. Eventually, the injustice that first fed on racism came back on those who had turned a blind eye to its wrongs the first time around.

"It will kill you dead. Hatred," Sydney stressed again with more conviction. "It eats you from the inside out."

Sydney's storm analogy captured what had happened locally with landownership. For the most part, everyone lost except the corporate-state. Since 1966, only 13 percent of the land stayed within a family, black or white, while 87 percent of it changed hands, according to surname.[24] Yet within that loss, there were some surprising gains. More black-owned land stayed within the family in the tax districts where Raleigh and Sydney live. Black families that owned land in 1966 and still own it today count 9,360 acres to their names. In contrast, white families who managed intergenerational transfer held on to only 6,311 acres. In those fifty or so years, white families' share of the intergenerational land has decreased by 58 percent, while intergenerational black family holdings have increased by 23 percent.[25] All were dispossessed to a large extent, regardless of race. But white families from that time have even less to show for it now, an example of majority cannibalism at work.

* * *

Majority cannibalism is fundamentally backed by the utilitarian orientation of the Hobbesian democratic state. This is a basic backdrop for the enactment of tyranny. Yet even as dispossession mounts and violations of the shared moral economy of democracy pile up, divisions between "more" and "less," "minority" and "majority," help maintain its rule.

Vorice Inman once felt a fuller embrace of majority benefits. As he invited me to sit on a couch by the front door of his trailer, he explained how his family had moved from being tenants to owners.

When Vorice's father returned from serving in World War II, the Federal Land Bank gave him a loan to purchase the 115 acres that we were sitting on—the only land that he still owned. Before the war, 58 percent of white farmers in Burke County were tenants. By 1956, with the help of such policies, the trend reversed, and a majority of white residents were farming land that they owned.

"We had another place further back that was 253 acres," Vorice explained, with a shake in his voice. He had just returned home pale and weak from a bout of chemotherapy.

"Was that by the river?" I asked. To get to his place, I had woven around on a bright red Georgia clay road toward the muddy waters of the Savannah. After knocking on the wrong door down the wrong road a few times, I finally found my way back to his white double-wide, nestled between the trees and the cotton fields.

He nodded. "Well, Georgia Power has it now. Well, the state [Georgia] bought it, and then they got it. The state sold it to the power plant."

"Did the state make you sell?" I asked.

"Yeah, they wanted it for Georgia Power. It was to build that plant back there in the early seventies when they started. It has had a real impact on the community down here."

"Tell me what it was like growing up here," I said.

"Well, you worked for what you got," he said. "You had to get out there in the field and work to try to make a living. It was tough times. Picked cotton, hulled peanuts, pulled corn. We had to work, all of us had to work. It was just a time back then in those days that you had to work for a living. There wasn't no such thing as a handout. It is like the Bible says, if you don't work, you didn't eat."

Jesus seemed to be in agreement, as he stared up stoically from the front of a gold and cream Bible resting on the coffee table between Vorice and me.

"But now, there is so much government giveaway. That is what is wrong with the world today. Too much giveaway," he said, pausing. "But it is hard times now, too. The dollar don't go anywhere. Just the cost of stuff is so high, and the dollar ain't worth a third of what it ought to be. It is just something else. And it is just because of the government. The government has their foot in everything. Too much control," he said pointedly. "And it don't seem to get any better. It is awful."

"But this thing back here," he said, motioning behind his head in the direction of Vogtle, "it was an impact on us when they first started with it. You got more people here, more crime. It is just different from what it used to be, just 100 percent. You used to go off all day long and leave your front door open, and nobody never come in. But, do it now. You won't have *nothin'* when you come back. Because they'll *break* in."

"I looked at some of the numbers," I said. "And Burke County has a higher rate of violent crime than the county housing Atlanta."

"They don't do nothin' to them when they put them in and sentence them," he replied. "If you are in the clique with the good ole boys in Burke County and Waynesboro, you can do anything you want to and get by with it. You just got to be in the clique. It ain't nothin' but a money game. If you got the money, you can get by with anything. That is right," he finished with a nod.

The clique, otherwise known as the elite insiders pulling the strings, surfaced in lots of local talk, including that of Sydney, Vorice, and many others. In describing the loss of land rights, black and white interviewees used words and phrases such as "good ole boys," "corrupt," "system," "we don't count," "government control," "clique," "money game," "no power like Georgia Power," "greed," "didn't need us," and "shysters."

The prevalence of corruption was agreed upon across races, but the linguistic understanding of blame diverged markedly according to race. Elijah Anderson and his coauthors stress that moving forward from the racial caste system of the past means "meeting head-on the assumptions held by blacks and whites themselves, framing them within a racial structure and historical context and then suggesting ways to move forward."[26] White residents attributed land grabbing to government failure and corruption; for black residents, the situation was much more entrenched—a system, likened to endemic minority vulnerability beneath that crushing majority.

"Do you remember what it was like when Vogtle came in? Did you get to hear about it ahead of time?" I asked Vorice, trying to figure out whether, as with Sydney, when his land was taken, it was unclear who was doing the taking.

"No, no!" he said, furrowing his brow and slightly shaking his head. "There was talk ten years before it ever started that they were going to build something back there."

"But it was just a rumor?" I asked.

"Well, yeah," he said matter-of-factly. "And then they started to buy up parcels of land."

"And who were they? Was that Vogtle or the government?" I asked.

I was having trouble tracing who the purchaser of the land was. Who or what was to blame was critical—a piece of what sociologists study to understand what gives rise to collective action. Diagnosing and understanding a problem rests on what you attribute it to, and eventually shapes how people try to deal with that problem.[27] The landownership ethic carried across the color line from Sydney to Vorice; the two men shared emotional attachment and a deep sense of loss in relation to their land, a big chunk of why people sometimes come together to push back against a wrong they share.[28] But when it came down to pinpointing blame, their pronouncements were wrapped up in their racial majority and minority statuses.

"They was the state," he told me at first. "See, the state turned around and sold all this land to the power company. I know there was one fella back there, he is a distant cousin of ours, he had a big ole fish pond back there," he said, gesturing to where a few rusty tractors rested in the sandy front yard by the dirt road that headed toward the river. "And he held out as long as he could, but they finally made him sell. I mean it was a *nice* place back there. When the government get behind something, they condemn everything. You got to sell. I thought one time they were going to take this here. They come right almost to the line back there." He pointed out the back window, east to west. "They didn't come quite far enough."

Vorice seemed to be suggesting by his use of "they" that the government was to blame for the taking, in line with his comments about the government's meddling control. He had just mentioned that the government did the condemning. Certainly, it made some sense. Without eminent domain, Southern Company couldn't claim the land.

"They own the ground all the way back here?" I asked, matching his general descriptor. We were sitting nearly five miles from the plant.

"They own a good chunk back there," he said. "Then the state owns most of the hunting park back there. They've got a wildlife area back there."

In a matter of two sentences, Vorice switched the meaning of "they." He referred to the government as "they" when talking about condemnation. But someplace after that, without clarifying, he switched to "they" meaning Georgia Power. He clarified as much when he said, "Then the state owns . . ."

Vorice had linguistically merged private interests with public authority. Indeed, the need for distinction had in part evaporated. But his linguistic choice to attribute blame to the government, rather than the corporation, is a significant one. It reflects one majority status he enjoyed through the democratic state, simultaneous with its more recent rendering of him into another type of minority. The government stood apart from the system, corrupt as an actor of control, but not an actor within a pervasive climate of oppression. For Vorice to recognize that his experience of injustice was couched in perpetual minority exploitation, he would have to recognize racial oppression. And Vorice did not. Vorice still felt some semblance of majority authority through his skin. Further, the government had helped his family—enabling his father to get land through a low-cost loan. Unlike Sydney, he did not bear the persistent reminders of slavery. For Vorice, the government was an enabler as well as a disabler that had recently played a part in dispossessing him. The state's condoning and enabling of the power plant transformed it into a force for taking and controlling rather than protecting and empowering.

"Why did they want all that ground?" I asked Vorice.

"It used to belong to a big timber company, back in the early days," Vorice said. "Probably in the forties. And they sold out to another timber company. And they went broke, and then they sold it to the state for a wildlife management area. The state started the wildlife management area, and then Vogtle came in, and they got part of it."

Here is what is so powerful about the rule of numbers and the eventual majority cannibalism. Some people are always treated as the Other, but they do not stand alone for long. Profit regularly seeks to capitalize upon the next group possessing something it can gain from. To rationalize the treatment of some group as lesser, majority cannibalism relies on "othering" strategies employed by the majority. The majority's othering of injustice can make sacrifice out to be something that the minority deserves, as in the case of slavery or, today, rural targeting. Othering creates what the scholar Kimberlé Crenshaw calls a "straw man." In the case of affluent white domestic violence victims, she points out how some say that they didn't expect to be battered wives. They imagined domestic violence in the lives of the poor and racial minorities.[29] Black families, as Raleigh casually reported, simply receive a lesser amount, no questions asked. But when the injustice comes at the doorsteps of white families, as it did in Vorice's case, the blow is less expected. The blow seems to be a shock, when in fact the system's capacity to enable such blows in the first place rests in the same utilitarian state that has long demanded black sacrifice.

"There were a lot of little, small farmers back there where that *thing's* at," Vorice said with visible disgust. "They bought *all* of them out."

"I don't understand why they wanted that land," I said, still bewildered. Like Sydney's land, Vorice's rests well outside the range necessary for plant operations, although in a different direction. Further, a power line on one farm does not take up hundreds of acres.

"For expansion," Vorice quickly replied as he continued to lean back knowingly in his recliner.

"You think they are going to expand all the way down here?" I asked.

"Oh," he said, moving his hands from the arms of the chair and resting them on either leg of his polyester pants and rocking forward "it won't *ever* be enough what they've got back there. Once these two reactors get there, that ought to be the limit. There isn't enough water flow down the river. There was an article in the paper about these, and the ones in South Carolina, they are the last ones going to be licensed for a while. But you know, that can change any time. It's not a done deal."

"That's just politics," I said.

"That's exactly what it is. Politics and money. Just like I said, if you are in the clique, you can get anything you want, and get it done."

"Did you know when your land was taken that it was going to be used for Vogtle?" I asked him.

"No!" he exclaimed, shaking his head. "Nobody knew. There was nothin' ever told about who was buying the land until it was done to us. There were a lot of those folks that didn't want to sell." He paused. "It isn't nothin' but ole sandy dirt." His voice got a bit louder and the shaking increased. His blue eyes began to swim as the sorrow threatened to take him over. "But to a lot of people it was home."

"Of course," I said softly. As with Sydney, it had been decades since the takings. And as it did for Sydney, the pain of loss remained terribly sharp.

"They come in there wanting to buy all that land, and Southern Company probably bought some of it themselves. If they can't buy it, they'll get the state to go in there to condemn it. And then what are you going to do? You can't do nothin' with it. It's just like, I give you what I want you to have for this land, and you just get up and move. 'Cause we are gonna have it to do what we want to do. The dickens with you.'"

"That must have broken some people," I said.

"You know, it's not right." He looked away from me. I tried to give him a moment of peace by resting my eyes on the carpet below my feet.

"It's not," I said, to him and to myself.

"But there ain't nothin' you can do about it," he said. I looked up and the tears had backed away.

★ ★ ★

Vorice's and Sydney's absolute sense of loss, even helplessness, suggests something shared: a violation of their most treasured rights, a transgression upon their moral economy, a corrosive sadness, a betrayal by authorities.

Where they diverge substantially is in their pronouncement and enactment of blame through the tools and language that the democratic state provides. Here, the recent nature of the wrong of land loss, versus the long-lived accumulation of perpetual loss, is the critical difference in Vorice's and Sydney's experiences. Patricia Hill Collins defines oppression as "any unjust situation where, systematically and over a long period of time, one group denies another group access to the resources of society." She goes on to clarify that "race, class, gender, sexuality, nation, age, and ethnicity among others constitute major forms of oppression in the United States," especially when these forms of oppression "converge."[30] What is critical for understanding oppression is how long it has lasted, and how it builds up and perpetuates systematic losses, as Sydney describes. For generations, Vorice's family had been poor, but they bounced back after World War II, only to lose again.

Amid this substantial difference in oppression, I find it crucial to explore what about Vorice's and Sydney's dispossession is also shared. In the five-mile radius around the Vogtle reactors, 66 percent of the population is white, and 28 percent is black. In the larger context of Burke County, 49.6 percent of residents are white and 48 percent are black. Thus, an interracial understanding along with a racial understanding of majority encroachment on rights is necessary in order to find shared opportunities to confront such injustices in decidedly mixed-race communities. To do so, I find it helpful to pinpoint another type of utilitarian rule taking place across the color line, what I call "profit's majority," the marketized majority of money that increasingly constitutes "public purpose" as well as "private rights." Leslie McCall writes in her assessment of intersectionality studies that there is some danger of falling prey to categories at the expense of complexity in understanding oppression. Recognizing this risk, I emphasize that this type of vulnerability in for-profit democracy is not fixed, but shifts according to utilitarian demands. Bentham's logic

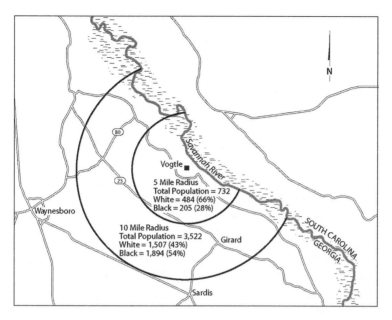

Racial and population demographics around the Vogtle reactors. Bill Nelson.

knows only an upward trajectory, moving from a majority of people to a majority of profit under an imperative of "best for all."

In a situation of public for profit, the worth of all communities is beholden to revenue. In a sense, it is similar to the slash-and-burn orientation of rainforest cropping systems. The rich forests are harvested, the land planted hastily with crops for a few seasons until the soil has no nutrients left to give, and fixing the situation would either require an investment of inputs, or a change in production regimes. Both of those methods cost, and so the tiller moves elsewhere, leaving a barren land that was once rich in ecology, and moving elsewhere to feed its insatiable appetite.[31] Such an analogy is symptomatic of the modern US economy. Profit extracts while there is money to be made, only moving on when there comes a better deal. Countless empty storefronts in countless communities attest to the thirst for short-term profits that drives a whip behind American society today.

This incessant, moving, and consuming characteristic of profit leaves even local elites vulnerable. Comfortable majorities can suffer minority status when they have something that profit wants. Those US citizens most accustomed to majority status, such as David, a white man who is president of a prominent political council and owner of a well-respected enterprise, can find themselves falling prey to profit's rule.

"Vogtle has been sort of a mixed bag," David Horsnby said, as we sat across from each other in his shop. "Not everybody thinks that all of the change has been progress. It has had a down side. This used to be a sleepy little town, and now it has more going on. But that is not unlike other areas that don't have nuclear plants, I guess. But we've got a lot going on without Vogtle."

"Have you had any land taken through eminent domain, or land that you had to sell when the plant came?" I asked David boldly. Patty had recommended that I speak to David. She had cheerfully informed me that finally someone else was going to bear the burden of Georgia Power's transmission lines this time around. And David was one of them.

"Funny you mention that," he said. "I am going to make a call today to a man. They are putting a high line in that is going across our farm. I expect to be in litigation with Georgia Power, or Southern Company, whatever, over that."

"You are going to try to stop them," I said, assuming litigation meant prevention. David had money. He had political power. He must be waging a battle to keep his property, I thought.

"I know I can't stop them," he said. "I just don't want them to pay me nickels and dimes."

I sat quietly, stunned. With years of racial majority status behind them, white citizens generally have substantially more resources. In stark contrast, Sydney and Mr. Bailey have a heritage of centuries of oppression, leaving them with significantly less money or the political means with which to level a fight. Vorice, whose family for generations were poor white tenant farmers, falls somewhere in between, as Nancy Isenberg compelling establishes.[32] Distinctively, those who are poor or are of a racial minority have known what it is like to live without the rights afforded to those of greater means or of a different skin color. David, however, had credentials that suggested immunity from injustice.

In the for-profit democratic condition, though, minorities are not exclusively long-lived ones. Tocqueville once suggested there existed a series of restraints on majority rule for the white men who constituted the citizenry at the time that he wrote, in the 1830s. America lacked a centralized administration to serve the demands of the crowd. Because the country was large, it was difficult for the majority to centralize its power, or for the majority's passions to take the country by storm. Tocqueville saw America as a place of middle people: no common center, no vast metropolises, no immense wealth, and no extreme poverty. Equitable distribution tempered the majority's will. People could empathize with one another. Because numerous people were morally invested in maintaining the rights of all, the political scientist Louis Hartz thought minority protections were well taken care of: "The American majority has been an amiable shepherd dog kept forever on a lion's leash."[33] Tocqueville did not. If all else failed, he saw lawyers and the courts as protectors of individual rights in cases when the majority wasn't up to the task.

Much has shifted since Tocqueville's time. Few factors remain among those he saw as integral to tempering the majority. American bureaucracy has expanded dramatically, becoming inseparable from the democratic state's administrative apparatus. America remains large, but a majority of people are now concentrated in urban areas, and only a dwindling minority lives in rural places. The switch has been dramatic. The United States in 1880 remained largely rural: 72 percent of its fifty million citizens lived in the countryside.[34] Thirty years later, in 1910, rural dwellers still held a comfortable majority: 54.4 percent to 45.6 percent. By the 1920 census, urbanites were the majority.[35] The developmental project has left rural people relatively few in number. Forty-six states now are majority urban, with only Mississippi, Maine, Vermont, and West Virginia having majority rural populations.[36] Overall, only 15 percent of the US population lives in rural areas. People have concentrated in the cities—changing the dynamics of majority power and minority interests.

Further, those rural places are regularly treated as a write-off in the utilitarian codebook. The infamous Cerrell Associates Report, commissioned by the State of California in 1984, explicitly encourages the targeting of rural places: "Not surprisingly, the profile of the 'least resistant' community goes something like this: small, rural town of less than 25,000 population; with many residents employed by the polluting facility, therefore deriving significant economic benefits from it; politically conservative, with a free market orientation; disproportionately above middle-aged, with a high school education or less; and with nature exploitative occupations, i.e., farming, mining, low-income."[37] Rural places are poverty pockets sought by industries.[38] The government has legalized the explicit targeting of rural places. The *Code of Federal Regulations* stipulates that nuclear power plants can be sited only in rural places, to control for risks.[39] Only 732 people live within five miles of the Vogtle plant, and 3,522 people live within ten miles, meaning the number of casualties would be fewer in the event of a meltdown. Rural people, relatively few in number, are rendered insignificant by the rule of numbers.

And America's wealth disparity is now significant. In 2010, the 400 richest Americans had a combined wealth of $1.37 trillion. The wealth of the poorest 60 percent, or 100 million American households, was $1.26 trillion. The United States has the most unequal income distribution of the twenty-six OECD (Organization for Economic Co-operation and Development) nations, once tax policies are taken into account. In the 1920s (the first decade for which these figures are available), the United States was one of the most economically egalitarian countries, giving America the image of the land of opportunity. In comparison, most European countries, such as Britain, were more wealth stratified at the time.[40]

And what of lawyers and courts? As chapters 2 and 3 detailed, for-profit motives have come to wield public authority over individual rights, even those of white property-owning men. Corporations are treated as individuals. A long trail of rulings upholds their authority over the sanctity of the human. The collective of the people, otherwise known as the public, is legally synonymous with profit. The judicial system too, it seems, has morphed into a tool of utilitarian dominance.

As Tocqueville's Middle America has faltered, and the reign of profit has taken over the meaning of the public good, any person who formerly enjoyed majority status can come to know a minority's plight. With the rise of profit's transient minority, one of Tocqueville's greatest fears has materialized. He warned that if the majority lost its "exclusive privileges" and was forced down from the "high station to join the ranks of the crowd," the government might not be able to handle the uproar, or even the anarchy, that would ensue.[41] Those who once knew higher status, even white property-owning men, can be deftly forced into a sacrificial position.

The fall for those formerly warmed by the embrace of democracy's rights is a steep and hard one, as David describes: "We have a lot of land that borders the highway," he explained. "In my lifetime, it won't be sold and developed. But I may have kids or grandkids who want to turn it into an upscale subdivision fifty or twenty-five years from now. And having a high [power] line certainly diminishes that value, even though they say, 'Oh no, it doesn't hurt anything.'"

"Who are you working with on it?" I asked. "Is it someone out of Vogtle? Or is it out of corporate headquarters?"

"They have hired people in the vicinity to handle it," he said. "And I have known the man handling it for years. They are using people that have some tie to the area. They are not having someone out of corporate that is cold and prickly. They want someone that has a little more warm and fuzzy glow about them than corporate. They didn't get where they are at by being dumb."

David took a sip of coffee and sat down his mug. He went on to explain that Georgia Power was offering him $3,000 an acre for thirty acres of his land. While $2,000 an acre was the average price for ground in the area, he thought the price was inadequate. It failed to cover what he called consequential damages to the farm and land after the lines went in. He will never be able to farm it, place anything on the ground over twelve feet tall, or put a permanent structure on it. David believed he should receive significantly more—$5,500 an acre.

"In fact, when they put a railroad in during the early seventies when they developed the plant, they more or less condemned about as much land on the northern end of the farm and put a railroad across it. So now they are going to go across it with a highline." He added, "And I know I can't stop it."

Neither of us spoke. David started to rustle his coffee cup on the table. His voice and gaze were smooth and even, devoid of emotion. He was hard as a rock.

"Does that make you angry?" I asked.

David laughed, and shook his head. "There again, all change is not progress," he said.

I later interviewed Georgia Power's land acquisition agent, a local forester who had an office in Augusta and whose family formerly owned land in Burke County. He told me that he was irritated with requests coming from those who were more affluent in Burke County, particularly "one individual," whom he left unnamed: "When I see people, it doesn't make a different to me who they are. Whether they make $15,000 a year or $1 million. We are going to treat them the same. And I get a little more peeved at people that think we owe them something than the ones that are realistic about it."

It wasn't always that way, David explained.

"What happened the last time they took your land?" I asked him.

"I think at the time they paid the going price for it. Daddy didn't want to sell it. It was a field. The first proposal they had for where they were going to locate the railroad was going to be near the house. It was going to devastate the farm. It would've come right through the whole farm."

"Did you get them to change it?" I asked.

"I didn't, no. And I don't think daddy had a whole lot of pull in it. I think there was a landowner also involved in the situation that had more political clout than the Butler family that made it be moved."

"Who would have that political clout?" I asked.

"Well, at the time, it was John Hurt."

"I haven't heard that name," I said.

"John Hurt was an attorney and a prominent Burke Countian. By then, I guess he was state court judge. I think his influence is what made it be moved to where it is now. And it is a more sensible location than down there, but I think Hurt is the one that did it. Of course, Judge Hurt is about ninety now, and has dementia and Alzheimer's. He doesn't know he's in the world."

"Would anyone have that political clout now?" I asked.

"Apparently not. For whatever it is worth, I can take what I'm fixing to tell you and a dollar and a half, and get coffee almost anywhere. But you are talking to the president of the Savannah River Regional Council."

"If anybody should [have the clout], I would think it'd be you," I responded.

"I would think so," he replied.

For-profit's appetite knew dollars and cents, not David's political title.

Nor his long-lived ties to the community. Nor his relatively comfortable income. He, and even those of substantially more means, can fall prey to profit, for there is never enough profit. Dispossession, even for David, could not be avoided under the rule of numbers in democracy.

"Does Vogtle approach you about different things?" I asked David. "As a council, do you have much interaction or control?"

"Control," he said, raising his eyebrows. "None," he said sharply. "They invite us to these [Nuclear Regulatory Commission] hearings. You know they want council members to come and combat the anti-nuclear people. The NRC and the Southern Company moderators at the meeting, they know them. If they stand up back there, they'll say, 'Alison, I'll get to you in a minute,' or, 'Hold on, Frank.' They want us to come and say, 'We really want Vogtle, and it's been a great part of our community,' and dah dah dah." David added, "I have been on the council soon to be twenty years. And when I first got on, there was more of a relationship with Georgia Power, Southern Company if you will, with the council then than there is now. They were more engaged. With this last round, it was more like they didn't need us."

"Why would they behave that way?" I asked.

"They didn't feel the need to do it, or the desire to do it."

"You'd think that could be kind of suicidal," I replied.

"Well, it's kind of like stopping that power line on your farm. What can you do about it? In fact, let me go get you a document and show you something."

David disappeared into a hallway, his leather boots, softened with age, clicking slightly on the cement floor. He returned with the formal offer from Georgia Power for his land. He handed me the letter. The letter warned: "This final offer is presented solely as a compromise for the purpose of concluding this matter without litigation and represents Georgia Power's effort to reach a negotiated settlement for this transaction easement." It continued, "If I have not received a response from you within ten days of this date of this letter, I will forward this letter to our legal counsel to initiate litigation proceedings to acquire the necessary interests in the above mentioned parcels."

"Oh, man," I said to David. "What a presumptuous letter."

"That date is April the tenth. Now on April the sixteenth, I get this," he said, handing me a shiny postcard inviting him to a Vogtle open house. "I guess because I am a member of the Savannah River Regional Council."

David watched me closely as I reviewed the documents. Red writing and a bright picture of future Vogtle Units 3 and 4 graced the front. An elegant calligraphy said: "In Celebration."

"They need to work on their housekeeping," I said to David. He nodded in return.

A month later, I was enjoying lunch at a pizza parlor with Patty when David walked by.

"Hi," Patty said. I echoed, "Oh, hello!" delighted to see him. He tipped his head toward me. Patty didn't waste any time. She turned around and said to him, "Did you ever settle with Georgia Power?"

"I did. They got the land." His dark, burdened eyes held my own for a moment. My delight collapsed.

Patty turned back around to face me and continued to eat her pizza, without a second remark. I watched David's back as he walked away. I looked down at my pizza and across at Patty, steady as always. I, for one, had lost my appetite.

A loss of a right was, indeed, a loss of a right.

Immunity from the rights-taking tentacles of for-profit democracy was hard to come by. Money ruled money. Utility ruled rights. Corporate power, allied with state power, trumped local authority, even for politicians. Patty, Lela, Moses, Veeona, Jamal, Sydney, Vorice, and David—at the end of the day, the rights of each fell to profit's demands. While the forced forfeiture of rights under for-profit power spread like wildfire, the shared denunciation of that forfeiture burned out, stagnated by the seductive yet fleeting embrace of the majority.

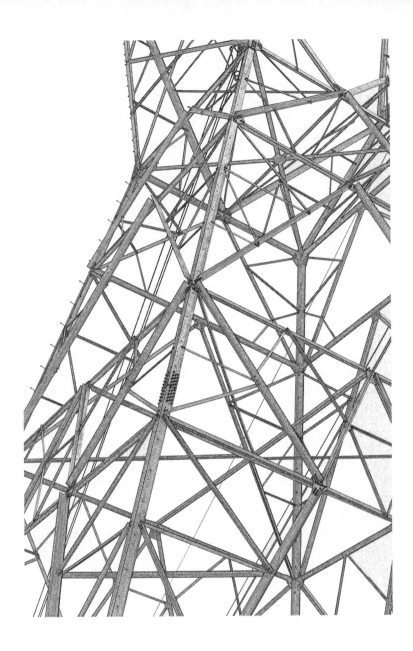

# Fallout

They call it progress. That's a word I've never really learned.

—William Gresham

When I first saw William Gresham, he was sitting on the sticky vinyl seat of an open-cab John Deere tractor, drenched in sweat and covered in specks of dirt and wood chips. Limbs and soon-to-be-logs of the pines he came to clear lay freshly cut on the ground. Behind his tinted sunglasses and the pulled-down ball cap, he was hard to read. Michael Brown's apprehensive introduction suggested something a little bit wild.

"Now, Loka, I am going to give you William's number," Michael said after he introduced me to William, dipping the L of my name to the point that it almost sounded like an R. William looked down at us as we sat clean and pristine in the shaded shelter of the golf cart Michael had driven across his property to check on William.

"You can give him a call if you'd like and arrange an interview," he said, carefully putting the ball in my court.

"I'll be free *any* time!" William replied, with a goofy grin that about ripped his reddened checks in two. Michael grinned back at him. I couldn't help smiling either. It was contagious.

"Want a beer?" Michael asked him. He had a loaded cooler in the bed of the cart.

"Nah," William said. "I'll wait until I'm finished."

"All right," he replied. "We're going to head back to the house."

"Nice to meet you," I called out as we buzzed off. William was still grinning. I heard the tractor start up again behind us.

"William knows more about Shell Bluff than anyone I know," Michael assured me as we drove away. Michael's wealth and education had gained him entrée among the local elite, while some of his friends were poor and working class.

"He's a good man," Michael said of William. "We've been friends a long time."

A few days later I arranged to meet William at the Burke Byway Store for an interview. Patty had begrudgingly given a kind review of William. He often stopped by her house to help with any household problems and to check on her. But he and those he ran around with would "shoot at about anything that moved," Patty complained, often with little respect for property lines. William's reputation for hunting was such that Patty bragged he had even taken a former governor hunting.

When I pulled up to the shop, I couldn't quite recognize the man I had seen before, his eyes then concealed behind the glare of the sun. Today, he was drenched from head to toe, meddling with something in the back of his massive white GMC truck, oblivious of the steady torrent of rain. His khaki cargo pants were sopping wet, and rain had soaked through his blue collared shirt to the white T-shirt underneath. His hat and sunglasses were gone. I halfheartedly waved, not certain whether it was him. As he returned the wave, I quickly parked the car, threw on my jacket, pulled my hood over my head, and hustled over to him.

He watched me approach, and we shook hands quickly.

"You want to go ride?" he asked me, leveling a steady stare as I paused.

"I'll grab my things," I responded, running back to the car to gather up my steady companions: a recorder, a phone, a notepad, a pen, and Mace.

I returned to the truck, took one giant step onto the foot rail, pressed in the metal button on the handle, and swung in, resting myself on the damp vinyl seat. William started up the truck, rattling it in and out of gear as we headed away from the store.

"You like sweet corn?" he asked.

"I do," I replied, studying his profile. He was older than I first thought. Gray was edging out the brown in his mop of hair. From the side, his profile looked like inspiration for the Greek statues of old.

"I've got some sweet corn and tomatoes in the back I want to drop by to Ms. Dessie, a real good, elderly black woman. She lets me fish and hunt on her ground."

William's daddy had taught him the streams, banks, and fields of Burke County. And he always taught him to share what you hunted, to give back to those who kindly allowed you on their land. "It's taken me years to earn the trust of the black community," he said. "They don't trust white men."

"I can imagine why," I said, thinking of the horror stories of rape and molestation I had heard from some older black women, and the undercurrents of race that ran through most of my encounters.

"That's right," he replied, looking over and catching my eye. "I have their trust now, and I've worked hard for it."

I, on the other hand, had yet to earn William's trust. It took an awkward, pointed conversation over the phone for me to assure him that I didn't work for Southern Company or DuPont, the former operator of the Savannah River Site, a notorious nuclear weapons facility. He figured I was fishing around on their behalf. And he was always busy. If I didn't accompany him to a job, most of my encounters with him would occur in the rain or the dark, the only times I could catch him free for a moment from work, fishing, or hunting.

"I still think you're a spy," he said, leveling a look at me from two thickly lined, drooped, amber-green eyes.

"Really?" I asked.

"No!" he said, smiling. "But you'd be a good one."

"You think so."

"Yeah."

"Why? I don't think I'm a very good liar."

"You don't have to be a liar. You just bring the truth out of a man."

I shook my head at him with a dubious look. "You haven't told me everything yet, I am sure," I returned, in what would come to be regular banter among William, me, and other men of the river, as some called them. A director of a local nonprofit had recently warned me that if I wanted to meet the men who spend their time on the waters of the Savannah, I would have to get used to the standard, overtly eager flirting. She said I could either put up with it or lose the connections. She noted that her husband could no longer stomach accompanying her to the river and listening to the remarks. Plus, she always had in her extended cab truck a furry, four-footed, hundred-pound companion.

The dark sky lit up with lightning as William drove down the red dirt road toward Ms. Dessie's place. When he reached the end of the road, he stopped at a small, tidy, one-story white house.

"Wait here out of the rain," he said to me. He jumped out and knocked on the door. There was no answer. I watched from behind the wipers.

As he waited for an answer and knocked again, I pulled up my hood and hopped out. When I walked up beside him on the steps, he raised a silver-flecked eyebrow at me.

"Looks like nobody's home," he said as the rain dripped off his nose. He hung the vegetables on the doorknob, and I followed him back to the truck.

"So what do you want to ask me?" he said as we drove off. Before I could answer, he tagged on a few more questions. "What do you think of Vogtle? Do you think it has a positive or a negative impact on Burke County?" I dreaded when this type of question was thrown at me, and it had happened fairly often when I first arrived. At this stage, I had been living in Burke County long enough that I really couldn't give an uninformed or neutral answer. The dilemma for me was how much to share with William.

"It seems like the results have been pretty mixed for folks. Some people have very-well-paying jobs, but it seems like a good number of those people live in Augusta. There is a lot of money that comes in from taxes." I paused, and William didn't say anything. "A lot of people lately have been telling me about the land that they lost to the plant," I added.

"Do you want to know what will shut Vogtle down?" he asked me brazenly.

I looked at him in shock and then stared at the foggy windshield, disarmed by the question. I could feel his eyes on me. He wasn't going to do the talking. He waited for me to respond, sizing up my intentions.

"Well," I said. "Yes. Can I turn on the recorder?"

"I'd rather you didn't," he responded.

"Okay," I said, wondering whether a little bit of suspicion still lingered in his mind.

"I am happy to take notes. It's no problem."

William was one of many former workers at Savannah River Site (SRS) who would talk to me only after receiving hearty recommendations from friends they knew and trusted. Most workers refused to be recorded. For Vogtle workers, trust in me came easier, and none whom I interviewed had a problem with being recorded. But those who regularly made the drive over the Savannah River to South Carolina and worked at what locals called the bomb plant were wary. Their experiences had taught them to be. Steve Pratt, a contractor who consulted for SRS and was an exception to the no-recorder rule, said, "If you rocked the boat, the first thing they would do was put spies on you."[1] Steve explained that the idea was to facilitate fear; if it wanted to, SRS could get out-of-line workers in legal trouble.

Having Vogtle across the river from the SRS, a producer of plutonium during the Cold War and now the largest nuclear waste repository in the country, made sense to planners of both facilities. The area was poor, rural, and there was plenty of land and water. SRS, though, is especially notorious for pollution. The Environmental Protection Agency has it registered as one of the most polluted sites in the country.

"What you really need to be looking at is the Savannah River Plant," William said, using the old name "plant" rather than "site." I started scribbling madly. "That water is completely radiated, from the swamp to the river," he said.

Sewage flowing downstream from Augusta and waste from nearby paper mills and a chemical plant only made the situation worse. Ashley Andrews, a white woman who works at Vogtle, said much the same about SRS. "That is just a cesspool over there. And of course, now the Savannah River. You can't eat fish out of there. When we were kids, we used to swim in the river. We skied there, we swam there, we fished. Sturgeons used to live there. You could catch them and get the roe out and the caviar-type stuff. It's just made a mess of the river."

"It's sickening," William said, grabbing a soiled shop cloth off the floor and wiping the fog off the windshield. "One of my friends made a statement once, 'I've never seen William swimming in the river.' I replied, 'I don't swim in sewage.'"

William began to rattle off a torrent of acronyms and titles: the burial grounds; the high-level caves; C, F, and H areas; Par Pond—all of which were foreign to my untrained ears. After about ten minutes of frantic note taking, the vocabulary he used to describe his work at SRS began to hamper my accuracy.

I decided to appeal to the southern gentleman. "My hand's getting kind of tired," I said, stretching my fingers.

"Oh?" he said with concern. "Go on and turn that recorder on."

I smiled a bit, and he smiled back. William casually pulled off the road, away from the bustling Vogtle traffic on River Road. He parked the truck under a large carport-style shed. Summer rains that would end a three-year drought in Burke County continued to pour down on the tin sheltering us, but the heavy pounding on the truck finally ebbed.

"It was an hour coming and an hour going," he said, describing the journey across the state line to South Carolina. No bridges connected Burke County to South Carolina, although from where we were sitting, the SRS property was only a few miles across the river.

"And there was so much politics involved," he said. "So much paperwork. Somebody was always trying to cut your throat. Nobody did a damn bit of good work, and they were all sitting there drawing a big salary."

"They have *billions*," he said. "They have to spend the money. They are giving it away! That's the government. A bottomless pit."

Like Vorice, and most other white residents I spoke to, William placed blame for the overbearing waste, land loss, and corruption squarely on the shoulders of the government. After William opened

for me the Pandora's box of SRS, I would come to hear similar complaints from fellow white workers about the dishonest use of their time and taxpayers' dollars. A former SRS maintenance worker, Landry Axson told me that she and a friend were instructed to drive the 310-square-mile site (198,344 acres) for entire afternoons to make sure the cars racked up enough miles to sustain government funding. Steve described some workers as openly saying they "did nothing," and despite attempts to seek out work, they often remained delegated to menial and unnecessary tasks. Steve Pratt said, "The federal government, me and you, we're the ones left picking them up." Between SRS employees, Vogtle workers, and local residents, disenchantment with the government raged throughout the countryside.

"What was it like working at SRS?" I asked William.

"When you stepped across that painted line into what we called an RDZ, a radioactive danger zone, the whole world around you changed in your mind," William said. "Everything on that side of the painted line would kill ya. But you could eat a honey bun and drink a Coca-Cola on the other side, and you're okay. That's hard for me to believe," he said with a brief, pointed look and slightly raised eyebrows. He didn't buy that an open space with a painted line in the middle could have one side safe and the other full of radioactivity. "But that's the way it worked. I've had several instances when I thought I was crapped up. That means you possibly got an exposure, contamination."

Once, when William was working with a sump pump that contained radioactive waste in an RDZ, his coworker let go of a discharge hose, and the water spilled all over him.

"Hell, the first thing that goes through your head is, 'Oh my God, I am going to melt!'" he said, with a lively rendition, throwing his hands above his head as though the waste was falling on him. "Like the wicked witch on *The Wizard of Oz*." He tagged on a smile and a brief laugh.

"And you had your dosimeter on the whole time?" I asked, referring to a badge that measures worker exposure to radiation.

"Oh yeah," he said. "You had two, sometimes three different badges that would absorb or would read the exposure as to the area you were in. But if you had any question about them, you couldn't find an answer. It is such a channel to go through, no one person really has the full picture. He just gets a little dose until he's not worried about it any more."

By dose, William meant exposure to radiation. The more one was exposed, the more normalized it became in a setting that allowed no opportunity to question.

"Did you get to see your exposure records?" I asked.

"After I left, I went through every proper channel to try to get a report," he said. "I never got to see my exposure chart. *That* is SRS. *That* is the federal government. They can bury that information wherever they want to. And that's what they do." William and the state were not on good terms. He paused for a moment from describing SRS, apparently reflecting on the torrent of information he just told me. "I have never taken the paved road. I've always hooked it hard left. I hit dirt and kept getting up," he added with a chuckle.

"Is that strong independence?" I asked.

"I do not regret leaving SRS," he said, moving on. "It's been a struggle. I could have provided much better for my family. But in all actuality, I haven't done too bad."

"You're your own boss," I said, also trying to be more upbeat. "That's a big deal."

"No, I fire myself about twice a week," he responded.

"Like today when it was raining?" I asked. The downpour had finally halted as the morning worked its way into the afternoon.

"Well," he said. "You fired me today. You hungry?"

"I am a little. Are you?" I replied. He nodded. For lunch, William took me to a nearby gas station off a busy road surrounded by pine fields. So busy that once when I was filling my car, I saw one of the county's many stray dogs wander away from the overflowing garbage at a neighboring dump site and into the path of an oncoming logging semi, traveling at a speed well above the fifty-five-mile-per-hour limit. The gaunt dog tucked his tail between his legs and scampered out of the way just in time, unlike many of his less fortunate counterparts.

What a different aura the gas station bore when I was with William. The first time I went through the barred doors to pay after filling up my car, there were only curious eyes to greet me. As we pulled up, William hollered at two black men casually leaning against the wall, one tall and lean, the other wide and short.

"Hey!" William yelled, throwing his arm out the window as he pulled into a parking spot. "Got it close enough there?" he asked the men as he crept his intimidatingly large truck closer to the wall they lounged against. They laughed in return, slapping their thighs.

"No further!" the tall man yelled, waving his hands and smiling. William told me he wasn't on a first name basis with the men, since I was hoping for an introduction.

I got out of the truck, and William and I headed into the station. He opened the door for me and pointed out the food bar in the back corner. I walked over to an array of fried chicken, sausages, macaroni and cheese, and cornbread resting behind the glass. I looked back in William's direction and saw him casually chatting with a few other men.

"Tim Dillard, this is Loka Ashwood," William said as I walked back over to a tall blond man with a Vandyke beard wearing a white tank and cutoffs.

"Loka, this is Lester Brown," he said as an elderly man in soiled clothes shuffled by in his walker, and we made our way out the door.

William and I climbed back into the truck, our chicken selection tucked in a black plastic bag. He turned onto Shell Bluff Landing Road and followed it to the river. We stopped in front of a gateway that required a security code to enter. I had paused there a few times, wondering about the failure of the empty development, once intended to become prime riverfront property. The owner had gone belly up on the deal. William leaned out and punched in a security code.

"I told you there was nowhere I couldn't go," he said.

As the gate opened, I looked around with hesitation for any sign of life, wondering whether we were going to get caught, knowing that neither of us owned the land behind the bars. William, on the other hand, carelessly rolled his truck in, talking a mile a minute, filling up my silence. He showed no sign of fear of arrest. The law, I would come to learn, was dictated by corrupt and often distant government interests that maintained little legitimacy. This was the breaking of established rules and the making of new ones in Burke County.

Whether the land was corporate, state, or locally owned, William made his way across it, an open affront to the rule of numbers and for-profit democracy, and a point of pride that garnered local respect and admiration. William is what I understand to be a "rural rebel," a designation in part inspired by the work of the historian E. J. Hobsbawm. I use the term to capture the exercise of power outside existing institutions, and against state and corporate authorities that locals view as unjust and violating their moral norms. From my experience in Burke County, rural rebels are exclusively white and primarily male, pushing back against oppressive rules that have become unpopular locally, but maintained by the backing of a central state.[2] Rules like keeping people off the land that formerly belonged to them.

Although historians widely view rebels as something relegated to the annals of the past, the heavy-handed, unwelcome rule of for-profit democracy has precipitated their return.[3] Hobsbawm, writing in the 1950s and 1960s, figured that an all-powerful democratic government, with police at home and military forces abroad, left little space for the rebel. He described how the democratic state wields more power than any nobility or hereditary ruler that the world has known. It codifies formerly uncodified spaces through taxation. Its surveillance leaves no corner free from its gaze. Rebels and bandits like Robin Hood seem mostly like figures from a distant past who could no longer outmaneuver the all-powerful nation-states that ruled them.[4] The rule of the Western state in Hobsbawm's view was impenetrable by virtue of its discipline, true to democracy's bureaucratic production of hapless foot soldiers, as Weber and Tocqueville similarly contend. Hobsbawm briefly noted that the United States had its share of rebels in its formative years, thanks to the independent ethos of settlers and their access to arms, unlike the restrictions present in other Western democracies. Even so, Hobsbawm thought rebels were only relics of the Wild West. Citizens came to work for reform through their government, rather than outside it, even in the United States. Or so he thought.

Today as yesterday, the antistatist tendencies of the rebel leave it similarly understudied. Sociologists limit their analysis of protest largely to social movements that work *through* the government for reform.[5] Hobsbawm scolded scholars for ignoring rebels for so long, simply because they were conservative, and unlike themselves. After all, they were usually the dynamite igniting broader forms of protest. Even though solitary, he found them to be important figures in political life because they often represented a hero-like leader for broader rural collective resistance. The sociologists of today, like the historians of the past, overlook rebels because they exist "in spite of the state"—meaning that their protest is leveled against the existence of the state apparatus, rather than more moderately designed to enact change through it.

Hobsbawm's error, replicated in social-movement scholarship more broadly, lies in overlooking the moral economy of democracy that underwrites states in the Western world, like any other type of state authority. A bulky, barrel-chested state isn't enough to command allegiance, even in a democracy. The legitimacy of the state in Burke County was deeply shaken by the state's sanctioning of pollution, monitoring, imposition, and property claims. Therein arises the space for rebellion, even in the modern age.

William parked next to a picnic table overlooking the Savannah River. He pulled his poncho out of the truck and draped it across the bench so I could sit somewhere dry. He laid out a garden tomato, a squirt bottle of mayonnaise, and half a loaf of bread on the table. While I organized things on the table, he went back to the truck to grab a box of Indian artifacts to show me. Sitting amid the lush green of the riverbank, I began to relax. When he returned, he reached into his pocket and out came a rusty pocketknife. As he started to clean it with his shirt, I grabbed mine from my pocket.

"Here, this is clean," I said. He took it and examined the flowers carved delicately into the knife's wooden handle. Screwed on top was a piece of metal engraved with "Loka Ashwood." "A friend got that for me as a bridesmaid present," I said. He seemed curious, but I didn't say any more. William pressed the knife into the skin of the tomato.

"What have you been cuttin' with that?" he asked. "Your husband?"

"No," I said, laughing. "He's been good so far," I said to William with a smile. "Haven't needed to use it."

"Sure is dull," he said, keeping his eyes on the tomato. "Want me to sharpen it for you?"

"No," I said. "Thanks, though."

Rebels, according to Hobsbawm, are "men who make themselves respected," with a good shot or a sharp knife.[6] There were historical exceptions, like the female Bavarian robber Schattinger, who kept to the family tradition of robbing. But she didn't have much local support for her endeavors, unlike the heroic and legendary status afforded the male rebel. (In part that was because she didn't bother to please the locals.) And in return, they did not provide her quarter when she was most in need, leading to her death. At least that is how Hobsbawm tells it: a warning to women and those indifferent to local customs and concerns.[7]

William managed to saw a few pieces of tomato onto each of our slices of bread. I dug into my chicken. Rough clouds started to roll in over the line of trees arching on the shell-studded bluff behind us. We were both quiet. I watched the sky, and William turned his head away from the river and watched too.

"I think it's coming for us," I said.

"I think so too," he answered.

A shower started rolling in over the tree line, rumbling over the forest. We jumped up, grabbed the mayo, the poncho, and the chicken, and headed to the truck. We left the artifacts to their cardboard cover, and the bread to its plastic cover, finishing our meal within the shelter of the truck.

★ ★ ★

Many words have been applied to the rebel, and none are typically used in a flattering fashion. Primitive. Archaic. Backward. Antiquated. And that blend has its everyday counterparts. Hick. Hillbilly. Redneck. Cracker. White trash. Hotheaded fighter.[8] Even stupid.[9]

Such terms denigrate the environmental embeddedness of the poor they are used to describe. Those whites laboring in the beating sun gained the epithet "rednecks" because of their burnt skin, which never had a chance to regain its paler color. "Hillbilly" traces back to the sand hillers of North Carolina; it was at first local slang to capture rural white people as poor and lazy—even a separate race—and gained further popularity in the characterizations of Appalachian and Ozark poor.[10] "Cracker," as mentioned earlier, described the poor white men who, around the time of the Revolutionary War, slashed whips at the backs of the cattle that they drove to market. Now, "cracker" is sometimes endearing and other times derogatory slang for southern white men who have a strong streak of country. "White trash" dates back to 1845, when a newspaper used the term "poor white trash" to describe the rural, backwoods, and squatter people who attended

President Andrew Jackson's funeral.[11] Ironically, disparaging terms like "redneck" and "hillbilly" carry a mainstream popular appeal. As the developmental state has directed the outsourcing and elimination of labor embedded environmentally, the admiration of white men who continue to engage in hunting or fishing in harsh conditions has in some senses grown in today's popular culture.[12]

But not academically. Such monikers stood for, and in large part remain tied to, political conservatives and the traditions of their environment, and opposed to the notion of progress that the state demands. Progress remains, 150 years since Karl Marx wrote, profoundly urban-centric.[13] Leaving the rural for the urban embrace of money and position still remains the gold standard for American success. Those who live and stay rural are labeled "left behind" and "lazy."[14] Perhaps most offensively, this is sometimes called the rural brain drain. A founder of sociological theory, Émile Durkheim, is still heralded for his almost century-old work on religion. In his writings, he labels pagan faiths with environmental idolatry as primitive and, consequentially, as less developed than their monotheistic counterparts. Even Hobsbawm, with his use of "primitive" and "archaic," opposed rebels to developed types of protest informed by the capitalist reorganization of society. His extreme positioning suggests that civilized protest happens through an urban developed state with centers of legitimacy. Modernity thus renders backwoods outlaws obsolete, Hobsbawm contended. Out of fashion and out of time, the rebel takes on an antiquated air or, in Hobsbawm's description, one that is "pre-political."[15]

I find such thinking to be rooted in a series of mistaken and interdependent assumptions: that the democratic state is modern and in some sense superior to states that preceded it; that modernity precludes environmental embeddedness; and that, consequently, protest in the modern democratic state is inclusive, collective, and, by virtue of its collectivity, urban. Such thinking develops the mistaken notion that rural rebels do not exist and, further, that there is no need for them to exist.

But in fact, rebels do exist.

First, they exist because all states have their problems, even democratic ones. All operate on a presumption of hierarchy and rule, by which a select group of politicians chooses for all, rather than all choosing for all. Second, they exist because people are environmentally embedded, and they have never ceased to be. Climate change has reminded the world of as much. Third, rebels exist because the democratic state is not all-encompassing in its representation. Minorities have always sacrificed, as they continue to. Lands have been taken. The state has been compromised. And the minority burden weighs heavily in Burke County.

Rebels, despite Hobsbawm's claims, are not prepolitical. They are anarchist. They are anarchist because they rebel against and outside existing channels of power and corruption. They act against the intertwined hands of those with the money and those who rule in for-profit democracy.

An anarchist basis for understanding political action reveals assumptions behind some of the prevailing theories of power and politics. The political scientist John Gaventa ventured into the realm of rebellion to document spaces where the traditional culture of Appalachian people provided the temporary impetus to stand up to corporate coal barons and moneyed elites. Much of his classic work aims at making participation possible in formal decision-making processes (often governmental ones) by identifying three dimensions of power. He is especially concerned with the types of information and rhetoric that keep people from participating, with the presumption that they should.[16] Taking the for-profit democratic state at face value prompts an understanding of rebels as something other than apolitical, prepolitical, or misguided malcontents. If the state is seen as complicit in the creation and persistence of the coal industry, the nuclear industry, or any other corporate industry that could not exist without the government, rebellion becomes less an unfortunate barrier to successful political action. It rather takes on its own legitimate basis of political reason by working entirely outside a state that sanctions exploitation.

I once asked William about his politics. "Politics? I don't have politics," he answered. "I do not care for them. I watched my father try to maneuver through politics his whole life and never break through."

William followed with a long story about integration-era politics, when politicians bent toward self-gain manipulated voters without conscience. William took issue with the power given to authorities, who then turned their authority into power over the people, rather than power for. He said that he didn't care about voting. That served to reinforce the state that had sucked so many of his neighbors dry.

What does William stand against? For-profit politics. He stands against conjoined corporate and state corruption that violates his ideal of hard, honest work, embedded in everyday, manual, resource-intensive labor. His beliefs about power and status play out in the rural hinterlands rather than in the organized spaces of the city. To be against for-profit politics, William stands against the politics of his state.

★ ★ ★

The next time I saw William, I tagged along with him on a job. That day, he needed to cut a pine tree resting precariously close to a house bordering the riverbank. I stood in sight of his review mirrors, helping him back his bucket truck into a narrow space. The truck hesitated as it met a series of tree stumps. William got out, cut them down a few inches with his chain saw, and got back into the truck. I ran over and picked up a chunk of the freshly cut wood to move it out of the way.

"Don't pick that up!" he yelled at me. "You'll get splinters in your hands."

I ignored him and moved the piece out of the way. "I'm fine," I yelled over the truck. "I've done plenty of this kind of work."

The few inches he sawed down left just enough room to park the truck masterfully close to the pine. He left the truck running and jumped out.

"You stay up there where it's cool," he told me, ushering me onto the porch as he roped himself into a series of straps. He returned to the truck, lowered the bucket, stepped in, and levered it toward the sky. A half a dozen times, in between cuts, he yelled at me to grab a drink for myself while he worked beneath the mercilessly beating sun.

William rose toward the top of the tree, rocking back and forth. He held the chain saw in one hand, slashing it forward easily, working from the outside of the tree's crown to the inside. Sometimes he grasped a large branch in one hand and held it while he cut so that he could swing it to a spot where it wouldn't meet anything during its long fall to the ground. The bucket looked solid but waved uneasily, sometimes hitting the tree before it rocked off to one side or the other. The chain saw dug into the wood, and its chokes and hums vibrated off the water and nearby houses.

William dripped with sweat, drenching his third shirt of the day. The scraps of wood shot off toward him. He wiped some of them away, while others drew blood. He arched higher into the air, handling large limbs barely within his reach. One started to break off and rock back toward him, and he avoided it with ease. He told me before he went up that cuts had to be precisely made to guide leaning branches in the right direction. But branches lurch unexpectedly. His bones ached. He avoided doctor trips. But he remained doggedly determined to work in the elements until his death. Even though he was a grandpa, his pride and identity remained closely tied to his labor.

When William finally stopped for a break, he came up to the porch and I handed him an icy bottled water that the thoughtful home owner had left for him in an outside fridge. William sat down on the steps in the shade, looking exhausted, and I felt a little shameful about peppering him with more questions.

"What is your favorite thing about this place?" I asked him.

"This area?" he responded.

"Yeah," I said. "What makes it home?"

"It used to be the creeks and the water," he said, as we both faced the Savannah River. We were at Stony Bluff, about fifteen miles south of where we last saw each other, on the riverbank of Shell Bluff, but still across from SRS property. "The biggest problem that is facing this county, I'd say the Southeast, is way worse than any radiation. It's erosion. Erosion in farm fields, from dirt roads, county employees scraping these roads right down to the creek so the rain washes the mud into the creek."

"I prefer dirt roads to any paved road. No government rock," he said. "That's what we call it. Rock the government loads up and ships in. This flint here on Stony Bluff, that's from the Indians. They broke it off to put the rock in the road. Those roads don't need grading. Let them decline with the flow of the land. Because of government mismanagement, every creek in Burke County is silted in. And it's a sin, and it needs to be stopped."

Over the flames of a late-night pit barbeque a few weeks earlier, William's neighbor Coleman talked about his preacher's recent message. He had referred to the passage in the book of Revelation about heaven's streets being paved with gold.[17] He son, unimpressed, announced over Sunday dinner, "If there's gold streets in heaven I don't want to go." Coleman pulled back in surprise and asked, "Why not?" His son responded, "There should only be dirt roads in heaven." The Georgia red clay rivaled in color any precious stone or metal.

The government altering timeworn paths, some of them predating the Revolutionary War, broadly agitated white men I spoke to. Another resident of Shell Bluff told me, "When I was growing up in Shell Bluff, none of the roads were paved. I don't think [Highway] 23 was paved then. I think it was a dirt road. That shows you how long ago that was or how primitive we were even fifty years ago. If it was up to me, they would not pave another foot of dirt road. We've got enough paved roads." Paving over the road in part symbolized the government running roughshod over local traditions, even those self-described as "primitive" but still preferred.

"Before it silted in, DuPont had the boasting privilege of having the second most diverse creek in the *world*," William exclaimed, "*In the world!* You couldn't have gone out in a Third World country and seen what I saw. It didn't exist. Every saltwater fish that swam in the ocean had come up the Savannah River to spawn in Sugar Creek. Flounder, mullet, rockfish."

Although the government technically owned the property, William understood DuPont as holding the reins. In the early 1950s, three

towns were forced to relocate for the bomb plant. An elderly shop owner and former veteran said people moved out of loyalty and duty to the United States. None of the thirteen workers whom I spoke to understood their work at SRS as patriotic, though one woman told me her father, who wore his work at SRS as a badge of honor, would likely be ashamed of her talking to me about its shortcomings.

"So why would Sugar Creek have silted in?" I asked William.

"Because of the construction up the creek. Constant construction and the poor practices DuPont put in place," he said. "You can hardly get a boat up there, and back when I was a kid, you could run a big motor up there because it was so deep and clean and natural. Now it's just full of sand. Erosion is killing our waterways. It's absolutely destroying this earth. There is no way that anybody coming up behind me, in this area, will see a fraction of what I've seen. Number one, they'll never be able to spend that much time in the woods. Number two, it doesn't exist anymore, and it never will again."

"What else, other than the streams, is gone that used to be there?" I asked.

"Timber. The trees," he said.

"The old timber?" I asked for clarification.

"It's no more. That's as old as you are going to see around here," he said, turning to point at some young pines surrounding a pond. William didn't cut the massive plantations of pine trees that filled much of the Burke County countryside. He eked out a living by working the trees in places where others couldn't earn a profit large enough to justify the risks and costs.

"And those are the most common, those planted pines. The big timber is gone. But there's a few places that it does exist, if you know how to find it," he said. "The most important wildlife in Burke County was the bobwhite quail."

"I heard about the quail," I said. Mobley's, a local favorite for fried chicken and hot meals, had pictures of champion bird dogs posted all over the walls. At least it did before the tentacles of the Great Recession penetrated deeply into the Waynesboro economy, and the longtime local favorite closed its doors.

"Burke County is the 'Bird Dog Capital of the World,' self-proclaimed," William said. "That's all we ever did, was hunt quail, train bird dogs. You could go anywhere and kick up a couple of quail. They eat good. It was the ultimate sport, so to speak. They still have bird dog field trials in Waynesboro, but they have to buy quail and throw them out there on the ground and hope that they cooperate."

"What happened to them?" I asked.

"Pine trees. Planted pines," he said.

"Why don't quail like them?" I asked.

"A baby quail, when he is born, his diameter is smaller than that Chapstick," he said, pulling a tube out of his pocket and pointing to the end. "The temperature change drastically affects all wildlife. But a baby quail, it affects the most. If you look around this Burke County area, there is a lot of sandy land. It's just real poor land. You go in there and destroy a piece of property by logging it and then planting pines, those pine trees start growing and dropping pine needles. Quail is a game bird, number one, and they scratch. When they can't scratch the ground, they can't get to the sand they need to eat to help with their digestion. They need to get down in that warm sand after these cold rains, and stay warm."

"And those pine needles mean they can't do it," I said, letting him know that I understood. He nodded.

Sitting quietly with William, I looked out over the Savannah River, admiring the beautiful markings of two white-faced, white-bellied birds about the size of a hawk, sporting black wings and double-pronged, scissor-like tails, shining in the sun. William caught me staring, and explained the bird was a rare swallow-tailed kite that migrated seasonally from Brazil. Hobsbawm wrote off such place-based knowledge as belonging to formally uneducated, and consequently primitive, "persons of purely local range and horizons."[18] What he forgot was that the rural rebel's dependency on the local land could produce expertise on its history and on spaces difficult for the state to code. This intimacy, wrote the prolific naturalist Aldo Leopold, belongs to those who live by the land, not simply on it.[19] William aptly captured those sportsmen who live on, but not by, the land. He called them "Wal-Mart hunters."

"If I could, I'd burn down every single one of those pine trees," William said, interrupting our silence and staring stonily into the distance. "But who cares about a quail? You've got paper mills everywhere buying timber."

"The biggest ones in the world," I answered him. International Paper calls its Augusta site "one of the most productive paper mills in the world"; downstream, the Savannah Union Camp plant was the largest paper mill in the world until International Paper bought it out in 1998 and reduced the labor force.[20]

"And they are polluting the river the most," he said of the mills.

For centuries, "landlords, usurers, and other representatives of what Thomas More called the 'conspiracy of the rich'" have motivated the occasional rise of rural unrest.[21] The story often shows the ruling government as the primary villain, stealing from the poor to further line the already-full pocketbooks of the rich. In past centuries, rebels sprang up to counter the unchecked takeover of their land as well as the forcible end of their farming and subsistence lifestyles. In the modern world, William finds the defenseless to be not only human, but also those voiceless life-forms in need of defense. The woods, open fields, lakes and streams, and inhabitants—quail, snakes, waters, trees—conjoin with disenfranchised humans to constitute what William sees as the defenseless rural poor, eager for a champion to overcome the conspiracy of the rich.

William saw his actions as a defense of the earth, hidden from the eyes of authority and inspired by a close relationship to the land handed down through the generations. The term "environmentalist," signifying someone explicitly engaged in green politics as part of formal governance, doesn't fit. William clarified to me that he "ain't no tree hugger." The rural rebel defends what I sense to be "environmental honor," a poignant protection of what is seen as a defenseless community of ecology. Such a treatment relates to the long-lived imagery attributed to nature as a feminized "mother" that "cleans up" magically, without any effort, but simultaneously cannot stand up for itself.[22] Gender plays a role in environmental domination, as it does in its defense.[23]

For environmental sociologists, frustrated with the inaction of rural and resource-dependent men, environmental honor helps make sense of the gendered treatment of the environment as a defenseless ecology in need of a savior, in contrast to moneymaking and outside exploiters. The environmental sociologists Shannon Bell and Richard York note how women in the Appalachia mountain regions join together to fight mountaintop removal visibly through democratic channels, whereas the men seemingly stay silent.[24] Environmental honor helps make sense of the spaces where men can and do protest, maintaining their sense of power and authority through acts of rebellion outside for-profit politics. As rebels acting in the environment's honor, men retain an aura of power beyond the grasp of state authority. It is harder to spot because it doesn't work through the formal channels that those embedded in the state anticipate. But the rebel's acts serve to maintain hunting traditions tied to masculinity.

"Why are there so many farm trees now?" I asked William.

"Farm program. Farmers were going broke," he said. "They didn't have anything."

William began to describe the Conservation Reserve Program (CRP), a federal initiative first implemented in 1985, during the height of the farm crisis, to encourage farmers to remove environmentally sensitive land from agricultural production and to plant species that help improve environmental health and quality. Officials designated pine trees as a long-term vegetative cover that would help improve wildlife habitat and soil fertility, and prevent soil and nutrients from running into waterways and degrading water quality.[25]

"You got a check from the government for leaving that ground dormant with pine trees," he said. "Now," he whispered, lowering his voice, "I don't want to be talking too much about farmers. There are a lot of them around here, and most of them, they've got big houses, big cars. I have never known one not to be pretty self-sufficient using government programs. But you've got to be in the clique to get it."

There the clique appeared again—that wealthy clique of beneficiaries. Farmers making use of government programs received a similar reception in most places I found myself, and descriptions of them echoed the language used by white residents to recount their land loss. Over a homemade dinner shared with Michael, his wife, and another couple I became friends with, they talked about how farmers farm the government. Jamie Gott, an elderly white woman who owned over two thousand acres of land, said that farmers and their families now seemed to sport the very finest of fashions. It was a sort of luxury lifestyle her farm family had never advocated, and she didn't either, but one that she now saw as provided in part by the government. Those managing the ground (working it was more a thing of the past) had earned themselves the label of high-living elites, courtesy of the taxpayer, she said. Like DuPont, Georgia Power, and the government, they violated the local moral code.

"I didn't realize that pine trees could get CRP funding," I said to William. The ignorance I bore as a by-product of my Midwest roots sometimes pained me.

"Oh, yeah," he replied. "Most definitely."

"But they are the reason the quail . . ." I said.

"They don't mind about the quail," he interrupted me. "They don't care about the sportsman. They call it progress," he said carefully. "That's a word I've never really learned." Progress, or as the political scientist Barrington Moore put it "the violence of gradualism" in the case of those forcibly removed from the land in the English countryside, serves as the enemy of the rural rebel. Hobsbawm reminds us that an action against progress is "no less revolutionary because it takes place in the name of what the outside world considers 'reaction' against what it considers 'progress.'"[26] That was what troubled William: progress in the name of what, and for whom?

"If you put a boat in the creek, and there is shallow water, and you start to see some shiny rocks, if you pick them up and put them in your boat, you may have an Indian artifact, broken property," he explained to me. "If you come to the boat ramp, the game warden can make a case against you because that is owned by the State of Georgia. But there are big plantations down here with seven miles of creek, and they can block it off, because they own both sides of it. Does that mean that they can dig arrowheads out of the creek? I mean, it's a double standard. If it is the State of Georgia, and they own the water, then they ought to be getting money from people pulling the water out of it. Right? Why not?"

I shrugged my shoulders.

"But they don't," he said, changing the topic to the massive amounts of irrigation in the region. "That water ought to be worth fifty cents a gallon to the state. And every state around here is in a bind." With visible irony, he said, "I am no politician. I am no farmer. I am a washed-up old tree man."

The bending of William's back in his self-chosen toil serves as an essential piece of his resistance against corporate and government control. He is not part of a roaming group of outlaws. Nor is he a member of a mob. He is in fact rare, and has the admiration of a following that stubbornly stands against the moneyed interests that he sees destroying his homeland. Unlike the historical conceptualizations of the rebel that are the rule in the literature, the modern rebel is not limited to the young, who are not bent in the labor of tending crops at home or trapped by a family with children, and consequently have the freedom to roam farther afield.[27] Today, the roles no longer stick. Those who go farther afield do not have the same place-based deference for the land. Part of being a rebel can be staying at home—that in itself is an act of defiance against the state, which demands urban migration.

William's stubborn position of independence at first garnered only my admiration and respect. His strength in brawn and spirit seemed an impassioned subversion of all the forces encouraging him to bend to the will of the government and its wealthy contractors. But as we spoke more often, and our months of friendship stretched into more than a year, I would find him working while bruised and sick because bills needed to be paid. Taking the dirt road bore costs I had not fully imagined. William was an aberration according to the powers that be, and he paid for it in sweat and blood.

"Where does Vogtle fit into all of this?" I asked him.

"Erosion, dropping the water levels in the river. It's the good-ole-boy system," he said. "They are going to acquire thirty thousand acres of land for this project that they are going to want to take back in from landowners. It is hard for me to see . . ."

"Where did you get that number?" I asked, bewildered, and interrupting him. Already, the plant and the state owned 14,692 acres within five miles of the plant. He stared at me and shook his head. The sweat had finally dried off his face, although it still clung to his clothing. Despite the work that cut and stung his body, his face remained smooth and unscarred.

"Have you heard that number before?" he asked.

"No!"

"That's the number I was told. Thirty *thousand* acres," he said slowly.

"Is that for the power lines?"

"No, no," he said. "That's for security. Takin' in the land around the plant. And they are going to do that by takin' some of the land they didn't get the first time. That was before 9/11, and [before] Vogtle was educated on the system." He burst out, "Vogtle don't need that bullshit now! They ain't gonna to give you what it's worth! Now, for ultimately security reasons, they just throw something down there on the table and let everybody divide it up like they see fit. That is going to create some chaos," he said, speculating on the future. "One man is going to get his hands on it, and he's going to say, 'The hell with the rest of 'em.' It's going to be, sure enough, something ugly going on in Burke County. Because greed is about the strongest thing in this earth. Somebody gets a dose of it . . . ," he trailed off and shook his head.

If William was looking for a reaction, he got it. I sat paralyzed in dismay. My gloomy pondering was not to be long-lived. The quiet from the silence of the chain saw started to attract locals, who wandered out of their trailers and houses to see the finished task.

"Whenever you fall a tree, people always come around," William told me as neighbors began to approach. Soon after, William drove me back to my car.

"You want to go see Sugar Creek?" he asked as I hopped out of the truck. "We can do some fishing."

This time I didn't hesitate.

"Sure," I said. "Give me a call whenever you're free."

★　★　★

When I pulled in to meet William for our tour of Sugar Creek back in Savannah River Site territory, he was sitting under a newly constructed dock, with an overhang and a thick railing all around it. I spotted him as my Honda bounced through hood-high grass.

I was late, and William watched as I approached. He stood up and shot me a look. He turned toward the river and walked down the steep pier in his usual clothes: laced-up leather boots, cargo shorts to his knees, purple T-shirt, camouflage ball cap, dark sunglasses—all were part of what Hobsbawm describes as "the rural tough's outfit," "a code which reads: 'This man is not tame.'"[28] Finally joining William for a trip up the Savannah to Sugar Creek, I was about to see his defense of the environment's honor: taking it back in order to practice the traditions his community privileged.

"Here's a back rest. You can sit here," William said, as he wrapped a cushion around the handlebars of a wooden box resting in the middle of the boat.

"Don't lean to the left," he said as I sat down. "Don't lean to the right. Don't get up. And don't put your fingers over the side of the boat. You'll smash them."

I leaned to the right, turning my head to look at him, trying to gauge just how serious he was. It was then I noticed the .22 resting comfortably on a couple of hangers off the inside of the boat.

"Can you swim?" he asked.

"No."

"Really?"

"No."

"I've got to get you out a life jacket," he said, motioning for me to get up.

"I'll be fine," I said. I took the smallest opportunities to push back against his authority.

"Can you swim?" I asked him.

"Yes, I can swim," he said, untying the laces on his boots.

"Why are you taking off your boots?" I asked.

"I need to get you if you fall in."

I looked at him with a bit of disbelief.

"Nah," he said, finally. "It's more comfortable in the boat without my shoes on."

William, in his white socks, turned the engine and started the boat up the Savannah River. The storm retreating south of us tumbled in the distance. The motor's roar drowned out our chat, and the cool breeze of the rainfall's aftermath flapped my shirt. An incoming front's dark billowing clouds started to open up over the wide curve of the river.

"That's the ole peachy state of Georgia," William smartly yelled over the roar of the motor as he waved his arm to the right. He motioned to the left: "And there's ole South Carolina."

I turned to the left this time and gave him a sharp look. He wasn't taking our fishing expedition as seriously as I hoped. Then again, he had cracked open his second beer, and he threw me a cool one.

"If anyone comes by, I'll hide mine," he said with a wide smile. "And you'll be fine." His windblown hair stood on end, his black Oakley sunglasses gleamed, and his self-satisfied air was set on agitation. In pushing my limits, he was enjoying himself all the more.

William worked around a bend and butted the boat against a muddy bank under the cover of a few trees at the mouth of a creek. He announced, "This is Sugar Creek, one of the most widely studied streams in the world. It was once the finest fishing spot in the state of South Carolina. It's been destroyed by erosion, building upstream from the reactors dumping chemicals and radioactive material all the way down."

At the moment we reached the highlight of the tour, the boat died.

"There go my dog chains," he said, getting up and starting to fiddle with the motor. "We gonna have to improvise."

The boat started to float downstream with the Savannah, and we drifted farther and farther away from the mouth of the creek. I began to wonder what fate was in store for us if we couldn't get the boat started. I spotted only one paddle resting among strung-out fishhooks haphazardly thrown around the hull of the boat.

He rummaged around and came up with a few pieces of flat rope. As we continued to float away with the current, he tied a couple of pieces together and fastened them onto the starter. He pulled, and the pieces fell apart.

"Damn," he cursed as he retied the bits of rope. We drifted farther downstream. He pulled again, and the engine roared to a start. He parked the boat underneath the shade we had drifted away from, and began to work some tackle onto his great-uncle's long golden cork fishing pole, with four double hooks at the tip.

"Watch out," he said as he finished, and rested the pole back in the boat. "You ready to go in there?" he asked me.

It was a moment of truth. Would I, too, willingly, become a rebel?

"I want to do what you do," I replied.

William grinned. "All right, Professor," he said. This was the cheeky nickname for me he used with his buddies. A few of them rang him while we were out. "I'm on the river with the Pro-fes-sor," he would say, drawing out each syllable. I would shake my head. Sometimes I would ignore him.

"Do they have cameras out here?" I asked, scanning the arch of tall trees the creek led us into. The government first contracted SRS operations out to DuPont. Later, Westinghouse. At that moment, Savannah Nuclear Solutions had won the contract, a limited liability corporation owned by another series of corporations: Fluor, Newport News Nuclear, and Honeywell.

"They're too lazy for that," he said of the contractor. "They'd have to come check them. I've never met anyone in a government job that wasn't physically lazy."

There again was the government as the culprit.

"Well lookie there," he said, pointing into the trees. "They've got a few new signs up," he said, scanning the bank as he steered the boat. "I'll be damned."

Most of the postings were worn away, some completely covered over with muck and mud. But a few fresh white signs stood out from the green. I read one out loud. "CAUTION. Unauthorized Entry Prohibited. Chemical or Radioactive Waste May Be Present." Tagged on the end was "Call 1-800-248-8155."

"That is disrespectful to the bald cypress, nailing that into a beautiful two-hundred-year-old tree," William said as his voice became serious and stern. "They're too lazy to stick a damn post in the ground." Pointing to a fallen tree that clearly bore the straight cut of a saw, William said, "Somebody's keeping it clean."

"Do you think it's SRS?" I asked.

"SRS wouldn't do that. Too lazy," he said. "No, some poacher's keeping it cleaned and fishable."

I didn't think of it at the time, but now as I look back, I wouldn't be surprised if that poacher was William. The word "poacher" carried such negative weight, and William bore the stigma a bit regretfully. During some times of the year, the managers of SRS issued permits and allowed hunters to take to its 198,000 acres of pine forest and swampland.[29] But not when William regularly went out alone or with others to fish its waters and hunt on its land.

The environmental historian Karl Jacoby called poaching environmental banditry when rural dwellers trespassed on land forcibly taken from them to create Yellowstone National Park. The setting aside of wilderness at the expense of local residents beckoned rural crime.[30] Noodlers in Missouri to this day fish illegally by grabbing fish with their hands.[31] It isn't the radical rural racism and acts of violence that some focus on—but it is radicalism in the sense that laws are violated in order to stand up for the community's moral interests and traditions, against state rules and bureaucracy.[32]

"I always thought that'd be a good place to leave a skeleton," William said, pointing out a cypress nearly as wide as my Civic in the middle, roots like bent knees filling the inside. "Scare people a bit," he said. The creek lay low in a landscape of swamp that stretched as far as the eye could see. Dozens of branches tangled just above our heads as we drifted through cobwebs. From the front of the boat, I pushed aside low-lying branches that threatened to hit us. "All these logs we are going over, and the ones on the side of the bank, have been here for most of my life," he said. There were massive, fallen cypress trees and a few oaks, some of them probably five feet in diameter and some mostly submerged. Standing trees stretched to the sky. William moved the motor up and down over logs that we bumped over, the silting having left the creek much shallower than it was in his youth. The mella bugs thick on the surface of the water didn't seem to mind us.

William showed me some old wood duck boxes from SRS monitoring in the 1970s, now decrepit and swarmed by wasps. "That's one fine wasp nest," he said. I looked over my shoulder as we passed by an open hive the size of a baseball glove. He guided the boat close to a smoothed hole where a gator had wallowed on the bank. From its size, William estimated that the creature was probably eight feet long. We hit a fork in the creek, and William wedged the boat up against a tree with a burst from the motor, and turned it off.

"Here is the biggest rockfish hole in the state of South Carolina, right at the intersection of Sugar Creek with Island Creek. The fish love the murky water coming in. You ready to catch your first rock-fish?" he said, enlivened.

I got up, rested my lukewarm beer between the rickety ridges of the boat, and walked across the hull, as quietly as I could, to where William was sitting with the reel. I carefully sat down on the cooler directly across from him, trying to stay light on my feet.

"Look!" William said in an excited hush. I saw a fish burst from under the boat and shoot across to the deep hole in a flash. Its spiny rays and thin fins shone close to the surface of the water. We were in a rare spot—one where the saltwater fish from the ocean came to lay their eggs and hatch. The shadows of dozens of enormous fish glided below the surface.

William explained that they ran to this hole twice a year. "The good fishing will be in the full moon of August and September when the females are beginning to lay their eggs. The male fish will protect the nests." This was called the fall run of the striped bass, their spawning season.

"When I was a kid, you could see ten times what we are seeing." He explained that a tile gate put in by the state had prevented the striped bass from migrating up the stream. Decades later, Georgia realized its mistake and demanded it be removed. "No one cares about the sportsman," William said. "He is the last on everyone's list."

He pulled back the pole and, in a seamless burst over my head, cast the line out into the stream. The line flew out just above the water and landed in the deep hole where the creeks met and the fish were flocking. William barely let it rest in the water before he reeled it in at a rapid pace, jerking it from time to time as it got closer to our boat so that it would not catch in the bottom of the stream. He got a bite as the line approached us, and he pulled up strongly in response. The fish didn't catch, but two opaque scales the size of the end of my index finger glistened in the sun as the hook came into sight. I took them off, and the silvery white flexed durably between my fingers.

William shifted in the boat for a better cast, and his weight broke the boat away from our wedging point. We started to drift down the stream, and William struggled again to get the engine started. The thunder began to roll dangerously close as the sky darkened.

"We're going to push pretty good now," he said as he wound up the boat to leave, and we rushed back through the creek. "When I come out here at night, an owl always says good-bye in that tree," he said, slowing down for a moment before we returned to the Savannah and pointing at a wide cranny in an old cypress. William cracked open another Bud Light. "That owl is always there."

We pulled out of the creek, and huge billowing clouds opened up before us. The lacy edges of the storm ruffled, carrying a dark mass behind. The tree line started to bristle as a strong breeze stirred. We sped rapidly, and the bugs on the river began to sting my face.

"See those leaves of the maples curling over?" he yelled as I gazed at their light underbellies. "That means a storm's approaching."

We flew up the river with the clouds moving in behind us.

★ ★ ★

A rebel is, in a word, rare. He attracts a following—adherents who take on roles like mine, following him into the woods. With the backing of admirers, William held a key position as a moral gatekeeper. An "exception that proves the rule" of rural rebellion, as Hobsbawm states. The rebel is to his people a hero, a champion, an avenger, a fighter for justice, tailor-made for the ethos of rural people in the countryside, who often resent the city and understand themselves as "separate as a collective group."[33] William's leadership, though muted, was an aberration that attracted admiration. This less showy, explicitly quiet, but perpetual rural anarchism stands in contrast to the armed insurrections of Ammon Bundy and other militants. So too does it diverge from prototypical urban anarchists, who attract the most attention today—the kind that visibly takes a stand in the broad daylight of Wall Street's gaze.[34]

The rural rebel reflects what Katherine Cramer Walsh talks about as a growing group-based "rural consciousness" in the American countryside, shaped by an understanding of the government as elite and withdrawn from their everyday concerns. She argues that rural politics are informed by a sense of "distributive justice": rural people are indignant about being sacrificed for urban needs and feel politically alienated as a result of decreasing representation.[35] With that loss of legitimization comes space for anarchy. The rules of the numbers game no longer apply to those players who chose simply to withdraw after regularly seeing cases of acute favoritism practiced in favor of centralized people and profit.

After William rested the boat against the dock and tied it up, he pulled his rifle out to give me a lesson. He nailed a lily pad a few times about twenty-five feet away before the gun jammed.

"This is not my day," he said, ramming the bolt back and forth, trying unsuccessfully to get the weapon to work. Giving up, we made our way back up the steep walkway and perched under the shelter, watching the storm clouds. William pointed to a sheltered area of trees where I could relieve myself. He had toilet paper ready. I took him up on the deal and headed into some distant trees.

I returned and sat down across from William in a chair, and we opened up fresh cans of beer. Multiple fronts rolled through, but the rain stayed at bay. William's phone began to ring. A few of his buddies had sighted us rushing back up the river.

"Where are you?" I heard one ask over the phone.

"At the river with the Pro-fes-sor," he said. He got off the phone, and we sat quietly, watching an aged SUV crawling at a snail's pace up the dirt road running parallel to the river. After it passed, it turned around at the tree line and came back our way again before heading out to a paved road.

"What are they doing? Wondering who you are," he said, answering his own question as the mosquitoes started to bite. "You want some bug spray?" he asked. Again, I refused his help.

The SUV returned about ten minutes later, making its way for us, like a vulture swinging back for roadkill. It parked a distance away. Two men stumbled out and made their way toward us.

"We heard y'all shooting. Thought William had finally got what was coming to him," a man in his mid-thirties said as he walked up.

"Loka Ashwood, this is Chester Chanders," William said.

"We heard one bang, followed by a bang," Chester said. "Figured you had taken him down and then finished him off."

I smiled.

"We went by, and I said, I never seen a woman down here," said the other, who introduced himself as Daryl. He was around William's age but stood a head taller. "We had to stop. Women don't come down here to the river."

"Never did see a woman," Daryl Edmonds continued, looking me up and down, as I checked my desire to leave. Daryl had a full beard, a head of thick brown hair, a heavy frame, and broad shoulders. He wasn't the leader, but the same rules about women prevailed. Maybe, though, it wasn't as bad as all that. I looked over at William and felt that we were perhaps friends. We were now as thick as thieves.

"We went fishing in Sugar Creek," William said. They had quietly been waiting for an explanation of who I was, and when they finally got it, they didn't seem pleased.

"You did what?" said Daryl, visibly irritated. "Why'd you do that?" he asked William. William remained stoically in his lawn chair, his shoulders filling up the width of it. The silence bore down heavily. William's eyes were hard to see under his ball cap, just an expressionless almost frown. He sat so still and upright that I wondered whether his back was bothering him.

Daryl turned to me and asked, "You aren't going to tell anyone about that now, are you?"

I didn't say anything, following William's lead.

"Not just anybody gets to see that," he continued. I stayed quiet, uncomfortable and uncertain how to explain myself. Most of those I knew who were lucky enough to travel Sugar Creek earned that right by inheriting insider knowledge from friends and family. One of my favorite Burke County pictures shows Michael sitting bare-chested on a plaid lawn chair in a pair of shorts, holding a beer in a koozie in one hand and draping the other casually over the trigger of a rifle lying on his lap. Behind him is one of the frequent SRS "No Trespassing" signs. His face glows with an obstinacy all too similar to William's. Whoever snapped the photo knew well the dissent it captured. Unlike Michael or William or the other men and one woman who told me of their illegal fishing and hunting trips, I wasn't from Burke County. On top of that, I was from the North. On top of that, I was a woman.

"What did you think of the creek?" Daryl asked, becoming reasonable as he calmed down beneath William's silence.

"It's amazing," I said, thankful to have the opportunity to give a confident response. "Beautiful."

"William, we like to think of him as Forrest Gump," Chester said, changing the topic. "He's this ordinary guy who does all of these incredible things."

"Run, Forrest, run!" Daryl said as the guys laughed. The Forrest Gump analogy puzzled me at first, but William later explained it to me: "Those guys see Forrest Gump as their hero." The constellation of factors necessary to facilitate the existence of the rebel is precisely why songs and legends build around them. Certainly, the stories about Robin Hood cannot be proved true. But the accounts of such legends span centuries, creating their own reality.

"You know he took the governor hunting?" Chester asked me. I nodded.

"Bill got me on the phone and said, 'Hey! You want to take the governor hunting?'" William said, retelling the story. Bill was one of his friends I had yet to meet. "I said to him, 'Hell, no. I don't want to be no babysitter.' Then he said, 'Hey, William, I've got him right here with me.'" William blew out his cheeks and his eyes got big as the guys all laughed, likely not the first rendition they had heard.

"I told Bill, 'Well, sure, I'll show him around.' I didn't have much of a choice then," William said, taking another swig of beer.

"Where are you from?" Daryl asked me, shifting the topic again.

"She's the Professor. Come down here from Illinois," William answered for me. Where I was from was not my home institution in Wisconsin, but rather where I was born and reared.

"Illinois?" Chester said, including the *s* in the pronunciation on the end, as did almost every Georgia person I had met. "Do you know Pike County, Illinois?" This gathering didn't focus on Chicago, but rather the country. More often than not, people would disparagingly bring up Obama.

"Yes, it's a few counties below where I grew up," I said. Pike County, located in the western part of Illinois, boldly calls itself the whitetailed deer hunting capital of the world. The stories started to excitedly roll about hunting and habitat before working back to me. Gradually, a badge of rural righteousness was starting to come my way.

"What are you doing way down here?" Chester asked.

"You're home to the first new nuclear reactors built in over thirty years in this country. Your case is a distinct one. That is, in a nutshell, why I am here."

"Have you discovered two types of people?" Daryl asked me. "There are two types of people here in terms of Plant Vogtle."

"I'm not sure I know what you mean," I said. I braced myself for a tirade about the differences between black people and white people.

"There are those who make money off Plant Vogtle, and those that don't," he said, talking as much to the other men as to me. "Those, like us, that have been here for generations taking care of the land

and looking after it, and those who will sell their souls for anything, you know."

The weight of local conventions steers the moral compass of the rural rebel, something that the foreign state or regime often has little regard for or knowledge of, according to Hobsbawm.[36] Of all the characteristics that define the rural rebel, the most important is that the rebel does not violate any code or law considered locally important. The rebel is deemed such only when "judged by a criterion of public law and order which is not theirs."[37] Putting a nail into a tree or taking land for a power plant may have seemed practical to those working for a foreign state, but it proved offensive to those whose familiarity with the environment came from their families, who taught them about the land. William's defense of environmental honor was what had gained him local respect and a following. But by "local," Hobsbawm and others who have discussed rebels refer to a community that is rather monolithic, without majority and minority dynamics shaped by race and the vanguard of the democratic state.

Most simply, William didn't trespass with his black friends. When I asked Veeona, who lived only a few miles away from William, about the trespassers, she laughed in enjoyment, saying, "Those are just some crazy white boys!" She wasn't bothered by it, and neither were her sons, who explained that they would hunt sometimes, but always stayed within their property line. Sydney told me he liked to hunt rabbits, but the younger generation of black men "wanted to play video games." Another black man, a former politician, explained that he enjoyed hunting, but like Sydney, could not get younger men to join him. And when he did hunt, it was with permission.

Moreover, black men couldn't risk the illegality, at least to my knowledge. While William mentored men younger than himself and took them hunting and even trespassing, they were young white men. William mentioned that he hunted rabbits with a black neighbor, and I knew he worked with black men cutting trees. The alliances stopped there. By virtue of his race, William could break the law with less risk of arrest and could avoid getting shot for trespassing. Although the profiteers—the plant, the state, and rich absentee landlords—faced local disdain across racial lines, poaching was a viable response only for the white male majority. Not the black male minority. For them, the risk was too great.

"We've looked after this land our whole life, like our families did," Daryl said, talking directly to me. "Appreciating it. Hunting in it. These guys come in here," he said, with pronounced slurring. "They don't care."

"That's right. Chester's had that same experience. He has their lines running directly through his property," William said to me as he headed down the dock to get the guys more beers from the cooler in the boat.

"We bought it in the 1980s when it had already got the lines through it," Chester said, joining in. "But it will never be the same. We never know what they are going to do. And if they want more, they can condemn it or whatever," he said. "They may get a lawyer out here to force you to sell it for less. Every last bit they can get, they're here to take it."

"That's what you are writing about, right?" Daryl asked. I nodded in return.

"Isn't this the most beautiful spot in the world?" Daryl asked me. "This spot right here? Look at that river. Look at where you're stand-ing. Most people are never lucky enough to be a part of this crowd, standing by this river. You are one of the privileged few that has ever been welcomed into this group."

As the men began to understand me less as a predatory foreigner and more as a counterpart sympathetic to their plight, my pres-ence became a bit more acceptable. In tracing who becomes a rebel, Hobsbawm writes, "Admittedly almost anyone who joins issue with the oppressors and the State is likely to be regarded as a victim, a hero or both."[38] I earned some credibility for writing about land loss. In addition, when locals found out about the $650 a month I was pay-ing, plus utilities, for my rickety old trailer, they cursed Jesse White-head and set out to find me a better and more reasonably priced placed to live. Truth be told, that is why eventually I moved to an RV on an occupied homestead: to save money, to feel safer, and to meet more people in Burke County. The fact I had been slighted, just like them, gained me stripes in William's eyes and consequently in his followers'.

Daryl opened up, and our conversation turned to the greed of Vogtle and land taking. An air of gloom quickly settled.

"What can we do about [the land taking]?" Daryl asked the guys.

"You sit back and wait for them to take it," Chester answered.

"Thirty thousand acres. That's what they're taking," said William.

"You are kidding me," Chester said, shaking his head.

"You still haven't told me where you heard that," I said to him. Slowly, I was starting to see verification of what William told me. The river, the creeks, the landscape. But thirty thousand acres was one figure I was still having a bit of a hard time swallowing.

"And I won't," said William. "All you need to know is the number." He was reminding me, and his buddies, who was in control. And it wasn't me.

"We got to throw you a party," Daryl said. His slurring seemed to be becoming more pronounced. "You like steak? We'll cook us some steaks."

"I'll probably be next," said Chester, ignoring Daryl. "We're butted up right against them."

"I don't think they are going to take more of your ground for the power lines," I said to Chester. "From what I've heard, they are going through a different area of the county with the new set of lines."

"We got to have you a party," Daryl said again. "Isn't this the most beautiful place in the world?" I smiled, realizing that the night was starting to wear on me. Another buddy arrived and promptly pulled out of a cooler resting in the bed of his truck a dead five-foot rattlesnake with fifteen rattles. He had inadvertently run over it the day before when he was leaving William's place. Shortly after running my fingers reluctantly over the rattles, I decided it was time to leave.

"I'm going to head off, guys," I said. William got up from his chair.

"I didn't run you off, did I?" Daryl asked.

"No. And, Burke County is the best place in the world," I said, appeasing him as I shifted away from the light of the shelter and into the ease of the dark.

"I'll walk you to your car," William said. He shined his phone toward our feet so we could keep a lookout for any snakes in the thigh-high grass, and we both had our heads down as I walked out to the car. He stopped as I swung open the door to give us some more light. The men watching from afar had grown quiet.

"Thank you for showing me around today," I said. "I'll never forget what I saw."

"I enjoy your company," he said in return. "Be careful driving home."

★ ★ ★

A person trying to serve justice in a democratic state faces a fundamental challenge. If the majority rules in its own interests, as Aristotle warned long ago, it can quickly discard the broader good.[39] A major component of that broader good is the defense of rights—the assurance that every person retains some fundamental protection based on moral grounds. If one person enjoys those virtues encoded in politics, whereas someone else doesn't, it reeks of injustice. Why should one enjoy rights to the land and not another? If not underpinned by the landownership ethic, the moral backing of property access and trespass becomes unclear.

"This land is your land," William sang, beginning the first lines of Woody Guthrie's famous song. We had just finished a long morning tour of his property. As the notes went higher, I started to realize that William could hold a tune. And that the bit of gruffness in his normal speech rolled away when he sang. "This land is my land." He stopped singing. "And then you know how it goes? From California, to the New York Island. From the Redwood Forest, to the Gulf stream waters." William paused again. "This land was made for *you*," he said, pointing my way, "and *me*," he said, pushing his bandaged thumb toward himself. He had cut it when his saw kicked back two days earlier. He wrapped it in paper towels and black electricians tape to keep the deep cut from bursting open.

William had stopped, but Woody Guthrie continues:

> Nobody living can ever stop me
> As I go walking that freedom highway
> Nobody living can ever make me turn back
> This land was made for you and me.

Sounded a lot like William.

"They can take my land," he said, hardened and staring straight ahead. "Come take it all. I do not care. Come take all of it." It was like he was goading them to go ahead and try.

With his challenge, William lost me. The morning tour of his four-hundred-acre property showed its careful tending. William knew the composition of the sand that the quail burrowed in to keep warm. He had stacks of wood as forage for rabbits. He left his overfarmed fields fallow for fifteen years to grow brush and hybrid grass as a habitat and feed source for the wildlife. His oaks, plagued by diseases not of his making, left ample acorns for wild turkeys and other foragers. He kept the growth of pine trees to a minimum so that the quail could stay warm rather than die in the cool rain, as they did elsewhere. William saw himself as the mediator of his land, keeping the balance between wildlife overpopulation and harmony. How could he let it go?

"It will still be there," he said to me. The sun shone on half of his face. The other half was slightly shadowed by the shelter of the Jimmy SUV we had been driving around in. His hair hung loosely, cupping his forehead, and he looked slightly drowsy. "And I'll be back. A deed's only a deed."

Indeed, a deed was only a piece of paper bound to the legitimacy of the state, upheld in courts of law. Like William, Michel Foucault sees legal doctrines as a tool used by the elite to maintain control over those on the margins of society. For those excluded from the wealth of for-profit democracy, the deliverance of justice is not abstract. Rather, justice relies on, in Foucault's description, "their own experience, that of the injuries they have suffered, that of the way in which they have been wronged, in which they have been oppressed."[40] For the rebel, the delivery of justice, rather than being entrusted to the state and its many apparatuses, is carried out directly by those avenging grievances. For William, retribution for wrongs came through what I call "direct justice," not the justice of the state, but the justice of a community responding outside of bureaucracy to personal oppression. In some senses similar to David Graeber's notion of direct democracy, direct justice is determined by the collective moral economy of the people and delivered accordingly. A justice of anarchy rendered against an oppressive, for-profit democratic state.

"You have to understand how it works," William said to me with his eyes almost closed.

"How what works?" I asked, watching his face for signs of jest or insincerity. But there were none. I didn't understand what he was suggesting.

"The security," he said, opening his eyes. "How they watch the land. I know exactly how the security works. I know who runs it. I know the helicopters that fly over." He nodded to reassure me. I must have been looking a little dubious. "I know when they take their shifts," he said, with a grin and a wink. "I've seen those helicopter lights up close. And they are bright. I was sitting on my truck, tailgate down, beer in my hand," he said, pausing. "Now again, I think it was a bottle of liquor," he said to himself. "Yes, it definitely was."

I chuckled at his gall.

"That helicopter hovered over my head, pointed down at me. I mean it was so bright, I was shielding my eyes from above and below. The reflection was coming up off of the tailgate. I was saying, 'Ahhhh!' It was blinding! I couldn't see a thing."

"They were just messing with you?"

"Hell," he said. "We were messing with each other."

"Have you gotten caught?"

"Three times," he said. "And put in jail twice."

"Don't they have to warn you?"

"They've got the signs up. That serves as warning," he said.

"Why don't they catch you now?"

"They couldn't catch me if they wanted to. They can't find me.

And if they did, they wouldn't want to. They know me now," he said. "And I know them."

"There's something I'm trying to figure out about you, William."

"What's that?" He seemed a little wary. I did ask a lot of questions.

"Why aren't you scared of going on that ground?"

"What is fear?" he said, turning his head toward me and looking at me. "Fear of what you don't know? I've had sixty years of learning the hard way. There's only three entities around here who won't let me go on their property: Jesse Whitehead, SRS, and Vogtle," he said. "So you know what? I go on there that much more. I get that many more turkeys. Come here, I want to show you something."

William led me into his one-bedroom hunting lodge, which sported a kitchen, a washer and dryer to the right, and a bed with a bright quilt of arched purples, whites, and dark green tucked in the near corner on the left. There were a few beautiful antiques scattered around the room. A dark table with massive clawed feet centered the space, and it was surrounded by a few old couches, one with duct tape on one arm and a DeWalt drill resting in a case on the far end of it. A tan wool blanket covered the other couch, and the cement floor had been recently swept. The big table was covered in papers and reports on SRS, some of them browned and crimped, showing the age of the details on soils and wildlife in the county. A curved yellow dresser with painted bouquets of flowers on the front filled the back corner. Along the perimeter of the room where the walls met the ceiling were tacked countless turkey beards.

"The guys kept telling me that I needed to show off all these turkey beards, so I put them up around the place. Now they keep falling off," he said, picking up a few and placing them on a shelf.

I counted eight bucks mounted on one wall, and there were antlers scattered in other places throughout the room. We kept wandering around, and William showed me beautiful tortoise shells and collections of wide cypress boards and ash, oyster shells, and artifacts that he had found on his adventures. An open-mouth bass hung over the fireplace.

"I have a hard time throwing anything away," he said as I sat down on a couch. William's place wasn't crowded with remnants of junk or knickknacks that had accumulated over years from needless purchases. His house extended Shell Bluff into his living quarters.

And then, of course, came the introduction to his guns. "I've got guns all over this place," he said. "There's one here," he said, pointing out the shape of a gun resting under a blanket on the back of the couch. "Then I've got one under that cushion." He happened to be pointing to the cushion my back was resting against.

"Here?" I said, getting up from the couch and starting to feel behind the cushion.

"Oh yeah, that's right, I took that out to the truck," he said, taking a look himself. Guns were as much a part of Burke County as the pine trees.

"You know what that is?" he asked, steering me over to see the reason why he first invited me in. Dangling was what looked initially to me like some sort of pink and bone-hued artifact. The roped treasure seemed a little too freshly vivid in its colors to be an artifact.

Without waiting for a reply, he said: "Those are turkey spurs."

Upon closer look, there were innumerable examples of what almost looked like one- to two-inch-long teeth that darkened to a charcoal point. The spurs were attached to the dried pink skin from the wild turkey's scaly magenta leg. Spurs protrude from the back of turkeys, and William had two dozen feet of them, looped around four times, hanging from the ceiling. That meant William had probably killed at least three hundred wild turkeys in his time, quite a feat for any hunter.

"That's what happens when they try to keep me out," he said. "I take that many more." He nodded.

William didn't wait for the state to mediate justice. In for-profit democracy, it wouldn't, anyway. He and his companions took justice into their own hands. One of William's buddies had said, "I'd follow him anywhere." I was starting to understand why.

"There's good and bad in this world, and it's kind of like black and white," William told me, explaining the context of his hunt. "And there's some shades in between."

"Vogtle is bad," William said, looking me square in the face. "It's as clear as that." He nodded at me in the silence. Dark as that moment hung, with a spur, he turned toward something bright.

"Let's go catch some squirrels," he said.

And we set out into the woods.

Nowhere have I ever found in the scriptures
where God said, "Ask the government."

—Reverend Samuel Franklin

"Southern Company and the government, they are after the same thing," the Reverend Samuel Franklin explained to me, his chestnut skin set off by the slight sheen of his lilac dress shirt. In a black leather jacket and pair of snakeskin cowboy boots, he stood out from preachers and laypersons alike.

"Why are they after the same thing?" I asked him in the quiet solitude of his church office, free from the echoes of the sanctuary.

"It doesn't matter if you're talking about Georgia Power or any electrical company," Samuel explained. "The government has provided the money to cause these companies to come into existence and to keep them going. If you remember correctly, even most recently, the Obama administration guaranteed the loans for Southern Company. So technically, they are one and the same. Even the regulators are controlled and financed by the government."

"What about the government? Do you find any hope in democracy?" I asked. Since he was one of the few willing to stand up to the power plant in collective spaces of protest, I wanted to know how and why he did it. How could he stand before the state when he thought government reform futile? Why bother? Samuel was perpetually among the few local residents—sometimes the only one—that I observed willing to speak out against the plant at public forums.

"We talk about the government," he answered me. "And we talk about democracy. And we talk about government of the people, by the people, for the people. I think that is perhaps answered best in this day and time since the Bush and the Obama administrations talked about the recession in our country. They seem to think that it is a situation that is going to affect everybody. But it doesn't affect everybody. Not the rich. If we do have a democracy, it doesn't function very well."

"Then who do you see pulling the strings?"

"The people with the money."

"What hope is there then for reform?"

"I am a Bible person," Samuel said with patience and sustained rigor. With two years of observation under his belt, he had me figured out—a skeptic about religion, but a local sympathizer. He knew he needed to concentrate on the former. And the former happened to be both his job and his calling.

"I've pastored for forty-three years," he explained. "I've been in the church all my young and adult life. Nowhere have I ever found in the scriptures where God said, 'Ask the government.' Okay? So therefore, if you want change, if you need change, you ask God. God has a way of changing things, and doing things that seem impossible to us. But he does it so easy, so simple. So yes, there is change. Yes, Plant Vogtle will be stopped. I sincerely believe that. But it won't be because of the government. At some point in time in the not too distant future, so will some of the other reactors."

"What gives you that kind of faith that change can come?" I asked, my curiosity whetted as my struggle to understand his countenance continued.

"Okay, Loka," he said, slowing down with a sign of fatigue after six back-to-back questions. "Loka. Between the year 1900 and 1912, here in the South, there was recorded five hundred lynchings. And we actually have no idea how many there was during that period. God has made some change when we were the kind of people who were serious about our faith. Not our religion, our faith. That's a difference. Religion leads to spiritual consciousness. Once they reach spiritual consciousness, religion is irrelevant. When we came out of slavery, my people bought by 1914 fifteen million acres of land. Now that we are counting on the government, we own less than three million."

"Faith," he said with a big booming laugh, stressing the simplicity of his point. "We had hoped one day that all men could walk equally together. But we did count on the fact that there would come a time when men would change the system. We did not count on the fact that it would be how much money you would have rather than your skin. The system is real good at manipulating the minds of the masses, and causes us to depend on the system, when there is no such thing as assurance when you are depending on someone else."

Samuel treated the government as "incidental" to his protest. His protest centered on overcoming the system, of which he saw the government as a part. For Samuel, reforming or fighting the government is not an end in itself—as Vorice and William and Patty believe. Systematic racism, rather, overarches and penetrates it. Thus, Samuel saw his faith as above, beyond, and cutting through earthly matters like governance.

Politically, I am usually a voter, sometimes an organizer, an analyzer of policy, and often a beneficiary of majority rule, and my mind has been fine-tuned my whole life to believe in the government as a route for change and reform, regardless of political leanings. If you want to convince people you are right, you do so democratically through the proper channels of authority, or so I had grown accustomed to assuming. To understand the full fallout of for-profit democracy, I had to begin to understand a simple truth relied on by those perpetually disinherited in the Burke County black community: God, not government, would deliver justice.

Then the LORD said,
"I have observed the misery of my people who are in Egypt;
I have heard their cry on account of their taskmasters.
Indeed, I know their sufferings,
and I have come down to deliver them from the Egyptians,
and to bring them up out of that land to a good and broad land,
a land flowing with milk and honey."

—Exodus 3:7–8

"The walk is by faith," Samuel said. To understand his walk required more than a simple documentation of him stepping forward.

He did a great deal of that. I saw him at Nuclear Regulatory Commission meetings, usually flanked by one or two fellow black reverends. There he appeared as an organized representative of Shell Bluff Concerned Citizens, a small group of mostly preachers and a few churchgoers—all black—that kept tabs on Vogtle. Dressed in a sharp suit, he would take to the microphone to ask questions about domination and oppression that were sometimes particular but usually more overarching. At meetings hosted by white out-of-town activists, I saw him show his support but make it clear that he had little hope in the efficacy of their go-through-the-government ways. Still, he worked to improve disaster plans for those in the evacuation zone by talking to Southern Company. By all appearances, he seemed committed to democratic reform by engaging in processes that the state sanctioned. That is often the sign that scholars look for in documenting a democratic protest: showing up and standing up.[1] Protest is supposed to be a cornerstone of a healthy democracy, reforming and reshaping the government when it goes astray.

Reckoning with the full fallout of majority tyranny in for-profit democracy requires rethinking the assumption that people showing up or standing up signals faith in the state they seek to reform. For Samuel, showing up didn't signal faith in the democratic state, a part of the corrupt system. It signaled faith in God.

"What the system has done is gotten very sophisticated," Samuel explained to me, folding one long leg over the other and leaning back with ease in his rolling desk chair. "Most of my people do not understand the system. They think I'm one of the worst black men they've ever seen in their life. Black folk and white folk. Because I understand the system. You've millions of people who are at the lowest on the totem pole, lowest economic status, who could wreck havoc on the system. So what's your best method? You've got to maintain racism. That's the mission. We have to learn, you do not look at a person by the color content of their skin, but the spirit that possess them."

The scholars C. Eric Lincoln and Lawrence H. Mamiya write that the black Baptist church has traditionally stood as the "most important and dominant institutional phenomenon in African American communities." Samuel preached to those accustomed to a rich regional history of black Baptists. Just up the Savannah River, on the South Carolina side, rested Silver Bluff Baptist Church, one of the first known black churches in America, which dates back to the mid-eighteenth century.[2] During two centuries of slavery, the church—that is, the white church, which slaves attended with their masters—offered the sole collective space for southern blacks to gather with some semblance of freedom. Most importantly, the church offered spiritual "survival" amid "extreme dehumanization."[3] After abolition, black churches were founded apart from white ones so that black worshippers could gain some independence from persistent discrimination and inequality. Black Baptist churches actively encouraged their members to engage in the political process and to vote.[4] The sociologist Aldon Morris writes that the black church and its message "functioned as the institutional center of the modern civil rights movement."[5] Often, the church was a singularly safe collective space for the black community, serving as a bank, a site for rallies, a school, a site of creativity in music and the arts, and a place for everyday action of community building like gossip and stories.[6] The church by many accounts was not just overtly political, but also a major catalyst for change.

Samuel, though, found himself and his fellow pastors often standing up alone.

"You know from day one that those individuals in your church can't stand," Samuel said. "Because if the system perceives them as a threat, they either lose a job, or blackball them. So somebody has to speak. Your congregation is back there. We talked about this in a meeting not too long ago," Samuel said, turning our discussion to a meeting that we both had recently attended. "What I said to the group: 'They are with you. They just don't want to come forward.' I said, 'Talk to them, and you will find out where they are. But they still are not going to come forward. Because they can't. They got to think about the job that they got.'"

At the meeting Samuel referred to, a handful of reverends and activists from the region had come together with a few black churchgoers to talk about water contamination, monitoring, and stalling construction of the new reactors. As we waited outside Aberlina Baptist Church (Lela's family church) for the meeting to start, Lucie Eagen, a supporter, pulled out that morning's issue of the county's main news source, the *Waynesboro (GA) True Citizen*. The headline said cancer rates were indeed higher, much higher, in Burke County than the rest of the state.

"It's all right here," said Lucie, who attended a different black Baptist church just down the road. "We're sick. This whole county is sick!"

"I am surprised they ran that," said the Reverend Cole, who headed a regional environmental group based in Augusta.

Lucie passed the paper over to the Reverend George Ellis, the head minister at Aberlina. He looked at it and said: "We already knew it! We already had the numbers. We been sayin' this for years."

"Nobody wanted to listen," said Samuel.

"I cannot stand up in church and say a thing, or they will shut me down," the Reverend Ellis said, directly addressing me. I had been sitting through his church services for months and wondering why the power plant never openly came up, not even in Bible study. "I have to keep my opinions to myself. If I don't, they'll be on me. They'll be on me like that," he said, pressing his hands together.

A black woman who formerly served as a local politician described the situation in dire terms: "Burke County is full of depressed, oppressed people. They are not activists. There is no active community association, or activist group of people. Or anything like that that is going to be able to. That is sophisticated and invested in the issue. Things are close to them, like their children, somebody gets wrongly jailed; something like that, social justice kinds of civil rights issues, you can mobilize people behind that." But not nuclear, she said.

"People do not want to come out to us," Lucie said, answering the Reverend Ellis. "They can't. They've got jobs. They're scared to come forward openly."

Those like Samuel, who, in his words, "came off the time clock in 1970," had a buffer from the system, but most others do not. Pushing back against scholars who blame "pie-in-the-sky" religion for black disengagement from the political system, Lincoln and Mamiya characterize the situation much more starkly: "The alienation of many lower-class African Americans does not stem from an otherworldly outlook but from the constant disappointments and daily betrayals they have come to expect from mainstream pragmatic politics in the United States . . . Their alienation is rooted in a deep distrust of a system that has constantly failed and excluded them."[7] In between absolute disenfranchisement and the promise of collectivity, the Burke County black Baptist churches can be found. There pastors stand up alone, entering spaces of hopelessness to speak the word of God, knowing that their people often cannot stand behind them in a system broken by the majority's rule.

> Ah Lord GOD!
> It is you who made the heavens and the earth by your great power
> and by your outstretched arm!
> Nothing is too hard for you.
>
> —Jeremiah 32:17

Stories of the system's iron-fisted rule ran rampant in Burke County. For black residents living around the plant, and even some who are white, Lela's troubles and her family's land loss were a well-known example.

"I am not fighting Georgia Power," Lela said as we spoke together at her home in Augusta. She often came home to Burke County, but the city was where she had spent much of her adult life. "I am standing on that word and that spirit of God that has sustained me. I haven't been about no nuclear, never. But for Jesus."

The last time Lela and I saw each other was at a protest against the plant hosted at the Aberlina Baptist Church, the only publicly displayed protest that took place during my stay in the area. The Georgia Green Party was there. So was a mock nuclear waste cask, pulled by a truck sporting the sign of a regional environmental group.

Among the displays was a poster with the message "For Humanity: An Urgent Call! End the Nuclear Danger." On the display, a red-hot mushroom cloud billowed eerily into the air, and destruction and death followed.

A busload of Atlanta activists, free from the local shadow of profit, had arrived to commemorate the reactor meltdowns at Fukushima, which had happened a year and a day earlier. A few local women came to sing, and then left, but Lela was more familiar with the folks there. She embraced a religious leader and activist from Japan.

"That's why I'm in the trouble I am in now, because I did do something," Lela explained to me.

Lela described how four years ago, Georgia Power told her that she needed to update her fuse box to meet current code. When she couldn't afford the update, Lela told me that the company turned her lights off. Since then, she has lived without power. To keep cool, she settled into the basement of her brick home. When I visited, we spoke by the light of the afternoon sun streaming through her screen door. Some air moved through at night to capture the cool, the door's iron bars still providing some security. During the day, Lela kept a towel hanging against the screen to provide a bit of shade. She didn't have a refrigerator or a stove. She lit kerosene heaters by the furnace to warm food and provide light at nighttime. She washed her clothes in a bin stored under the sink. A pullout couch served as her bed.

Lela believes her activism against the Vogtle plant, partially owned by Georgia Power, is to blame.

"So therefore in the speaking, I came upon this," she said. "Before, I never would have said the things like I told you or have said. I was afraid of white men."

For Lela, racism was synonymous with whiteness and the masculinity she saw as driving the system. She explained how she had long borne interpersonal oppression executed by white men. "To the white man, as a black woman, as a black girl, you are just a sex object to them," she explained. "See, you have not been molested by the candy man as a child, while my mother and father was in the field." Explaining her faith, she said, "There was a power that kept me through that struggle. Because at that time, you just accept things. But the power of the Holy Ghost has kept me and strengthened me so that I can speak about it. Because even though it happened to me, there are thousands, millions of women that have gone through the same trauma. But they cannot overcome it until you deal with that issue. And it is not just the white man. Then you have to deal with your own race. Black men. So then you have to change yourself further. It's not the man—it's the devil himself. He comes to steal, kill, and destroy. And he don't care about color. I promise you that."

Lela used the Bible to understand how the system could be transcended. By "transcendence," I mean how faith can enable liberation from the state when injustice permeates governance. Here, I hope to add a slight addition to the rich scholarship on black religion, seen, in C. Eric Lincoln's words, as "a relationship with the Divine that transcends all human accidents and considerations."[8]

I want to be more explicit about what is transcended: the minority burden, interpersonally and institutionally, in the for-profit democratic state. Transcendence is the language of hope for those living under multiple and perpetually compounding minority statuses. When Martin Luther King used a language of love, he transcended racism. In doing so, he defined a part of the collective response of the civil rights movement through the hope of love, an ideal that could resonate with anyone.[9] Thus, faith helped Lela step outside and above the state, and consequently to stand up to it. Like Ida B. Wells, a black woman who stood against lynching in the 1890s South, Lela found her strength in faith.[10] Transcendence offered a counter to the institutions of majority rule and everyday political ideologies, which often leave people of color suffering.[11] In a moment of transcendence, one could enact a moral economy of democracy for all, one in which people were out for the good of all and freed from the politics of self-interest demanded by the state.[12] In a sense, in her moments of transcendence, Lela was an anarchist—not the kind resorting to guns and violence, which often captures the media's imagination—but one ruled by neither money nor the state. Lela was ruled by her own conscience.

Lela's fight was thus transformed. Rather than fight her molester, Georgia Power, Southern Company, or nuclear technology, she fought the devil. To her, the devil represented hate, achieved through racism, the ultimate master of oppression. She attributed her ability to speak against the devil to the Holy Ghost, which has protected her since her mother taught her the scriptures in her youth. She said its light allowed her to stay strong while "nigger" was yelled by the white children going past in the school bus as she and her brothers stayed in the fields picking cotton. Lela, her sister, and brothers stayed in the fields through September while the other children's schooling began, trapped in a system shaped by caste and race. In those days, black children started school only when they had finished the harvest. She placed her strength and her loyalty in the word of God; the particularities of democratic politics did not guide her engagement. Those politics long had failed her and her people. As with the Reverend Franklin, her walk was by faith.

"Race is a way to keep people divided among themselves," Lela further explained. "But just like it was in the Bible days, God took care of those Israelites."

Centered in the main room of Lela's basement was a table adorned with ornaments commemorating her faith. White ceramic angels formed a candelabrum holding up sparkly round tea lights, resting beside a Bible and a radio buzzing with soul and gospel. Voices raised to praise Jesus reverberated around the room as we spoke. The walls were yellow, like the shutters on her brick home, and there were photos and awards posted throughout the room. One was a Martin Luther King Jr. award that was a patchwork of fancy scrap paper and computer text. Another was a certificate from completing a theology course, and another, a financial course. She had a tribute from one of her pastors hanging on the wall, a series of overlapping photos in a square, premade and printed on one sheet. She had another award with a picture of her husband. She had lost him nearly two decades ago.

"God is not making no more dirt," Lela explained. "So you go back into the biblical part of it. It is just like in the days of pharaoh, when the children of Israel were down in Egypt and they were in bondage, the Hebrew children. They were God's chosen people. They died in bondage. But the key was to get them up out of the land. Because if you don't have a place to stay, you don't have a job, you don't have a church home, then it creates all kinds of psychological, emotional, physical discord within that group of people. So you what? You homeless. What do you do? But Jesus. Jesus."

The Exodus story told of God delivering a suffering and chosen people from slavery and oppression, from a land of bondage to a land of comfort, food, and shelter. W. E. B. Du Bois characterized Lela's homeland in much the same way: "How curious a land is this,—how full of untold story, of tragedy and laughter, and the rich legacy of human life; shadowed with a tragic past, and big with future promise! This is the Black Belt of Georgia . . . and men once called it the Egypt of the Confederacy."[13] The Exodus story was similar to Lela's past, her family's escape from slavery and their sustained struggle to buy, and later keep, the land. Nuclear was a drop in the bucket of evil oppression, and Lela saw her aims as much grander than altering the politics of the plant. Her guide was not governmental politics, a scripted action defined by bureaucratic rules and NRC meetings. It wasn't a pathway forward measured by democratic engagement. Her life trajectory of systematic oppression turned to a life-altering source for strength and reform that delivered the chosen people.

"That is my faith," Lela said.

> But you are a chosen race, a royal priesthood, a holy nation,
> God's own people,
> In order that you may proclaim the mighty acts of him
> who called you out of darkness
> into his marvelous light.
>
> —1 Peter 2:9

Transcendence afforded tremendous power. By being outside, above, and through the system, it provided a framework on which to stand publicly against powers that seemed ominous.

But that boundless biblical power came with a bounded and biblical catch. Much of the Bible describes the delivery of the meek, poor, and oppressed from bondage, identified as a "chosen race," according to the Apostle Peter. Lela coupled the indistinctness of transcendence with the distinction of a people.[14] She allied herself with the Israelites in their suffering and centuries of persecution. The Jews long struggled against the Egyptians and eventually saw justice exclusively through the hand of God, she believed. Therein was transcendence over unjust oppression. Therein, too, was the designation of what I think is worth pinpointing as a "people," a socially exclusive group defined by heritage. The idea is used in everyday life to sometimes create, sometimes reinforce, and at other times challenge social inequality.[15] For the designation "chosen people" implies that there are unchosen people.

In Lela's biblical alignment with the Israelites, being black meant belonging to a people who had suffered a long-lived legacy of oppression and one day looked for escape and rewards through a higher

power. Such ideas of deliverance and freedom define black Christian spirituality.[16] Concurrent with the transcendence of faith comes the exclusiveness of an oppressed, bounded group brought together in the black church. The two messages come to a head: God's people, of any color, as those who accept Jesus Christ, or as an oppressed group, specific to an ethnicity or race.

Followers of the Christian form of transcendence largely practice their faith dividedly on Sunday mornings. In Burke County, only twice did I see or learn of white families visiting black churches. Both were special invitations—one for a centennial birthday party and the other to celebrate northern environmental justice activists. I never heard of, nor saw, a black person attending services at the one white Shell Bluff church, Botsford Baptist.

Historically, white families have been free to enjoy the welcome of black congregations, but rarely has hospitality gone the other way.[17] This is where a major critique of Christianity comes into play. Michael O. Emerson and Christian Smith, in their surveys of and interviews with white evangelicals, find that white believers see racism as strictly interpersonal. Because of their inability to recognize the institutional impetus for black churches to break away from white ones, white evangelicals, the authors conclude, will likely continue to fail in their efforts to reduce racism.[18] Howard Thurman further attributes racism within the white Christian church to the decoupling of Jesus from his Judaism.[19] Consequently, the minority oppression endemic to the stories of the Bible is glazed over, losing the structure amid the story. The story of Jesus as the pristine savior replaces Jesus as the zealot and Jew.

Here is where "a people" versus "the people" can become divisive for those who share the same faith. The power of "a people" rests in its specificity—a distinction between oppressed and oppressor. That specificity ties into numerous global, state, and local enactments of racial oppression, including environmental racism, the legacy of the civil rights movement, and, more recently, the Black Lives Matter movement. As Kimberlé Crenshaw writes, "At this point in history, a strong case can be made that the most critical resistance strategy for disempowered groups is to occupy and defend a politics of social location rather than to vacate and destroy it."[20] Thus, distinguishing "a people" was critical to rendering the fight fair. But while moving beyond the local, "a people," forced in the first place by white majoritarianism, restricted the collective capacity of "the people" to combat the environmental burden in the mixed-race context of Burke County.

"Some whites want it. Some whites don't want it," Samuel explained to me about the plant. "That's where we are at. People are not unified. It's going to have to take something to come along and that bring them to that point of life where they be able to stand."

While knowing that radiation did not recognize color, Samuel still found great power in "a people," rather than the generality and cross-color of "the people."

"I was ten when my daddy died. Fourteen when my mamma died," Samuel said. "My grandmamma finished raising me. My grandmamma was a Cherokee. She'd say to me, 'Boy, stick with your own kind.' Said, 'Boy, stick with your own kind.' So I come up, all my children are from [those] women. It does not matter if you are Asian, Hispanic, African, white. No. We are to operate together, but God has made us separate or different. We have different ethnic makeup for a variety reasons."

Working across color to oppose nuclear power means facing the ideological tension between transcendence and the distinction of a people that Samuel believed in. In 2006, Lela and her family were invited to attend a meeting about the plant hosted by an environmental group. Lela was the only one in her family who came, and when she saw white people going into the room, she stayed outside, thinking it must be the wrong meeting.

"I thought it was black folk, like NAACP," Lela explained. "But I saw white folks with blue suits on. I saw them goin' in and out. But I didn't know that was the meeting until Reverend R. T. Stone came down. So I saw him, and I said, it was like I saw Jesus. I said, 'Reverend Stone, what you doin' down here?' He said he was coming to a preacher revival at the church over there on Few Street. I had been there about three hours waiting. We had a talk. So I realized that was the meeting in there. So I went in there, and I was sitting down, and I was listening and listening," Lela continued recounting. "And then this white nurse got up and said—because, see, if anybody know, the nurse and the doctor know. There are some white people in Burke County who have shown me the grace and the good of God. The nurse knew. When she said what she said, it clicked with what I knew."

What clicked for Lela and the nurse was the issue of cancer in the area. Although she first thought it impossible for white people to share her complaints about the plant, Lela witnessed a moment of transcendence when she went into a white-dominated meeting and saw a white nurse stand up in protest, who showed "the grace and good of God." Despite the other woman not being of her people, for a moment the distinction faded.

"That still small voice came to me, like you and I sitting here talking, and it said, 'Speak now or forever hold your peace,'" Lela said. Lela, for the first time, stood up and talked about family members and neighbors who died of cancer.

From that point forward, she saw herself as a walking target. "Now and forever since," she said, "whatever was said that night is what has brought me here to this point."

That point was where Lela and I found ourselves at that very moment: sitting together without the lights on, even though differing by race, geography, class, and age.

"Without the power working with me, then it would have just been Lela's word," she said, describing the centrality of her faith. "But it didn't happen like that. And I told. So I did, and after that. I have faith in that voice that spoke. I knew that I had been a target in that area, dealing with that land, my family. But then the fear of the white man was great. The fear of the white man was great, but the fear of the small voice was greater. To God be the glory."

A tension persisted for Lela. For while recognizing that evil did not always know color, it often did. Exceptions to this rule were not the norm. Transcendence at the time appeared momentary, not systematic. So she waited, leaving her faith in God for a yet unknown time when absolute justice would be delivered on earth. In the meantime, her faith helped her imagine great transcendence and recognize small acts of it. Small acts of resistance, like a mental and moral attitude that confronts oppression, matter. As Thurman describes it, it is more than simply a "force of arms."[21] The little acts were grace; the big transcendence would bring vengeance and justice suited to the long-lived oppression of her people. But that act would be the last one, delivered by the hands of Jesus.

Power thus split into the two fronts of transcendence and a people. One, belonging to a people, galvanizes social change based on distinction, as the civil rights movement aptly demonstrated. And the second, transcendence, removes distinction and blends humanity together, based on faith, as the civil rights movement also aptly demonstrated through love. Those powers competed with each other as Lela navigated her relationship with Mary Dunn, a white activist and nonprofit leader.

"Lela told me that her neighbors would say, 'You have just been led around by the white woman. White women want to just get in here so they can get into bed with black men,'" Mary, a petite blond who spoke softly and rapidly, explained.

"Whooooooooosh," Mary said with a wave of her hand good-bye. "You just have to keep on going. Some of that is probably true."

Lela once told Mary, "We have to live here. You get to get in your car and go home."

Lela and Mary experienced moments of transcendence. For Lela, they affirmed her faith. For Mary, who did not share Lela's faith, they affirmed her commitment to humanity. When Lela first stayed the night at Mary's home for an event that stretched late into the evening, Lela was terrified of Mary's husband. Lela had never stayed in a house with a white man, and she asked that Mary lock the door when they went to bed that night. The doors were then locked, with the blessing of Mary's husband. That night was one small step in cultivating a trust that continued to build over a decade, Mary explained to me in tears. Today, Lela greets Mary's husband with a hug, as she does mine.

Like Lela, Samuel had reservations about communication with white women. He told me that a few weeks prior, he had met with a young white female friend for lunch. While they ate and laughed together, a white man stared at them intently. The man followed them out of the restaurant and then tailed Samuel as he drove home. Worried that his friend could also have been followed, he called her and kept her on the phone as she drove home.

"Loka, do you think you'd be sitting here with me, by yourself, by myself, if you were uncomfortable with Loka, or I was uncomfortable with me?" he asked me. "Do you think I would be in here? I have seen what happens to black men that fool with white women."

Transcendence and a people formed a double consciousness for Samuel and Lela. Certainly, transcendence was possible, but always the distinction of a people would keep it from being fully realized. As W. E. B. Du Bois writes, the "veil . . . hung between us and Opportunity."[22]

And so an unfair burden rests upon the minority of minorities. To have some power, they must embrace distinction. But to gather the most momentum, they must transcend that distinction. In the meantime, much of the majority can afford to remain unaware. As for the majoritarian few who decide to join the minority cause, they must embrace the distinction of a people.

"There is no reason that black folks of Shell Bluff should trust white folks," Mary said, going on to describe the "nuclear-industrial complex," "racism," and "systematic oppression."

Mary spoke exclusively of racism as explaining nuclear targeting. Likewise, her group[23] labels Vogtle a case of environmental racism, distinguishing it by a people and finding much power in that framing. Media reports had presented it the same way: a case of environmental racism, with no mention that most of the residents who live within five miles of the plant are white.[24]

"When I am driving with Lela, and there's a shift change [at Vogtle], she tells me how many black people are in the cars. And out of maybe, like, eighty cars that pass, there's maybe one black person driving," she said, explaining how few local black residents have jobs. "All you can do is keep showing up and believing what you're believing in, and expose each other to different things."

Lela and Mary, in describing the authority behind the plant, spoke of it as white authority. There was power in doing so: color gave glue to the injustice of nuclear power in a poor community. Much of the environmental justice movement came from communities of color rising up to protest their disproportionate burden of pollution.[25] Because environmental injustice issues have been seen as most acute in the South, and because many of those who participate come out of the black church, the church has been treated generously as a catalyst for action.[26] So although racial glue has bound many discussions of environmental justice and racism, Laura Pulido has critiqued such an approach as "monolithic" in its simplistic approach to the role of race.[27] The environmental sociologist David Pellow argues, "Environmental inequality is more complex . . . It is much more insidious because it is the mechanism whereby interlocking systems of inequality serve to divide and conquer stakeholders who may be potential allies. [The environmental inequality framework] therefore reveals the much deeper workings of power in society . . . Until we understand the full ecology of production and consumption, our analyses of environmental inequalities will remain inadequate at best."[28] For those who have long suffered oppression, and form a group identity to find space for spiritual survival, the exclusivity of whiteness makes the possibility of "the people" profoundly difficult.

And so the system, conjoined with "a people," brandishes a double-edged sword: while it jabs at for-profit democracy's perpetual favoring of profit and the majority, and helps the dispossessed survive violence and cruelty, it simultaneously jabs back by using a dialogue focused exclusively on race. While empowering minorities, it disempowers the collectivity of "the people" across majority and minority statuses.

"Them whites, you see, they don't care about us no way," Lela said. "To them, we are just dogs. So you know, you accept it and you move on."

> Whenever the LORD raised up judges for them,
> the LORD was with the judge,
> and he delivered them from the hand of their enemies all the days of
> the judge;
> for the LORD would be moved to pity by their groaning
> because of those who persecuted and oppressed them.

—Judges 2:18

When democratic channels fail, and when the government is to blame—either as a part of the system or as a tool of wealthy oppressors—possibilities for reform turn to heroism outside the state. William represented an ideology of resistance despite his odds of success being low. In the context of a system informed by both institutional and interpersonal racism, leadership, too, is invoked. Like the heroism of the rebel, the heroism of Christ offers potential relief in a seemingly hopeless situation. Those who stand against the system become enshrouded in that faith, a nearly mystical part of another power. And for Lela, that included me.

Lela and I left her house after talking for a while, she dragging her bad leg slightly as she struggled to get into my car for a tour of the area. Hers was a beautiful neighborhood: ample green lawns with mostly ranch-style brick houses, some two stories, often well situated on hilltops. Yet the median house value at the time was only around $30,000. It was white flight, as Lela told me. She and her husband had moved in when the white people were still there. They could afford it with their steady full-time jobs, especially Lela's, which provided benefits. She said that as soon as the blacks came in, the whites left. So, too, did the home values.

Lela first took me to see a close friend and fellow congregation member who lived a short drive up the road. We pulled into the driveway and went up the back steps, across an open porch into the house. We felt the relief of the air-conditioning as Lela opened the door, and I spotted five little girls resting on mats on the gleaming wood floor. A three-year-old with green barrettes in her hair and wearing a denim skirt threw her arms up to be held. I picked her up, and she wrapped her arms around my neck. I followed Lela, carrying the little girl into the living room, where seventy-six-year-old Jamella Kilgore was lying on the couch. She wore a pair of sweat pants and a cutoff white sweatshirt with embroidered flowers on the front. Jamella sat up and introduced herself. Lela told Jamella that I was writing about Vogtle, and Jamella invited us to sit down on the loveseat across from her.

"What is your point?" Jamella asked. "What is your angle on this?"

I didn't answer for a while. The weight of Lela's loss hung heavily. "I'm writing about the community of Shell Bluff, how it has been impacted by the plant, and what has happened with Southern Company in the community."

"And who are you working for?" she asked. "Will this be published in a newspaper?"

I said, "No. I am a graduate student. I hope to put this in a book."

Jamella's suspicion somehow disappeared with my answer. "It is people like you that give us all hope," she said. "Lela has suffered greatly. They shut off her power four years ago. They said that her meter was on the wrong side of the house and that she was the first one who had to replace it, and everyone else would follow. When I found out, I went up and down the block on the cell phone with Lela. We called in and I looked at every house, and every single one of them had the meter on the other side of the house. Why did Lela have to change hers?"

"Jesus," said Lela, melodically.

"Southern Company has all the power," said Jamella, continuing without acknowledgment of Lela's reference to Jesus. "I told Lela that she is up against Southern Power, and she cannot fight them."

"Jesus. Jesus our Lord and Savior," Lela said.

"What about Jesus?" she said turning to Lela and then back to me. "She has stronger faith than I do. I wonder, where's Jesus? Why doesn't Jesus just turn the lights back on?"

Lela continued to pray, ignoring Jamella.

"But you, you give us faith," Jamella said. "We see you, we know the Lord is helping us. He is bringing you to help us. And I will pray for you. I will pray for the Lord to protect you. I can understand why white men try to keep people like us down. I can understand."

"Jesus," Lela said, almost as a plea.

"We are dogs. But when people like you fight them," she said, stopping. "You too are at risk," she finished.

"Jesus," Lela said, a little more pressingly.

Lela's faith was attached to a specific example and a specific savior. While her sense of transcendence freed itself from any rules but a moral code of righteousness, her faith also rooted itself in a hierarchy headed by Jesus. In Jesus, Lela saw someone representing those who, in Howard Thurman's words, "stand, at a moment in human history, with their backs against the wall." Those with their backs to the wall are "the poor, the disinherited, the dispossessed."[29] Jesus as a poor Jew fighting against the centralized wealth of the Romans resonated with Lela as a poor black woman fighting against for-profit democracy.

So too, though, did Jesus stand as a leader. In Michael M. Bell's words, he was considered "impartial," "loyal," "free of material and sexual desire," "separate from the state and economy." In sum he was, "a non-political divine."[30] With a bit of tragic irony, this non-political status as the one of purity and truth, and all others as sinful and filled with fault, facilitates hierarchy. There are those above and those below, making a savior conducive to the power of the state. Even though possessing important minority and rebellious aspects, a savior can reify the power of the state.

Jesus as a savior depoliticizes his status as a minority. Jesus stands as a superior, all-powerful leader above and better than those who worship him while also being eminently sympathetic to their plight. From this hierarchy can come, as Michael M. Bell writes, authoritarianism. So while faith in its transcendence borders on anarchy, Jesus at the top and others at the bottom reinforces the organization of the state. What I mean to stress here is that while faith challenges the aims of for-profit democracy, and Jesus as a minority gives moral authority to the oppressed, Jesus as a savior limits the capacity of people to work more nearly on equal terms, by reinforcing hierarchy and social control.

"You are in danger," Jamella said, warning me. "I tell you, someday the Lord will anoint you with a crown," she said as my eyes widened. "And that crown will fall down around your shoulders because your head will not be big enough to fit it."

I stayed speechless, shocked at their trust in me amid the loneliness of their loss.

Finally I replied, "I think you are putting me on a pedestal."

"We are thankful you are here. To help Lela and tell the truth. The world must know the truth," Jamella said.

Lela, becoming restless, asked for water.

"We all went down on a big bus when Lela's mother died, to see the land," Jamella said, returning with a bottle of water. "So much land! I mean here? There's just a bit of land. But there! The land goes on and on. They want the land. They did the same to me. To my family in Jacksonville. They took it piece by piece. We had 150 acres, and they took it piece by piece."

Lela stood up. It was time to go before Jamella's story ended.

We walked toward the back entrance through the toys and the children at play.

"The mamas can't afford to pay much, so I take them in," Jamella said.

"Thank you," I said as we left.

"Thank you for inviting us in," Lela said.

We got back in the car and Lela directed me to her church, regal and built of brick, with a large white steeple and a graveyard on the side, once a worship site for white families. The back of the church had two stories of offices, and the front majestically boasted big arched windows. We entered through the back door and found ourselves in a long narrow hallway. Shelby Small, the minister's wife, greeted us.

"Hello!" she said, surprised, and looked at me, letting out another surprised "hello." "How did you all get in here? Isn't it locked?" she asked.

"No, it isn't locked," Lela responded. On my way out later, I noticed the big bolt on the door.

Lela led me into the sanctuary, and I thought amid her silence that she was showing me where she worshiped. The blue pews in the enormous sanctuary stood out from bleached white walls. The words "Do so in remembrance of him" hung over the kneeling place at the front of the room.

"Kneel with me," Lela said as I looked around. I knelt beside her, my knees resting on the blue cushion, spotted with tiny white flowers. I leaned forward and clasped my hands in front of me. Lela sat to my right in silent prayer. Shelby came in, and Lela asked her to lead us in a prayer. Shelby rested herself to my left and took my hand. Lela grasped my other. They prayed for my safety. They prayed for my work. They prayed for my family.

After the prayer, Lela led us outside, and we wandered around for a moment—until she spotted a few others who worked at the church. I waited under the shade of a tree as Lela searched around for people to introduce me to. When they arrived, she asked for Bob, another member of the church, to lead a prayer for us all, but me in particular. Lela clasped my hand as the prayer began, grasping it strongly, pulsing my hand. She said, "Yes. Yes, Jesus. Yes." She told me after, "You can never have too much prayer."

We returned to her home as the day faded, and it was getting time for me to go to a meeting. I had arrived that morning before lunch, bringing with me some gumbo, quiche, salad, and brownies for us to share. With her diabetes, Lela wouldn't touch the brownie, and she worried about the mercury in the shrimp, but she said she could have the quiche and salad. She brought out some plates and utensils. I served her some quiche and salad with a plastic fork, and then myself. In my state of hunger, I dug in, keeping the fork for my own use.

I had forgotten to say grace.

"Please join me in a prayer," she said as I guiltily swallowed some quiche.

"My family would be ashamed," I said with a "sorry." The four prayers given since I arrived—not counting the ones that were like poetry, so interwoven with Lela's everyday speech—were not yet enough.

After the prayer ended, I returned to my feast, putting my plastic fork to work. Only too late did I realize, as some salad teetered on Lela's knife, that she had given me her only fork.

> I have also heard the groaning of the Israelites
> whom the Egyptians are holding as slaves,
> and I have remembered my covenant.
> Say therefore to the Israelites, "I am the LORD,
> and I will free you from the burdens of the Egyptians
> and deliver you from slavery to them . . .
> I will bring you into the land that I swore to give to Abraham, Isaac,
> and Jacob;
> I will give it to you for a possession.
> I am the LORD.
>
> —Exodus 6:5–6, 8

"God will tell you to do some strange things," the visiting reverend said melodically to the crowd jammed into the Aberlina Baptist Church for a summer revival in the Shell Bluff countryside.

"Yeah," a man sang in response, dressed smartly in a navy blue suit, his pitch in line with the charged ups and downs of the visiting reverend's rolling voice.

"Because he moves in mysterious ways," the reverend said, shaking "ways" up into a high note.

"Yeah," the man sang in return.

"I have been washed in the blood of the lamb," the reverend sang and spoke, beginning to move up in a fevered pitch as the piano and the clapping crowd joined him. "There are some here who do not know the blood of Christ. I need the blood of Jesus."

"Yes, Lord," a multitude of voices said in unison.

"I am so glad," he sang and spoke toward the ceiling as a piano joined in.

"YES!" the crowd cried, packed from front to back, every face of more color than my own. At the back pew, in the back corner, amid the excitement raging, my anonymity and late entrance allowed me to stay quiet.

"I've been washed."

"YES!"

"In the blood of the lamb.

"YES!"

"I'm."

"YES!"

"So glad"

"YES!"

"I've been washed."

"YES!"

"In the blood."

"YES!"

"Of the lamb."

"YES!"

"On Monday morning."

"YES!"

"In my bedroom."

"YES!"

"I look at my hands."

"YES!"

"And I've been washed," he sang, holding out "washed," hitting the climax of the afternoon. Transcendence did happen. Mary and Lela formed a strong friendship. Color lines could be crossed. Samuel clarified that "we must understand that nuclear, whatever it is, whether it is a nuclear plant or nuclear bomb, if it gives trouble, it's global."

Those acknowledgments and acts didn't seem enough, though. Overcoming the ominous authority of racism, nuclear power, the government, and money called for faith in something greater, a washing away of woes at the hands of Jesus—a savior equipped to destroy the system and render ultimate judgment. Faith in one another was deemed insufficient. People had been betrayed for so long, by so many.

"YES!" the crowd continued.

"I've been washed," the visiting reverend replied.

"YES!"

The piano sensed the leader's movement toward quiet, and so did the crowd. The pace slowed, and the clapping continued gently and sporadically.

"My brothers and sisters. As we are standing here tonight. There are some in this place. Who do not know Jesus as your personal savior. He said, 'Whoever believe in me, let them come. And the day you hear my voice, harden not your heart.'"

"Yes!" came cries and whispers in unison.

"He says to one of us, come clean or you are going to die dirty in the muddy water."

"Yes."

"And I need the blood of Jesus to clean me up, to wash me thoroughly. When it comes to the Christian experience, it comes to the baptism. There are churches who will get you where you want to go. We just want you to join the body of Christ tonight."

The body of Christ, a people, defined by their being born again, baptized into the community of Christ.

The choir moved to the front of the church and broke into "He's alright. Oh, he's alright. He's alright. God is just alright with me. He's alright. Alright. Alright." The older ladies singing at the front of the church wore two-piece skirt suits, sequins and pearls at the shoulders sparkling gently in the dim light. Vividly colored dresses marked the double row of singers. Reds and greens and yellows and oranges and stripes and solids and flowers and dots. The men in the front were all in suits, and some in the audience, too. They swayed back and forth.

That afternoon, no one came forward to be saved.

The congregation broke into applause as the piano thundered to a bluesy end. The Reverend George Ellis, head of the Aberlina Baptist Church, took the stage to offer praise following the visiting pastor. The next night the revival was moving to a neighboring church on the local circuit, all brought together for the yearly celebration.

"We continue on tomorrow night and hope to see all of you then. Amen?"

"Amen," the crowd responded

"Amen. God is good," the Reverend Ellis said in return.

The blood of Jesus, the acceptance of him, and immersion into the water to wash away sin could belong to anyone. I could have chosen to walk forward that afternoon. We all could be "saved." That saving, though, was left to one above us, rather than turning to one another for salvation.

★ ★ ★

The Reverend Ellis took pains to deliver subtle messages that spoke to me, as well as others, during the intimate Tuesday-night Bible studies that I attended at his church. One night he arrived a little late, which always received a few grumbling remarks from those waiting. But as he came in with his easy style, he offered full smiles to those there, and cold feelings retreated with his warm presence.

"The same spirit and Lord. The church is for all God's people," the Reverend Ellis said. The sun was setting, and the shadows rippled on his face. He made little eye contact with me during his lecture on the scriptures, but I sensed he was speaking as much to me as anyone else.

"At one time there was only one church. White and black. Botsford Baptist Church. They were one. Then the whites split off from the blacks," the Reverend Ellis said. Botsford was an old church, dating back to 1773, when it was founded by Edmund Botsford.[31] Then, slaves and masters alike attended the church, blacks sitting up top, and whites below. That history shaped two distinct approaches to Christianity: that of the oppressor and that of the oppressed. Such religion continues to leave believers far apart, as Gayraud S. Wilmore describes: "But it is a matter of serious debate whether a specific religion of a specific people can be transmitted *in toto* to another people—even in the same geographical area—without certain differences arising on account of ethnicity, nationality, social structure and many other factors. Especially is this true in the case of one people who are free and another people who are in slavery."[32] How to move toward "the people" and "a people" at the same time? Doing so requires recognition of what Jason E. Shelton and Michael O. Emerson call distinct elements of the black Christian faith, like experience, survival, mystery, miracles, and justice. Simply put, transcendence requires an absolute recognition of the physical and mental violence and terror practiced against black people by white people, like that practiced against Jesus.[33]

Fully realizing faith in one another, though, necessitates an understanding of Jesus as a human, even a zealot, with his own political flaws, as Reza Aslan writes.[34] Even the flawed can behold mysteries and miracles. Faith can build on the best of people, unlike the utilitarian principles that count on the worst. The rule of numbers can be counteracted by faith in one another's decency. As James H. Cone writes: "The Christian gospel is more than a transcendent reality, more than 'going to heaven when I die, to shout salvation as I fly.' It is also an immanent reality—a powerful liberating presence among the poor right *now* in their midst, 'building them up where they are torn down and propping them up on every leaning side.' The gospel is found wherever poor people struggle for justice, fighting for their right to life, liberty, and the pursuit of happiness."[35] Transcendence can and does become immanence.

As our Bible study ended, the Reverend Ellis brought all sixteen of us together, ten women and six children, in a circle at the front of the church for a final prayer. He prayed for husbands that that could not be there that night. He knew mine was gone. He prayed for all families, aunts, uncles, and cousins. He recited the numbers of the scriptures in his prayer, reminding each of us what we had learned. My hand tingled from my neighbor Iris's strong grasp, swinging me into the rhythm of the group as my arms drew my body back and forth with the melodic prayer. I was bound into a chain of "Thank you, Lord" and "Jesus, Jesus, Jesus" filling the gaps and pauses of the preacher's prayers. My eyes were supposed to be closed, but through narrow slits (I hoped no one would notice), I stared at the maroon carpet. The Reverend Ellis's feet moved around the inside of the circle as he spoke. The heat enveloped us as worshipers picked up their pace with the elevation of the prayer. The last remnants of the sunset streamed upon us through the stained glass.

"Did he reach you?" Iris Fewell asked afterward.

"It was wonderful," I said in return. I meant it. I hadn't paid attention in church for a long time.

Nathaniel, who hit above my knee, looked up and asked: "Are you German?"

"I am part Dutch," I said.

"German?" he asked again.

"No, I'm part Dutch. It's close to German," I replied.

He then said proudly, "Well, I'm one-fourth German!"

We smiled at each other. A moment of transcendence that allowed *a* people to become *the* people—enjoying our shared humanity, but dignified in our difference.[36] A moment of many consciousnesses. Fear declined in favor of shared humanity as we became the transcendent people. For in that context, I found myself guided by those around me toward a moral economy of justice and humanity that profit could scarcely understand. A morality that knew more than our state, our race, or the rule by numbers.

People are indoctrinated with fear.

—Walter Hamilton

Filled up with barbecued chicken, canned green beans, coleslaw, and six straight hours of church (the weekly 2.5-hour Aberlina service, plus a 3.5-hour special family and friends event at a neighboring church), I drowsily drove back with a friend to the relative peace of my trailer. Taking a familiar turn into the lane, I jerked to attention: my gate was wide open, with the lock dangling from the chain.

One way in, one way out, the corner storeowner echoed in my head. Months ago he had warned me, "If they come back there, they ain't coming to love ya."

I drove down the sandy lane and encouraged Sarah, visiting from Wisconsin, to head inside and turn on the air as I spotted a van sitting next to the pond behind the trailer. I finally remembered that Jesse had told me someone would be coming around to figure out why the pond was losing water at a rapid pace. Parking the car, I got out and headed towards the visitors. The water glared up from the edge of the path as I wove my way back. The sand made its way through the thin slits in my leather flats and gathered between my toes.

With my hand shading my eyes for a better view, I focused on a man in his thirties and a young boy a few feet shorter, both clad in camouflage, standing at the edge of the pond. They sported knee-high rubber boots and baseball caps in the same patchwork of greens and tans, and guns dangled from their hands, thankfully at ease by their sides. The doors of the van were wide open. There rested an assortment of weapons, tack, rods, and a cooler.

"Hello," the man, known as Bret Mooney, said to me as I neared.

"Hello," I said back. "How are you?"

"Doin' fine," he said. "I knocked on your door early when we arrived, but you weren't around," he said with a grin. His bright blue eyes were narrowed to half-moons beneath the slight shade of his cap.

"I just got back from a picnic," I replied. "How's the pond coming along? Are you going to have to replace the pipe?"

Bret began explaining that he would be digging up part of the pond to get to a leaking pipe. His son pulled out a large BB gun with a scope and pointed it toward my trailer.

"Whoa!" Bret said. "Don't point that at the trailer."

"Dad, can I shoot at the light?" his son Jimmy asked, looking up from beneath overgrown bangs.

"What brings you to Burke County?" Bret asked, ignoring his son's pointing of the gun toward the top of a tall light pole that overlooked the pond.

CRACK.

"Yeah!" yelled the child. I kept my eye fixed on the light, unable to tell whether he hit it.

"Does your husband work at Vogtle?" Bret continued.

"No," I replied. "I'm here writing about the area. What it's like to have a power plant here and what people think of the new reactors."

"Jesse worked at Vogtle before starting his business," Bret said, referring to my landlord. His mop of red hair edged out beneath his ball cap, which failed to shelter his fair skin, reddened from the sun.

"Look at the fish!" Jimmy exclaimed as the barrel turned rapidly toward the air bubbles that might have come from a form of life beneath the water.

BAM BAM BAM BAM.

No bellies up this time.

His thin arms continued to swerve rapidly around, Winchester in tow.

"Dad, can I shoot the turtle?" he asked with unhinged enthusiasm.

"Yeah," Bret replied. "He's got a lot of land around here," he said to me, continuing to talk about Jesse.

POP.

"I hear around 3,000 acres or so," I replied with distraction. Environmental honor was far from Jimmy's young mind. He had nearly as many weapons at his fingertips as William did, but his sport was altogether different.

"Lot more than that," Bret returned. "He owns up and down this road, all the way back to the turn by McBean."

"Look at that butterfly," Jimmy said. "I'm going to shoot it."

"No," Bret replied, halfheartedly.

POP.

"Hahaha," Jimmy laughed, his freckles crunching together.

"Hey, don't aim that toward the trailer," Bret said again, before redirecting. I had rights of rental, I thought to myself as my ire grew, but not property. Asking him to put down his gun wasn't an authority that I felt I bore. Jesse did, though, and he had given Bret permission to be there. "It's so beautiful out here," Bret continued, obliviously happy to be away from Augusta. "I love to hunt. I've been coming here since I was a kid. Now it gives my son a chance to shoot, fish, hunt, enjoy the peace and beauty of the countryside. Have you seen any more gators around here?"

"No, nothing except the sho . . ." I said, cutting myself off, realizing he must have known to ask.

"You mean shot gator," he said, reassuring me. With a quiet, pointed look at each other, I now knew who had shot my alligator. We both knew it was illegal. That gator was shot in the winter, well outside the hunting season.

"You seen any deer or hogs?" he asked.

"None. The only thing I see around here are possums and squirrels."

"Squirrels!" Jimmy looked up with rabid interest, like a video game player ready to turn the joystick for a quick shot.

"Oh, Jimmy will take care of your squirrel problem," he said.

But I didn't have a squirrel problem.

"Where are the squirrels?" Jimmy asked, eagerly, with a series of jumps, hindered only slightly by the weight of his rubber boots.

"What's that wild hog meat taste like?" I asked Bret, ignoring Jimmy.

"Dad, where's the Browning?" Jimmy asked, rummaging through the back of the van.

"Sorry, I must have forgot to load it," Bret said. "We're never short of guns in this van," he said with a smile. "If you need any protection, and this van is here, don't fear."

An irony, even folly, for Bret to suggest that the weapons aimed at my residence, and ecologies unable to point back at a barrel, could serve in my defense. The domino effects of fear coupled with guns played out in a space I called my own. Like my neighbors, I began to sense a need to protect myself against assault. Jimmy pointed into the lake at two turtle heads, knelt on one skinny knee, and POP POP.

My gun was inside. And that was where I headed.

"I best be heading back in," I said. "Good luck with the pond."

★ ★ ★

"Fear," Howard Thurman writes, "is one of the persistent hounds of hell that dog the footsteps of the poor, the dispossessed, the disinherited."[1] Of Georgia's 159 counties, Burke County in 2011 had the highest assault rate. The second highest in 2010, the fourth highest in 2013, and the fifth highest in 2009. According to the FBI, which compiles local law enforcement records from across the country, aggravated assault is when one person attacks another "for the purpose of inflicting severe or aggravated bodily injury . . . usually accompanied by the use of a weapon or by other means likely to produce death or great bodily harm."[2] The overall violent crime rate, which includes murder, nonnegligent manslaughter, forcible rape, robbery, and aggravated assault, is similarly high in Burke County: third highest in Georgia in 2010 and 2011, seventh highest in 2013, and tenth highest in 2009. These crime rates, even by national standards, are substantial. Burke County's 2011 aggravated assault rate—its worst— was more than three times the national average: about 8 for every 1,000 people, versus 2.41 per 1,000 nationally.[3] In 2010, its violent crime rate was more than twice the national average.[4]

These are not typical numbers for rural counties in America. Nationally, the violent crime rate in 2013 was 3.5 times higher in urban counties than rural ones.[5] For a county of 23,316, with only 28 people per square mile, the crime and violence in Burke County contradict widespread idyllic notions of the countryside and places identified as rural. Rural places have a reputation for being safer than cities, and preferable places to raise a family.[6] The rural sociologist Jennifer Sherman documents the substantial weight of morality in the community balance, where work and conservative values hold the most social currency.[7] So too does a moral privileging of self-sustenance, harking back to the landownership ethic that informs the moral economy of democracy. Much rural pride centers on a close relationship with the ecological world, which materializes in self-sufficiency and local know-how. Michael M. Bell calls this the natural conscience: rural people see themselves as being more embedded in the environment, and consequently on a higher moral footing than their urban counterparts.[8] Wendell Berry supports such a notion when he argues that the devastation of rural communities and farm life through industrialization is synonymous with the devastation of America itself. After all, in his view, culture collapses without a land-people dyad.[9]

If it were only a matter of lots of guns used in environmental pursuits, such moral-centric and idealistic framings of self-sustenance might stand in Burke County. The sportsmanship and hunting ethic could perhaps excuse Bret's tolerance of his son's liberal shooting.[10] Perhaps one could stretch matters to say that turtles and butterflies were casualties in the development of a certain kind of natural conscience. After all, there is ample evidence that rural people own plenty of guns. The Pew Research Center in 2013 reported that nationally 39 percent of rural people versus 18 percent of urban dwellers own guns. In open-country places in the Southeast, like Shell Bluff, that have no incorporated town, the numbers are even higher. Tom Smith, a senior fellow at NORC, found in the General Social Survey that 68.9 percent of households in open-country places in the Southeast have guns.[11] Even though such figures are high, from what I learned, gun ownership is even more widespread in Burke County. Of the sixty-nine residents I interviewed in the Shell Bluff area, black or white, all had rifles or guns in their homes.[12] Such pervasive ownership of weapons is unusual, even for rural people.

A plague of violence and crime had spurred a crisis of public health and conscience that was particularly acute in Burke County. But why?

★ ★ ★

In the weeks before I moved to Burke County, a pregnant white woman was killed by a single shot through the stomach. Her three children found her dead in their trailer. News and police reports provided few details about suspects in her death at the time, and three years later, the alleged killer or killers remained at large.[13] A Shell Bluff local named Cletus Wiley described what he believed to be the backstory as he drove me near the site of the tragic event. We spoke just a month after her death.

"I know exactly what happened. But they are not ever going to say it because it is racial. So it is not going to make the papers," Cletus said, as we drove through Girard, the town closest to Vogtle and the site of the crime. His surname had been in the community since the British Crown first awarded land grants.

"She had at least three kids before," he said, filling in the holes of the story with what he had heard around town. "They were two different daddies. She's white. She was currently pregnant by a black guy. But it wasn't the black guy that she was living with. You kind of get the picture. So the black guy that she was living with had told people, 'If I find out that she is pregnant and it's not mine, I'm going to kill her and I am going to kill him.' Well, somebody killed her, and if I had to bet money on it, I would bet that it was him or the other guy."

"Do you think the sheriff's office will get the killer?" I asked as we turned away from Girard and headed down a road covered by live oaks on our way to Stony Bluff.

"They'll eventually crack it," he said, keeping his eyes on the road. Cletus liked to drink, sometimes putting the hard stuff in Mountain Dew that he sipped from a Styrofoam cup. He said it made the short drive between his home and his web of family a little more fun.

"She had her morality issues," he said. "But she was apparently a very nice young girl. Shot her in the belly and killed the baby. It may be one of those they can never solve. I think they will, because when they get the two guys that are the most likely suspects. . . . Both of them took off. And they can't find them."

"Why wouldn't the paper report on that?" I asked.

"Even though a lot of people that write for it are moderates or conservatives, the editor is very liberal," he answered. "[The editor] doesn't want to put anything in there that is going to offend the black folks. I don't think it would offend the black folks just to tell the truth. Sometimes we don't give our black population enough credit around here for being able to determine facts."

"She was three months pregnant," he said again, pausing. He looked relaxed in his sunglasses and loose, untucked button-up shirt. "They don't have a great sheriff's department, because it's the good-ole-boy system."

"I have heard that from many people I've talked to," I replied.

"There's no doubt about it. Nobody can beat Greg, because as long as he wants to be sheriff, he will be sheriff," Cletus said, talking about the white sheriff who stayed in charge for thirty-six years until he retired in 2016. "He has most of the black folks who are influential, and he's got them. And that's all you've got to have in this county. Although the population has changed. It's probably at least

50 percent white now. It's not so much racial, as he overlooks illegal activities. Thereby, he gets the votes. A lot of things that I say to you today might come across as not racist necessarily, but prejudiced. But I am just telling you the facts as I see them."

Whenever Cletus and I spoke, he never mentioned white-on-white crime. Not at his all-white family reunion, not at the countryside bar and grill BFE (the site of a 2015 white-on-white murder), where we listened to a friend's son play music, not at a handful of late night barbecues, and not during the few times we met for lunch at Burke Perk or the Lakeview Restaurant in downtown Waynesboro. To Cletus, crime in Burke County was a black matter that white people were forced to deal with. He understood the "black population" as the Other.[14]

"Most southern boys are never far from their guns," he explained. Cletus kept his weapon tucked behind the seat in his Ford truck. A few of his relatives openly carried handguns in exposed, not concealed, holsters.

"If you want to shoot sometime, we'll do that too," he offered. That night, he insisted on trailing me back to my cattle gate to make sure no harm came to me. Most nights, if he knew I was out, he would text to make sure that I had made it home safe.

"Having a gun is fine," he said. "But if you don't know how to use it, basically it's a heavy paperweight. Most of the time, if some bad guy gets after ya, all you got to do is pull it out and he will run. If that doesn't work, all you've got to do is pull the trigger, and he hears the noise, and he'll run. So you really don't have to be that good. All you've got to know is how to use it."

That "bad guy" Cletus referred to was implicitly black. Our conversation created a contextual scene of black crime, black male murders, and black illegal activities overlooked by a white but corrupt sheriff. For Cletus, the southern white man stood in opposition to the threat of the black male, whose blackness stripped him of the honorability of "southern."

Here is the first and well-established answer to why Burke County residents have so many guns: white residents' prejudice against and proximity to black residents. Scholars have tirelessly documented the relationship between perceived racial threat and a rush to the gun.[15] There is a long tradition in the South of perpetrating violence against black people simply because white people perceived them as a threat, even when they were innocent. Lynchings are among the most infamous examples. These prejudices are dramatized by crimes that may have no confirmed evidence of black-on-white assault, but still agitate prejudicial fears.

On edge after a high-speed car chase a few nights before that ended in two deaths miles from their home on Highway 23, two white newcomers to the area, Bella Laverty and Finn Hunt, invited me to shoot with them in their back field. The *True Citizen* reported that a police officer, suspecting that two black men were drinking, chased them at a dangerous speed out of town. The car flipped, and the men, ages sixty-six and thirty-six, were crushed and killed. The newspaper reported anonymous complaints that the officer had acted out of line in the high-speed chase, but the chief of police, a black man, countered that the white officer had acted appropriately. In addition to the high-speed chase, Bella and Finn's black neighbors' rear car lights had been smashed the night before. They had called the police. All this took place just miles from Vogtle in the countryside, but around fifteen minutes from the nearest town. After all the chat about the recent happenings, Finn set up a series of targets in his backyard, an empty expanse of dried-up grass and thorny weeds. Formerly a pine field, the clear cut showed a few scattered signs of green recovery.

"I need to be able to shoot him from back there. If he comes into my house, I'm going to shoot him," Bella said as we stood in the warmth of the January sun. She set an imaginary scene for her male target.

"You won't be legal if you shoot him from forty feet away," Finn said while trying to hand Bella a handgun. "The law says he has to be causin' you probable harm. Twenty feet is close enough."

"Anybody could shoot from that close," Bella replied.

"Well, that's all that kind of a handgun's designed to shoot from. You have to use a rifle for further away," Finn quipped as logging machines to the left of us groaned behind a line of pines.

"All I know, is if they come into my house, I want to be able to shoot across the house and hit him," she said.

"The house ain't no more than fifty feet wide. And you're not gonna be able to see all the way across there," Finn said. Bella and Finn were what locals called "Vogtle-ites," in the area specifically for some high-paying plant jobs. They had built a beautiful new house, immaculately adorned with new decor, that I frequented as a dog sitter when they were away overnight.

"Twenty feet is as close as you need to get," Finn continued, who was something of a stately standout with his finely groomed mustache. "You probably won't even have to shoot, as long as you see him."

Bella was in no mood for Finn's reason. She was a superb shot. Finn filled me in on the many competitions she had won as a kid. She nailed the bull's-eye with the handgun and, later, a series of rifles she tried out. Finn couldn't keep up. I missed the targets entirely, regardless of the four weapons I tried, including a Beretta 96 Combat.

Finn and Bella did not explicitly attribute violence to race, as Cletus did. Yet in both cases, the trigger for shooting or talking about it involved black people. The preparation for violence, whether by taking target practice or making a mental laundry list of weaponry, came after events that either involved black people or were imagined to involve black people. I understand the extrapolation of threat from the pregnant woman's shooting, the breaking of taillights, and the high-speed car chase that killed two men, as "token events." My use of "token" here is inspired by the writings of Dana Cloud, who identified tokenism as the assumption that the dramatic success of a few minorities, like Barak Obama or Oprah Winfrey, means that all minorities can just as easily reach success as the majority.[16] Even when there was no definitive case at hand to back up Cletus's notion that black violence was a threat to white people, token events, such as a dramatic car chase or a violent shooting, could set off racial fear and preparations for attack. Certainly, crime rates were high in Burke County—but the racial tenor of blame that informed white residents' view of the culprits was sometimes based on perceptions: an extension of one event to denote the factors behind all others.[17]

The basic point is this: when bad things happen, whether at the hands of black people or not, racial prejudice plays a role in the rush to the gun.

★ ★ ★

A mind focused only on racial prejudice, though, misses the fuller context of gun ownership and violence. Although white ownership of guns is typically higher, a good number of black people also own guns in the Southeast: 56.2 percent of black households in open-country places, and 71.9 percent of white households.[18] Whether black or white, you are more likely than not to have a gun in the house if you live in places geographically similar to Shell Bluff. There was not a black person that I interviewed in the Shell Bluff area who did not have a weapon at home.

Fear, the Reverend Samuel Franklin explained, is the primary reason why. "I've been in some hell of places," he said. "Okay? Had it not been for my faith, I would be afraid. There was a time, I have to admit. And my head has turned white, my faith is stronger. But there was a time when I used to be armed. I had a gun that stayed with me all the time back then. Back in the seventies, when I was part of the civil rights movement, I went to Glasgow [Kentucky] one morning, and somebody shot out a tire," Samuel explained. "So I turned around, came back. Came back to Louisville. Had the tire changed. Then went right back to Glasgow. He got me by surprise, but this time I was lookin' too."

"Did they shoot again?" I asked.

"No, no. Didn't have any problem. I am so glad," he said, laughing. Because if shots had been fired, the Reverend Franklin had been ready to return them. Today, he keeps rifles at home for rabbit hunting. But he no longer carries one on his person or in his car.

The move toward weapons for protection grows out of a long-standing and persistent division between black and white community members. Ula Young's trailer was one of the roughest I knew to be inhabited, and the most rundown of any I visited. The roof was rusting, and on the bulging tin sides were some holes that had been hastily patched with gray sheet metal that stood out from the peeling blue and white paint. An old, rusted-through blue van was parked outside. Four two-by-fours were stuck precariously into some other two-by-fours to form unstable steps that led up to her screened porch, which hung off the front of the single-wide. There was no rail for Ula, now elderly, to hold on to when she went in and out.

I called out for Ula from the top step when I came onto the porch, since there was no doorbell or way to knock without entering first through the porch. She hollered out from inside the trailer that she was coming. The screen mesh on the windows of the porch was ripped and gaping.

Ula gave me a big hug when she came to the door, barefoot in a taupe-colored cotton dress that hit below her knees. She invited me to sit down on the porch where there was more light. Her electricity had been turned off when she couldn't pay the bill. Inside the porch, the linoleum tiles were peeling up, and ants ran across the floor. I sat down on a stained flowered cushion on a wooden chair adjacent to a long wooden table. She sat down on a plastic bench that she had draped towels over.

"We lived on the other side," she said as we sat down together, telling me about the area where she grew up. "They called this across the creek. Above the church. She'd [mother] tell us to go to the store and get her some thread. But she said if you hear a car coming, 'cause there weren't many cars back in the days, she said you all gotta hide in the bushes. So we would hear a car comin'," she said, raising her voice as a semi rushed past on the busy River Road. The plant traffic roared by incessantly. "And we would hide in the bushes. Because it was dangerous for us," she said. "They may snatch you up and do anything to you. Just 'cause you black."

Ula was never attacked, but she lived in fear of it. By the time she was eight years old, she was cooking for her family while they were in the fields picking cotton and peas, shaking the peanuts, and breaking the corn. She recalled with a smile, revealing two deep dimples, that on some Saturdays her daddy would let them take a bit of money and buy crackers or bologna at the shop. There was never enough to eat.

"We lived on this farm," she said, slapping a few ants off her legs and encouraging me to do the same. "The land we lived on belonged to Joe King. My father farmed half of it, and my uncle the other half. What they were doin', they were sharecropping. At the end of the year, they never made any money because the man would tell him, 'You know, Billy'—my dad was named Billy—'Billy you got so-and-so much fertilizer. You got this many seeds from me.' By the time he paid him, the seeds and stuff, my dad hardly had any money. We had to pay rent. We had to go to the spring. To a branch here and took water back to the house. Everything my daddy got, he thought he had to go through the white man to get it."

Her mother, though, didn't think the same. She purchased a house with about thirty acres. Ula is now in her late sixties, but that long-standing dominance of the white man, and fear and distrust, continues to shape much of her understanding of the interworkings in Burke County. Even though her own grandfather was white, he said, in response to her asking whether she was his granddaughter, "Where you all gettin' that from?" Despite disowning Ula as a grandchild, her grandfather stayed with her grandmother, whom he called "cook," until she died.

"I just didn't understand why people don't get along," she said, recalling her first job off the farm, when the full weight of the racial caste system hit her. "Why, why, why? Because I am one color and you another color, I've got to be judged by the color of my skin? Why can't you treat me right? Why you talkin' to me this way? I haven't did anything to you. I didn't understand it. [My employer] sent me to a psychiatrist because they thought I was crazy."

While Ula counted herself faithful, her beliefs were not enough for her to overcome her fear of white people. Nor was faith enough for Ms. Rayanna. Even though a leader in her black Baptist church, and a local icon of perseverance, hard work, and neighborliness across racial lines, she kept her shotgun handy behind her couch by the front door.

"When I first got married, my husband had a gun," Ms. Rayanna explained, her hair tucked under black netting and an apron pulled over her ankle-length skirt. "And you know how it is when you first get married you want to do some of everything the husband does. He was shootin' one day, and I told him, learn me how to shoot. But I didn't like the handgun. I liked to do the rifle."

"You could lean it against your shoulder and get better aim?" I asked.

"Uh-hmm," she replied. "And the little handgun, I am slow about pullin' the little trigger."

Local fears, while sometimes rooted in threat from the opposite race, also existed irrespective of color. When I dropped by for visits at Ms. Rayanna's impeccably clean gray house down a red dirt road, picturesque with well-tended flower beds, she always asked me whether I had locked my car doors. Even though her closest neighbors were relatives, and even though her house had never been broken into, she lived in fear of a black family that lived across the highway.

"Did you lock your car?" she asked after I pulled up one afternoon.

"Should I?" I responded. "Why . . . ?" I started to ask.

"I don't never want people to come, because the neighbors across the road have some young boys," she said, interjecting.

"Have they been in trouble?"

"Yes, ma'am," she said, still standing, and glued to the open door. "Well, maybe it's all right because the bus put one out. And maybe they've gone on home."

"I saw the bus," I said.

"Uh-huh," she replied.

"I was driving behind it . . ."

"I took some of your soup," Ms. Rayanna said, sitting down and changing the topic. She had been sick, and had frozen part of a pot of chicken soup I brought her. She talked about how she liked my hair and asked about my husband before leaning up from the corner of the couch to look out the glass door.

"Do you want me to close that door?" I said, wondering whether she would feel safer with it closed.

"You leave that door so you can see if anybody comes up," she replied.

"You worried because my car's out there someone is going to come up?" I asked.

"Well, they sometimes walks," she replied. "You knows how boys are. If they leave the house, I can see, because the road is right in front of my door."

"Are you worried about those boys bothering you?"

"No, I seen them before Christmas, and they don't come over here," she replied. "But you know how the devil is. He's everywhere. And I don't trust them. I don't never know when they might come this way. So I keep my door locked all the time. I'm not afraid of them. They seem like nice men. I heard they're not in good standin' with messin' with somethin' they don't need to."

Ms. Rayanna religiously raked her sandy yard so she could see any footsteps when she woke up in the morning or after she came home from getting groceries in town.

"There they go on back up the road. A four-wheeler, or whatever you call it. I don't think they have a car," she said, rigid on the edge of the couch with a keen look out the door.

"Huh," I said.

"I'm okay," she replied, sensing my concern. "They just runnin' up and down. If they don't have on a helmet, the law gonna catch them."

In the hour and a half I spent with Ms. Rayanna that late afternoon, she interrupted our conversation seven times to watch and report on the family across the road. She said she had considered moving to town so that she would constantly have people around, for she worried when her family left to go into Augusta for an afternoon or evening and she was left alone.

Ms. Rayanna's gun behind the couch, Ula keeping watch out for the white folks driving by, Cletus staying close to his gun, and Bella and Finn practicing their aim—all attempted to enact a freedom of sorts: a freedom rooted in fear and distrust. I call this "freedom under the gun," which affords some semblance of liberty through the self-defense of bearing arms. It often occurs when freedom for the moral economy of democracy has generally fled from sight. While related to token events and racial prejudice, freedom under the gun is not necessarily rooted in racial prejudice. I see freedom under the gun as a second trend, somewhat distinct from token events and racial prejudice, that helps explain why guns and violence saturate Burke County.

The philosopher Isaiah Berlin identified two types of freedom: freedom-from, the freedom to do what one wants against an antagonist perceived to be threatening; and freedom-to, a self-proclaimed liberty to do as one wishes by cultivating conditions conducive to that state. The first freedom, the negative type, seeks freedom in face of some sense of oppression; the second, positive freedom, enjoys liberty in a setting without the aggravations that shape the first.[19] In Burke County, the sense of positive freedom had collapsed under the utilitarian logic that sacrificed people and places to the majority's interest.[20]

In this way, Burke County is a window into broader problems plaguing the nation—the problem of having the freedom to do something versus the problem of having freedom against something. Burke County's freedom is set against the antagonistic conditions wrought by for-profit democracy and the perpetual burden of the minority.

The set-against notion of liberty couples with weaponry to give rise to freedom under the gun. Jack Katz describes how "unable to sense how he or she can move with self-respect from the current situation," a person can come to jump "at the possibility of embodying, through the practice of a 'righteous' slaughter, some eternal, universal form of the Good."[21] The most important point is that crime becomes the method of choice when people have few choices already—it thus becomes a way to enact control over an out-of-control situation, like that cultivated by for-profit democracy.[22]

"Can you tell me about the crime?" I had asked Ms. Rayanna on another occasion. "Has that changed over your lifetime?"

"Yes, Lord. Yes, ma'am. 100 percent," she said. "When I was coming up young, you didn't hear of nobody killin' nobody. You didn't see nobody prisoners. No young people who everybody was in prison. The only person that I remember seeing young, he was twenty years old. Back in those days they wore white clothes, with wide black stripes. And I was afraid of them. I was afraid of them stripes like I was [of] the people. And you wouldn't hardly see but five or ten in a group. And they would be beside the highway cleanin' up, cuttin' the trees, and diggin' the ditches. But now, you see a lot of fifteen- and sixteen-year-olds on the highway, pickin' up trash. That's a lot of changes. So much change. 100 percent. We didn't have no place to keep children back in those days. It just was a jailhouse. They didn't have no children in trouble back in them days. If your child did something underage, the parents would take care of that. Beat that child nearly to death. And that would be it."

Negative liberty, agitated by the absence of collective goods, by targeting, and by the erasure of rights, flourishes when the democratic state's legitimacy collapses. Ms. Rayanna's sense of security was under attack, as she sensed killings in Burke County to be on the rise. Token events gain increasing prominence, which reaffirms what I take to be an "anti body of logic" as the national and legal structures for a "pro body of logic" collapse. A key anti body of logic belongs to the exclusionary reasoning of race and racism—that one color is to blame for the problems of another color, versus a pro body of logic, by which all are entitled to human rights and prosperity, despite minority statuses denoted by skin color or class. Rather than freedom-to for all, freedom becomes something to seek against someone else.

But anti bodies of logic do not stop at racial lines. They are most powerful in any context when people sense that they have lost security. It was easy to be in favor of something when things seemed to be being created rather than destroyed. But when one feels under attack, one positions for self-defense.

"Why do you think there is so much more crime?" I asked Ms. Rayanna.

"The system. Parents used to could chastise and raise the children. You can't do it now in a certain way. You can't whup a child. You can whup him, but if that child call 911, they will want to put the parents in trouble about it. You go to school, some parents don't want the teachers to chastise your child. And that's givin' the child a chance to do what it want to do. So I think it's the system gots a lot to do with it."

There the system came up again, the utilitarian state, perpetually demanding that minorities sacrifice ideologically, institutionally, and culturally. Here is where my understanding of violence and gun ownership departs from much existing scholarship on crime and guns. I see rates of ownership and crime as directly connected with the state's validity. When centralized authorities are seen largely as invalid, either as part of the system or as part of the government, citizens need some way to cope with that insecurity. Guns hold power, power that expands beyond a person's reach. Gun ownership and self-defense become more important as state legitimacy wanes, and perhaps even further, as the state is seen as a threat. A sense of insecurity takes root, one agitated by racial tension.

Leon Lewis, a black man who lives within the plant evacuation zone, described himself as "just an ole country boy," adding, "I like to live in the country. But I am not like the rest of them. I'm strong union." He counted his relatives back five generations in Burke County, even tying his surname to former slave owners in the area. He felt that he had witnessed substantial improvements in civil rights.

Yet, Leon saw racial tensions flaring recently, in no small part because of Barack Obama's presidency. Leon said, "Most of the white
people, they hate him."

"The black male is just, in a sense, fading out," said Leon, a grandfather who placed himself close to the issue. "I read this article the
other day in the *Augusta Chronicle*, and they was talking about how
hard it is now to get young black males into education to teach
school. That used to be the thing to do. They just come out with all
these crazy laws and stuff now. All this shoot to kill, neighborhood
watches, and stuff. This shouldn't have been allowed and all. Some
state was trying to create some law to allow college students to have
guns on campus and all kind of crazy stuff. It's not just guns. If a gun
is available and a little argument they get into with somebody, that's
the first thing they are going to do is pull out a gun and shoot somebody. It's too much of that's going on."

"You've been keeping up with the case in Florida," he said with a
slow and steady delivery. I nodded. "It is really horrible. It is going to
bring such a racial divide and all. They not just protesting in Florida.
It is beginning to have protests now all over the United States."

The Trayvon Martin shooting was fresh on Leon's mind. In Florida, an unarmed seventeen-year-old was shot by a neighborhood
watch volunteer, who was later acquitted of his murder. The ruling
and shooting brought regional and national attention to an issue that
was festering in Burke County, too. Leon noticed a racial divide taking the media by storm. It was based on different notions of freedom: freedom from white oppression for some of the black protesters, countered by freedom from black violence for some of the white
protesters. Freedom to simply live was getting lost in the shuffle as
the racial rift capitalized on the logic of freedoms-from, fed by the
social ills of minority sacrifice for majority interest.

"Do you think there's more violence than there used to be?" I
asked Leon.

"Oh, yeah," he said. "With drugs and all, it is a lot more violent
crimes and all. A lot of people are so afraid of them and all. And
then, it's black-on-black crime too. Just like Augusta, it's an average

of probably thirty young black men killed per year there. Just violent crime. Some of them even be friends. And just get into a little argument and pull out a gun and shoot them."

Leon had guns, in part because he enjoyed hunting and in part to keep the intruders out. Leon related some of his personal history: "Back in the eighties I had a break-in. First, in 1985, someone broke in the house while we were at work. Then it happened again in 1988. Then I put in a security system, and I really believed that helped. That's somethin' you don't ever want to come home and find that somebody has broken into your house. I don't think anythin' else can give that kind of feelin' and all. You come in, and everything is just torn all up because I guess they were lookin' for money and all. Especially the second time. It just gives you this feelin'. Somebody broken in here while I was at work, came into your private dwellin', and did all this. After you had been home. They never did caught nobody or anythin'."

Since then, Leon has spent $40 a month for a security system, and his brick house, on a dirt road well back from a paved route, hasn't been broken into since. Unlike Cletus, Leon did not see the police department's corruption as due to its alignment with black folks, but he said, "Let me put it this way. I think that the Sheriff's Department and all could do a much better job than they do."

A perpetual fear had taken root in Burke County residents, white or black, centered on freedoms-from: Leon's freedom from intruders, Cletus's freedom from bad guys, Ms. Rayanna's freedom from her neighbors.

Leon did not put a color on his intruders, because they were never caught. Patty, who held at gunpoint two thieves she caught on her property, made sure to mention race in retelling that particular story, as well as other notorious crimes in the community. She saw money-eyed corruption, and what she called the "lawless" sheriff's department, as to blame, but not a general race. It is important to stress that not all white people resort to token events. Patty had enough interracial traffic to prevent her from using a token representation of criminal activity to make a generalization by color. But she also had enough experience to know that crimes were common, making her feel a constant need to be prepared to defend herself—a constant state of agitation cultivated by freedom-from.

The two burglars that Patty caught on her property were white and female. She attributed their stealing in part to an insider deal between a local white business owner and the sheriff, although she had no direct evidence. She retold recent cases of murder, including two white women accused of shooting their white husbands.[23] She described rape cases, some decades old, that she had heard about in the course of some of her volunteer work, mentioning the race of the rapist in each case (sometimes black, sometimes white) but not stereotyping by group. Patty kept guns on her property, and in her truck when she went out on her land, and cursed the power lines for allowing intruders easy, undetected access to her property and people's homes. She felt compelled to protect her freedom by carrying. The gun—the same size for women and men—tipped the power balance in what she viewed to be her favor. Her weapon provided a fleeting but tangible ability to secure freedom under the gun as fear flourished.

★ ★ ★

At the heart of gun ownership and violence rests a third factor, in addition to freedom-from and token events: an approach to people as naturally inclined toward violence. In a utilitarian state formulated around majority and minority, for-profit democracy fosters a for-and-against way of thinking that rapidly morphs into good and bad.

"With guns, with weapons, there is the fear of violence," Walter Hamilton explained to me. "If you mess with me, I might just mess with you. I might just blow your ass away. I don't care if it's black or white. The threat is there. People are indoctrinated with fear. Especially toward the black population. 'Keep them under control.' It's gotten to the point where, 'I'm defending my house, probably, from this black guy, from breaking and entering. I want to make damn sure I got my gun.' That's the level it's at."

"Was it that way before?" I asked him. Walter's family had been around Burke County for a while. His antebellum roots were more or less white and aristocratic.

"It's always been that way to a large extent," Walter explained as we drove through his fields, and he paused to show me the latest addition to his herd—a friendly bull named Murphy. "Hey, big guy!" he called out with a lopsided smile. "But it's been unspoken," he continued. "But all these terrible things that have happened kind of bring it to the forefront."

By "terrible things that have happened," Walter meant the widespread shootings of young black men, which were making national news and just beginning to motivate the Black Lives Matter movement. I asked Walter whether he thought there was more crime now than there was before.

"Yeah," he said. "Then who's doing the ramping? What is it? What is it all about?" he asked me in return, steering us out of the pasture and toward his field of crops. "I don't know. I am not a conspiratorial-type person. I don't think they are trying to do it. But I do think there are things that are driving the violence in the culture. Both white, black. White-on-white. Black-on-black. All of that is somehow just getting more and more tense. I kind of think of it like climate change. Our weather. Weather as opposed to climate. The question is of climate change. There is no question in my mind that the changes in weather are almost exclusively related to climate change. Now and then, you've got natural variation within the weather. The seasons change. It is going to happen anyway. The earth is going to turn even if there isn't a damn thing on it. And it is going to tilt on its axis."

Walter moved rapidly in the direction of environmental determinism to explain people's motives, what I pinpoint as a "naturalization of violence." Crime is simultaneously excused and accelerated by the belief that people are innately inclined toward such behavior. This is the third factor that I see pushing the rush to the gun in Burke County: the assumption that people are born with violent proclivities.

"But with all this carbon in the atmosphere that is already there, it is not a question of are we going to do it later," Walter continued, bringing the golf cart to a stop. We both got out and began walking, his thin legs catching the sun between his shorts and work boots. "It is only going to get worse. But if we don't start mitigating now, in some serious way, it's going to continue to boost everything. Ramp up, if you will, the everyday weather. It's just that much worse. In a way, it's the ramping up of violence in a community. You can look at it in a way like that. It is not a perfect simile. There is a certain thing of that. Human nature. Violence. Extremes in human relations. And then the weather. Driven by climate change. Ramping it up. It's not conspiratorial. But it's fact. The question is, are we going to be able to bring the globe to its senses? And really, we can only do it in the United States. Which begs the question: if we don't do it, who is going to?"

While seeing violence as part of "human nature," Walter also stepped back from such a contention. Climate change was about the earth and its ecology, but simultaneously it was agitated by people's actions. In short, while he depoliticized violence through recourse to the natural, he simultaneously recognized that people's intentions had something to do with it.

"This begs the question of where does the government come in," I said in return to Walter, trying to get him to further explain what he meant by the "United States." Our rapport was fast, intense. We both had landed on something that was unnerving, so much so that we had failed to talk about the crops we were walking through, a rare occurrence when the two of us spoke. "In terms of violence, what do you think of the law?" I continued. "Do people not respect the law?"

"They don't care," he said. "They operate outside of the law. You cannot have enough law enforcement people to stop the violence in this community. There is no way. It won't. Not any more than— again, go back to climate change. How are you going to stop that big storm coming down that's related to extreme weather? You can't. There is no way."

"You don't think putting people behind bars is going to help?"

Walter shook his head no.

"So why?"

"Effective law enforcement will help. You can't let people get away with murder. They may try to get away with it. But I don't think that is going to change the violent nature of people."

Walter again supported the same idea that Hobbes characterized as a dog-eat-dog world. And there Walter landed on precisely why utilitarianism continues to have so much power, even among democratic people who ultimately believe in their state for the good reasons, not the bad ones. Fear edges in; people come to believe that others really are fundamentally violent and self-interested. That we all are indeed just out for ourselves, as the state claims in treating us like mere numbers.

"Then you tie that [violent nature] in with their damn guns? Holy moly," Walter said. "This idea, 'I have a right to my gun. I have a right to protect myself.' There's all this fear, going back to this black thing. They fear that the blacks are going to break in. 'They are going to rape my wife and my daughters. They are going to kill or they are going to steal from me. I am not going to let that happen because I am going to blow that son of a bitch away.'"

Walter, while allowing himself to slip into a naturalization of violence, did not form gun-centered habits in his own self-defense. Even though he owned two shotguns, including an old .22 target rifle, he didn't bother shooting either of them. He never carried, and made a point of telling me so. "I am just not a gun person," he explained. "I did not grow up hunting. Now, Evaline grew up with guns all around."

When I sat down for a feast of Vidalia onion casserole and some fresh gulf shrimp with Walter and his wife, Evaline, they didn't disagree directly about weapons. The right to bear arms was something they both could agree on, that is, until the topic turned to carrying.

Evaline started by explaining that she had "a wonderful childhood growing up on the farm." She had horses, learned how to drive when she was twelve, got stuck in pastures full of Angus cattle, and played in the cotton fields and pecan groves. "I had a pistol and a rifle I kept in the jeep with me because we were always finding snakes and all kinds of critters," she described. But not anymore. "I have to find my damn gun because he won't let me keep it in the car," Evaline complained.

"I don't want it in the car, because she'll leave the damn thing in there," Walter quipped back, echoing Evaline's emphasis on "damn." "I'm driving her car most of the time. [A police officer] could say, 'Oh, I didn't know that was in there, this .38 revolver.' I'd say, 'Well, sorry, sir. It's her car. Her gun. And she has a permit, but she's not here. She's at work.'"

Thus, while Walter thought people naturally violent, he explicitly resisted making guns an everyday part of his life, even when his wife insisted that he should. He countered his own naturalization of violence by his explicit choice not to carry. He stood his ground by not carrying a gun.

★ ★ ★

Despite the processes pushing the rush to the gun in Burke County—token events, freedom-from, anti bodies of logic, and naturalized violence—Walter resisted the pull of the tide.

"You know, we've had this separation between blacks and whites, and not only here," Walter said, explaining his reasoning. "But everywhere. And they don't understand each other. The whites don't understand blacks. The blacks don't understand whites and what motivates them."

Walter told me that he saw the gun as a barrier to overcoming the suspicion and animosity that fed the beast of violence in Burke County. Freedom-to needed some "traffic," in his words, some traction to pull people together toward community goods, rather than apart toward individual self-defense. Burke County needed community that could bask in the moral economy of a democracy shared, rather than individuals desperately opposed in their efforts to protect themselves from one another. Studies show that less segregation is correlated with fewer black homicide victims. More generally, the more disadvantaged the community, the higher the level of crime—black or white.[24] Walter thought that people needed space to be people, to see one another more as humans and less as majorities and minorities strapped for resources and exploited.

Walter saw relationships as key to countering the fear that negative freedom counted on. He explained how his work in education, training, and public service helped him cross the color line. "There are so many people like me who do not have the opportunity that I had to learn," he explained, referring to his work as an educator. "I hate the fact that it is a black and white community situation. Why? I mean, we are all humans. A community of human beings. But it doesn't seem that way down here. It is something, to an extent, in the black community. And definitely," he stressed, "in the white community."

Interracial traffic was stalled by the segregated schools, according to Cora Beth Shaw. Cora Beth, a prominent politician, explained that she wanted to become involved in Burke County government to become an "advocate" for rural people. Cora Beth described Burke County as "very poor," with "very few opportunities" for youth, stemming from the still segregated educational system.

"You went from slavery, to sharecropping, to Jim Crowe," she said. "I finished Waynesboro High in Industrial School, which was a segregated school, in 1965. Schools weren't really integrated until 1971 there. In the meantime, when *Brown v. Topeka Board of Education* came down [in 1954], they built a private, segregated academy [in 1960]. Most of the white kids go to Edmund Burke Academy. The white kids who go to the public schools are the very poor or the very wealthy. There was a subset of [white] leadership who said we have to sustain our public schools. They were thinking about business, the community. So those kids stayed in the public schools. But the majority of white children go to Edmund Burke Academy. The interesting thing about Burke County is you have this division among white people between the public education proponents and the private ones. They fight each other tooth and nail."

The division was palpable. Burke County High School is 70 percent black; from what I heard from local accounts, Edmund Burke Academy is all white.[25] Hardy and Caroline Kessinger, two white outliers, faced ridicule for sending their children to Burke County public schools rather than the private Edmund Burke Academy. The intense judgment exercised against them by white parents resulted in subtle and overt methods of social exclusion.

"I went to public schools," Hardy said. "Both of our children went to public schools. I think that the powers that be in this community cause this to be two school systems, private and public. The private school is a throwback to integration times. It's just a fact. They'd like to forget that, but it is a fact." He continued, "I think it does a couple of things. Number one, that private school isn't free. People put a lot of money into it, into construction, building, all of these things. It also takes their interest away from the public school system. I have a lot of friends in the black community, and I've had some of them who were very active. And one of them in particular said, 'I don't give a damn about that private school. As long as I get that tax money for my public school. Why am I going to worry? As long as they pay their taxes.' But to me, that is sort of narrow. Really, it is the support of the [educational] system. I don't know if we had a single system that it would necessarily make the system better. As long as you've got that dichotomy. There are people who are going to say we have a right to go to private school. Now, with the private school, you have years of this thing going on, and all this alumni. I don't know if they will ever stop it."

"Do black kids go to the private school?" I asked.

"No," Caroline replied.

"None?" I asked.

"No," she said again.

"It's a segregated academy," Hardy stressed to me again. "They can deny that as long as they want. It is a segregated academy, created purely for that reason. Now, to do away with that, you've got all of this baggage that goes with it. School spirit. The EBA Spartans, as opposed to the Bears."

"Here is an interesting little tidbit," Caroline began. "All the kids that my oldest son went to preschool with had the birthday parties. We made the decision to put them in public school mainly because we couldn't afford to pay the private school. You write twelve checks at the first of the school year, and they deposit them like clockwork. When our son and Jim Weston's son and Jerrod Cox's sons both went to public school, all the little friends he had started to have birthday parties with, they stopped inviting him to them." She paused for a while, considering. "Just the fact that these kids who were our son's best friends last year would not even invite him to their birthday party this year because he went to a public school, and they went to a private school."

"This persisted?" I asked.

"Yes," Caroline replied. "The only thing that didn't totally ostracize us was the fact that the doctors did it also."

Caroline said that she "had no problem with integration": "[I] was raised with the blacks. For the first six or seven years of my life, all of my friends were black."

"Was that rare?" I asked.

"Back then it wasn't," Caroline replied. "Because if you grew up on a farm, you had all the labor that worked on the farm with you. And we had a black maid. The foreman was black. Between the two of them, they kept me out of more trouble. They were also there when my parents weren't. They kept us so much of the time. Fishing. They'd be right there with me."

Integration formalized racial mixing institutionally, but the privatization of education afforded a method of skirting the Supreme Court ruling. And as farming declined in Burke County, and the tenant-farming arrangements that accompanied it, informal integration—in which white and black people mixed through their everyday work—declined, too. While the retreat of paternalism was a welcome event, its exodus took with it perhaps a becoming attribute: casual mixing.

Somewhat anomalously for a region of the Black Belt, there is ample money for education in Burke County. Plant Vogtle's taxes pump millions of dollars into the public schools. By some accounts, the standard of education at the public schools seems good: eighth-grade testing scores show that 96.1 percent of students are meeting or exceeding standards in reading, 80.2 percent are meeting or exceeding standards in math. (Figures are not publicly available for the Edmund Burke Academy.)[26] The Burke County High School graduation rate is 94.2 percent. But the Georgia Department of Education gives Burke County High School a 62.3 on its College and Career Ready Performance Index, substantially below the state average of 75.5.

"When you talk about racism, it's an attitude," Cora Beth explained. "If you ask a typical white person in the community, why can't he do better on test scores and that, they'll tell you about the poverty, they'll tell you about the single-parent households, they'll tell you about the special-needs kids, the drugs. It's low expectations. It's like we have all these black kids in the school, so what you expect? That's where the racist attitudes come in. So because of that, there's not much of an effort to promote, to expand."

Cynthia Duncan, in her highly regarded book *Worlds Apart*, documents the central role of education in alleviating poverty in rural America.[27] When schools divide communities into the haves and the have-nots, children lose their potential for social mobility. Divided districts stifle the ability of the community to come together. Those who share a similar moral economy across races—the barebones of political, economic, and human decency—then have trouble crossing the road to create the traffic that Walter sees as critically important. And there festers resentment and budding animosity, as freedom to an education for all becomes freedom from the other school.

Treated to a Lowcountry boil and an ice-cold glass of homemade sweet tea, I sat with Thomas and Lacy Harold, two white residents, in their recently renovated kitchen. Our discussion of young people's difficulty in getting jobs at Vogtle quickly turned into a sharp critique of integration.

"They come out of school without the preparation to work, and the attitude to achieve it," Thomas said, without any specific racial attribution, but complaining about the qualifications of young people locally who wanted to get Vogtle jobs.

"Our schools have gotten terrible," Lacy continued. Both Lacy and Thomas had attended public schools. As for their children, they made certain to send them to Edmund Burke Academy, which they believed had a much better quality of education.

"The problem is they have pushed your A, B, and C groups together," Thomas continued. "The teacher, to make sure everyone achieves a passing score, pulls down the A group so that the C group can get on okay. Even though you have your very smart group at first, eventually they will be pulled down, too. They will lose that edge and intelligence. They have to pay so the others can come along."

The general discussion of students with different intellectual capabilities quickly became more specific. They were talking about race.

"We had the exact same thing happen to me when I went to high school," Lacy said. "They forced the integration of the schools. It was so terrible. I mean, nobody had a choice. The blacks had to go with the whites. They didn't have a choice either. I would go to school every day with a spray bottle of homemade disinfectant that my mother would make up. They disgusted me. I absolutely hated them. Every time I would sit down at my desk, I would spray the desk. I would spritz it all around and wipe off all of that kinky hair on my desk. I just hated those kinky black hairs." She continued, her momentum building, "There was one black guy who always sat beside me. He was the star basketball player, and he had a terrible lisp." She stopped here and imitated him: " 'Miss Lacy, Miss Lacy, what time is it?' He asked me the same question every single day at the exact same time. 'What time is it, Miss Lacy? What time is it?' I thought to myself, why in the world can't he know the time when he asks me the same thing every day? At one stage I asked him, 'Can you read the numbers? Can you read what the numbers are on the clock on the wall? Those two arms on the clock work together to tell you the time.' " She paused, watching me. "He replied, 'Miss Lacy, I can't read.' "

Lacy predicated her freedom to education on her black neighbors' freedom from her education. More simply, she saw her own capacity to get a good education as predicated on blacks' exclusion from that education. For most white families that I spoke to, the sense was that the private school enabled their children to keep up with the more educated elite. Certainly, money often can buy a good education and a ticket to social mobility, as Annette Lareau carefully documents in her study of children of different class backgrounds.[28] Especially for those who never had an opportunity to go to college because their families did not have the money, like Lacy and Thomas, the resentment leveled toward the public school system was acute. Rather than seeing shared opportunities for traction across races, and elevated education and community support for all, Lacy and Thomas founded their notion of good education on an anti body of logic. This negative freedom came to cultivate an attitude of resentment and, eventually, hate, as Howard Thurman describes: "Hatred, in the mind and spirit of the disinherited, is born out of great bitterness—a bitterness that is made possible by sustained resentment which is bottled up until it distills an essence of vitality, giving to the individual in whom this is happening a radical and fundamental basis for self-realization."[29] That distilled bitterness crystallized into thinking the very worst of people. Lacy told me a story about a black classmate explaining to her how integration afforded him a better education— the freedom to learn. He had gone on to college, but Lacy had not.

"Those four years after we were forced to integrate, I just floated," Lacy said. "We all didn't achieve anything. We just got through and got out. I didn't learn a single thing. The teachers were just trying to get us through and get us out the door. Nobody wanted it. In later years, black people in my class would come up to me and say I was the nicest to them out of the white people. I couldn't believe it. They said that, and I absolutely hated them. I just replied that none of us wanted to be there, but that we had to."

"The government forced it on us," Thomas added. "We didn't have a choice. They took away our choice."

Like Lacy and Thomas, Gerald Henry, a white man who lived in the plant evacuation zone, told me he "didn't have anyone to pay his way," and consequently he had been unable to attend college. He was insecure about his accent, and often slowed down or formalized the way he spoke so that I could better understand him. When he cursed, his accent would thicken again. I asked Gerald whether his children attended the Burke County schools.

"Noooooo," he replied, dragging it out.

"Private school?" I responded.

"Both of them," Gerald answered. "And if I had to work a double shift, which I did most of the time, they were not goin' to school with the niggers. Not in Burke County. No. No. My education was kind of, durin' the time when, in the South, we were forced to go to a black school. We were bused. First of all, I think I was in about the fifth grade. When I went to the sixth grade, they bused the black teachers from the black school over to here. And it was probably a lot like you listenin' to me talk. If I talk too fast, you don't have a clue as to what I am saying, because my slang, my dialect. Right? Isn't it different?"

"It's a lot different," I answered him.

"It was real different when I had to be taught by someone that I couldn't understand," he continued. "It never has been in the black community, very few that speak good English. And I find myself talkin' a lot like, with a slang, and cutting words. And I contribute that because of goin' to the public schools and just being able to communicate. I went to public school most of my life, those that would let me," he finished with a laugh.

From there, Gerald abruptly changed his message, seeming to sense the prejudice his words carried. "But I have a lot of black friends. Especially around here. Yeah. I help them," he said. "They live in little rickety shacks. You know they don't have no money. There ain't no way they can pay."

"But you do it anyway?" I asked, referring to the carpentry work he did in the area.

"Sure. I can help them out," Gerald replied. "Why wouldn't I? If I'm capable, if I'm able. I don't expect it, but you do somethin' like that for somebody, it's not forgotten. In fact, it will carry you a lot further than a dollar."

Like Lacy, Gerald recognized that integration benefited those who had long lacked the freedom-to that he had enjoyed. Those "black friends" who, in Gerald's words, "don't have no money." Those who were kept out of school to pick and plant cotton while he and his white friends got an education. Those whose work as slaves built big houses for the white man instead of homesteads for themselves. Gerald knew all that. Simultaneously, his personal education was situated within a nation that valued white types of education and white types of talking, and integration altered his participation in that system.

His bitterness at being denied freedom to the education he deemed superior hardened into freedom-from, a racialized hatred that demanded separation from black folks. And from there, hatred spread, with little to abate it.

Howard Thurman described such a process when he witnessed three black girls making hateful remarks about white people. He warns that hatred, although rooted first in a particular type of prejudice, as soon as it is released, quickly skips beyond any racial boundaries as it cannibalizes, like the majority, its own: "Hatred bears deadly and bitter fruit. It is blind and nondiscriminating. True, it begins by exercising specific discrimination. This it does by entering upon the persons responsible for the situations which created the reaction of resentment, bitterness, and hatred. But once hatred is released, it cannot be confined to the offenders alone."[30] Fear and resentment, once specific to a race, could quickly spread, creating a shared condition of freedom-from across racial lines while freedom-to faded from the sight of all.

★ ★ ★

Fear draws its lifeblood from resentment, the notion that one of us has done more than the other in enacting or righting a wrong. As Thomas and Lacy described, that resentment can harden into hatred. Born of a fear of having less than another—of paying an undue price—the worst of our intentions can fester. Even institutional integration only scratches the surface of simmering hatred. As of 2018, three white men, one black woman, and one black man serve on the Burke County Board of Commissioners. The mayor of the county seat, Waynesboro, was a black woman when I lived in Burke County. One of Waynesboro's most popular restaurants, Taylor's, known for its barbecue, has a mix of white and black folks lined up behind the cafeteria-style food counter daily. Black and white faces pepper the aisles of Wal-Mart. These places afford an appearance of freedom-to, while freedoms-from continue to prosper beneath the surface.

"You have to be so careful who you are talking to," Leon warned me as he went to leave my trailer, where we had spoken that particular afternoon. "Some of them are not going to be truthful." When I remained silent, he said again, "Be careful. You meet up on somebody there, or people. Just get away from them as quick as you can. When they are showing all this arrogance, they probably aren't going to be truthful with what they are telling you anyway."

Leon's freedom-from concerns didn't form simply along a racial line. He feared for my safety—me staying free from the surrounding threats. There was violence, stealing, and uncertain authority. Governance seemed to have left for brighter shores. Racial differences, although agitating the circumstances of distrust and cultivating negative freedom, didn't change the sense of fear, which crossed racial lines.

Leon walked a little further down the sandy lane in front of my trailer, looking up into the towering pines. "You aren't afraid to live back here alone?" he asked.

"I was," I said. "I'm kind of afraid of the snakes to be hon——"

"Be careful," he said for the third time, interrupting me. "When you step outside and all, they like to come around steps. But we don't have a lot of poison snakes in this area. Mostly rattlesnakes. And we've got two kinds of water moccasins. You probably would with the little pond." Leon then got back to what was really bothering him: people. "You know when you come in, lock your gate," he said. "Sometimes people are out just looking to go somewhere and do something, and see a gate open or something and just drive in. Just keep it closed. Probably nobody knows you are down here alone anyway."

"It's kind of you to be concerned," I responded.

"I am," he replied. "I didn't know it was this far off of the road. I thought you was close to the road. I had never been back in here."

I couldn't help but stand there wondering. What if Burke County residents came together, not out of fear, but affirmation—guided by their moral economy toward a new day of justice? What if the state facilitated more freedom-to rather than freedom-from—building on the best rather than the worst of human actions? Perhaps then the predication of majority prosperity on minority sacrifice could end, and democracy of the people could reign.

# Recovery

# eight THE MORAL ECONOMY'S FREEDOM

Try to love your fellow man.
Speak what is right. And keep on going.
But do it out of love.

—Sydney Jackson

"It's about money," Sydney told me as we sat in rocking chairs on his front porch.

A cold, indifferent truth stands out for the people of Burke County. Their lives are worth what the rule of numbers dictates. That happens to be not very much, and hasn't been for some time. First, it was the taking of land and the rendering of people into possessions to feed the industrial demands of pipes and looms in England. Then arrived the hope of self and land possession, only to be encroached upon again by the antidemocratic rationality of the corporate form. In the presence of abundant minorities—of rurality, of poverty, of race, and of region—the corporate form has made a majoritarian feast of the people of Burke County.

"From what I've seen and read, you always come where there's less resistance," Sydney softly explained, referring to corporations. "Down here, there's less resistance for them to be able to do what they want to do without any obstacles to block them. They can give a few dollars here and there. And brainwash a few people. Then they can move on in and do what they want to do. The first few plants, they got in the doors. This time they don't care about the people. It's not about the people."

Letting the moral economy of democracy reign requires escaping the clutches of the state, which has failed the democratic ethos. William turns to the forest to practice direct justice. Sydney turns to God to transcend oppression. In either case, the state is something to be overcome, rather than a venue for reform.

"The law has been manipulated," Sydney said. "People take the law and twist it and use it. But God said vengeance is mine. You cannot change that. God has that power."

Hope for all can abound by allowing the moral economy of democracy to reign. Then, the best of intentions—a freedom to do— could inform the structure of society, and people would not need to constantly reposition themselves for defense against the latest attack. A positive freedom would topple the inhumanity of the rule of numbers, under which subjects constantly scramble to seek some shelter from profit's tyranny.

"This world is a fellowship," Sydney said. "Try to love your fellow man. Speak what is right. And keep on going. But do it out of love."

★　★　★

"Good to see you!" I said, getting out of my car at Casey's Store, where I had been waiting for a good half hour. William was the late one this time.

"Good to see you," William said back. I had made a weeklong return to Burke County to check in and review a few things with those whose identities were particularly vulnerable in my descriptions. William was one of them.

I hopped into his latest truck, a $750 Ford steal that he had fixed up and got running again. I pulled out my computer, opening up a PDF of chapter 5 for him.

"How do you work this?" he asked, as I handed him the computer. I showed him how to use double fingers to move the screen up and down through the pad.

He pulled himself back a bit, appearing to stretch, with a sigh, pulling himself in sore places.

"Now look, anything you don't like, we can change it," I told him as he began to read. "Anything you think might help people determine who you are. Anything—just tell me."

"Nobody's going to know it's me," he said.

"Well, wait until you read it," I said.

"Who's going to read it?" he replied.

"The public," I said. "I'm going to try to write it as a book."

"Who'd want to read about me?" he replied. He began to read, and I watched his face closely at first. He laughed a little, grinning as he got through the first pages. My eyes had been over those pages so many times that I could anticipate what words were reaching him as he let himself into the text.

"I remember everything," he answered, not letting his eyes leave the page. He read a little further.

I tried to remain at ease in the truck, but I was glued to any signal of his opinion. He continued reading, and my nervous energy mounted. I began to restlessly move my foot back and forth.

"Do you feel that?" he asked me.

"I was just shaking my foot," I said. "Nervous energy."

"I thought someone was messing with me at the back of the truck," he replied.

As the pages began to pile up, I watched his face become serious and steadily focused.

"You're giving me chills," he said. "I haven't ever seen it in print," he said softly.

I stopped watching him and let my eyes rest on the gray wall of the gas station in front of me, brightly lit to provide a back way for employees to reach the dump.

A young, blond, kind-eyed cashier left the shop and walked in front of us. One morning she had thoughtfully warned me about buying an old newspaper. She waved at William, not recognizing me. He looked up at her without raising his hand, and she dropped hers quickly as his response stole away her smile. I couldn't read the look on his face, but it seemed somber.

"Hey," he said to me after a while, interrupting my solitude. "What are you thinking?"

"About what you're reading," I replied, finally looking away from the gas station wall and at him. He drew up his stained, calloused palm to wipe a hint of overflow away as soon as my eyes rested on his face.

"It's like you've captured what's closest to my heart," he said.

"Well, your heart's in the right place," I said without looking at him.

"Your heart's in the right place," he replied back to me.

Our best of intentions forged a moral economy of democracy. We both were quiet for a moment, and William pushed down the computer screen and pulled back with a groan.

"I have a cramp in my hand and a cramp in my leg," he said as he stretched out as much as he could in the truck and flexed his hand. I took the computer from him and sat it between us on the torn vinyl.

His Droid lit up, singing its robotic tune, flashing light through the spider web of cracks. He had abandoned the case, and as to be expected, the phone was on its last leg.

"This is my buddy," he said, looking at the screen, "A young guy I showed all the spots to. I've got to answer this."

"Hey!" he cried, answering the phone. "How's it going out there? Get anything?"

Pause.

"Is it dead?"

Pause.

"No, you can't shoot it," he said. "You've got to take an arrow and pierce it through the neck. Dig that arrow into his vein. Stop its pulse."

Silence.

"Where are you? How far away are you from the spot I took you to? You're in the pines? All right, that's not too bad."

Pause.

"Hey! You've got to put a rope around its neck and hang it up so it can bleed out."

Pause.

"I'm at the Casey's Store. I'll be right there," he said. "Just hold on."

William's young trainee had gotten himself a buck on somebody else's property. William had to help him get it out.

"I'm going to have to go," he said, hanging up. "Help him get this deer."

"All right," I said. "We got through a good bit."

"Let's finish this up tomorrow," he said. "I have a full day in South Carolina, a long day. I probably won't be back until eight. Let's do it then. I'll get to see you before you leave."

"I'm going to see Patty then, so I'll see you after," I replied, sliding out of the truck.

"Hey," he said, grabbing my attention as I closed the door. "I don't want to change a thing."

★ ★ ★

It was a long day by the time I met up with William again, my last evening in Shell Bluff before I headed back to the northern fall. He was preparing for another night-hunting expedition, and I met him out in a sandy lane by a plot of ground that he was going to enjoy that evening with a buddy. William had made his way through a portion of the text, but not all of it, when he received a call from the friend who was headed over for a hunt. I closed the computer, and William got out of my car. He shook one aching foot as he testily started to put some weight on it and began limping toward his bucket truck. His broad shoulders filled a brown shirt, and his camouflage pants met the top of his sandy laced-up boots. I joined him, leaning against the still-warm radiator of his bucket truck in the cool October air, waiting for the company to arrive.

"Listen to that," William said, straightening against the truck as his head pulled back and he lifted his chin. In a moment, he was transformed from the slouched, weary, and worn-out William into a daunting force, alert and ready. He had two guns resting in his truck, a revolver and a shotgun, both loaded. Hunting season had arrived.

"It's turning around," he said, listening to a car passing by on the main road. "Hear it winding down? It's going to wind up again in a moment. Can you tell which direction that's coming from?"

I was quiet, straining my ears to listen. I stepped away from the sandy lane and toward the tree line, pine needles crunching under my feet.

"South," I said. We listened as the motor quieted and the car turned around. By flashing their headlights on the deer, the hunters could more easily, although illegally, shoot the stunned animal.

"They saw a deer," he said. "That's the best way to hunt this time of year, driving up and down the road. Shoot them on sight." We were quiet again until he heard the deer coming through the tree line and alerted me.

"I'm going to have to go," I said. It was nearing ten, and the family I was staying with would undoubtedly be starting to worry about me.

"I know," he said. "It's getting late."

"So you are going to write a book," he said to me. "What are you going to call it?"

"I don't know yet," I said to him. After my recent visit, as usual, the intention and direction of the book had altered as people explained more to me about their thoughts and their responses to what I had written and would write.

"There other people in this?" he asked.

"Yes, there's other people," I replied.

He didn't say anything as I walked back over to where he was still leaning against the truck.

"My hope is that the book will do some good, that it will help," I said.

"It's not going to help a thing," he replied. "I can guarantee you that. It won't change a thing."

"Man, you sure can be cynical," I said with irritation, without looking at him. "Seriously, that is so cynical," I said, finally making eye contact.

"Maybe it is," he said. "But I *do* hope you get filthy rich from it. Filthy rich."

"You know what, William," I said sharply. I paused, and he turned toward me. "You're wrong. Things can change," I said.

William was silent.

At the end of the day, we wanted the same thing: justice of, by, and for the people. I hadn't quite given up on him or myself or Burke County or the nation. If we could believe in ourselves and our capacity to govern as a people of flesh, not dollar signs, the many corporate landmines in our path would be of little consequence.

A promise remained for the wavering democratic state: to let humans, all of them flesh and blood, have the structure they deserved to let their best intentions reign. To let their moral economy of democracy realize itself, regardless of the for-profit costs. Then the people, rather than the system and the government, could flourish in a democracy of direct action.

William's buddy pulled into the lane, blinding us in the darkness. We said our hellos and good-byes. I headed away from the quiet of the night toward the hum of the pavement, ready to go.

# APPENDIX 1: METHODOLOGY

I did not set out to write a book about for-profit democracy. My purpose initially was more modest. I headed to Burke County to study community responses to nuclear energy production in the context of rural targeting. In the broader context of rural environmental injustice nationally, I sought to understand how rural people experienced and lived with risk in a mixed-race community. By coming to know the people of Burke County and the misfortunes they bear, I found myself aligned with their standpoints, but uncertain about the place from which these troubles came. My search led me to the primary thesis of this book: that dispossession runs deep in the hierarchical roots of the democratic state.

I square the account presented in this book in four sources: archives, interviews, ethnography, and a conjunction of descriptive statistics and law. Archives serve as a textual representation of the state and corporate purpose while simultaneously providing a footing in the history of Burke County. Before arriving in Burke County, I reviewed environmental impact statements and assessments pertaining to the Vogtle reactors and others nationally. I followed the media coverage of the Fukushima-Daiichi disaster carefully, analyzing the reporting of the events and the state's response. I became familiar with the *Code of Federal Regulations*. All this helped prepare me for the kinds of representations of rural value and rhetoric that informed the Burke County case. Upon arrival, though, I realized that I knew little about the local history often invoked by those I spent time with. I then began extensive research on Burke County and the Shell Bluff area in dialogue with the local experts of the Burke County Archive Society. Their patient tutelage, along with my position at Auburn University, played central roles in the writing of chapter 3 as well as in my broader appreciation of southern history. My archival research helped me identify what I present as foundational minority sacrifice and majority rule. Then I began to pinpoint profit's role in slavery and the very kindling of the US democratic state.

Interviews were a critical first step for meeting people in the countryside. I started with two primary points of contact: black Baptist reverends and my white landlord, Jesse Whitehead. I met the reverends during my first visit to Burke County, in 2010, and Jesse two years later, when I moved to the community in February 2012. I kept residence there until August 2012, and then returned again for a month in February 2013. I made brief return trips in the fall of 2013 and the summer of 2015. During my stay in Burke County, I lived in three places: the trailer documented in the book, and also two RVs. I used my initial points of contact to meet other black and white residents. I met bureaucrats and regulators at formal meetings, which I then followed up with interviews. My interviews with local politicians and Atlanta activists came through phone calls made by residents who vouched for me, or by referring explicitly to the person who gave me a number. I completed eighty-nine interviews in total. Sixty-nine interviews were with residents: twelve black men, twenty-three white men, seventeen black women, sixteen white women, and one Latina woman. Those interviewed include twelve Vogtle workers or contractors, four nuclear regulators, six elected officials, ten local or state activists, and eight people who included journalists, absentee landlords, and former residents. These categories of interviewees are not mutually exclusive. To protect the identity of participants, I do not further detail combinations of roles with race or gender.

Interviews often prompted invitations into spaces where people interacted with one another and their environments in ways usually less structured than the contexts of my interviews. I use fictional names for the corner stores, gas stations, and churches that I frequented, excluding Botsford Baptist Church, because it is the only white church in the area. I walked a fine line between black and white sites of gathering. Notably, this book mostly lacks sites of interracial mixing that are not political or bureaucratic. This was my observation and experience in Burke County—I rarely saw black and white people interact, and I reflect this by presenting the experiences of black and white residents distinctly. I attended black churches regularly when I first arrived, along with white dinner parties and cookouts. I sensed a gaze upon me, wondering whether my parked car outside the Aberlina Baptist Church would catch the ire of white community members. Most notably, it never did. In such a rural place, people likely recognized my Illinois "Land of Lincoln" license plate regularly as they became familiar with and often commented on my Honda Civic. I came to hold an unusual position as someone with local connections who talked across racial lines about the injustices imposed by the plant. After I had known them for a few years, reverends who were members of Shell Bluff Concerned Citizens once asked me to solicit the support of white residents in protesting the construction of the new reactors. I told them at the time I would be happy to pass out materials when I visited people, but I did not want to take on an advocacy role. I made this decision in part because I sensed that engagement in formal politics could cut off my connections with those who were explicitly opposed to protest through the state and rather favored acting outside it. I reflect on this choice often. I tend to think it was the right choice because of the central thesis of this book— that an increasingly illegitimate state provokes protest outside it. By acting as an agent of state-sanctioned protest, I would have been acting against the white anarchist tendencies I document.

I use descriptive statistics and the law to situate the broader context of property rights, race, education, corporations, and poverty in the United States. Most notably, in chapters 3 and 4, I analyze current and fifty-year-old tax parcel data to better understand landownership around the plant. The loss of land—a topic I did not anticipate when I began research—plays a formative role in the book. I combine archival accounts with US Census statistics to pinpoint how much land was owned and by whom. I studied eminent domain jurisprudence in all fifty states to contextualize how the Burke County case is emblematic of laws across the nation. In addition, I analyzed Supreme Court rulings to better understand how profit has come to dominate rights in the United States, including the right to property. I place the particulars of the Burke County case in the broader national and historical climate of rights and laws.

In a sense, my squaring of methods is an attempt to refute claims that my book falls prey to the "ethnographic fallacy," as Mitch Dunier calls it. Ethnographies can be accused of taking too much from the particular without contextualization. My presentation choice moves between local and theoretical, global and particular, to form a dialogue between Burke County, national trends, and scholarship. More than simply "extend," in the words of Burawoy, my case to the broader context of democratic illegitimacy in the United States today, I work back and forth, both inductively and deductively, to make my case.[1] The work I present here required thinking outside state evaluation and data to study illegitimacy and acts against the establishment. Doing so switches the view from the gaze of the state to the steely resistance of the moral economy, an approach this book embraces.

My project received Institutional Review Board (IRB) approval from the University of Wisconsin–Madison. Researchers generally are required to solicit IRB approval in order to ensure that the rights and welfare of humans participating in research studies are respected. I obtained oral rather than written consent from participants, mainly because some people that I interviewed could not read. I used pseudonyms for all people in the book. I used the standard of plausible deniability to protect participants—that is, I fabricated something about each participant that was not relevant to the topic at hand, but allowed the person I was quoting to deny his or her participation if asked about it. Some participants reviewed pertinent material to ensure their comfort with its content. I transcribed my recordings. In the notes, I clarify which material came from recordings and which came from my notes. I took notes in two ways: reporter notebooks filled with written notes taken while I interacted with people and ecologies, and computer journaling. I mainly used the first method during interviews and ethnographic observations. I did not take notes on my phone, because doing so was considered rude and inattentive. When alone, I elaborated my written notes into a journal electronically.

My IRB protocol stipulated that all interviews and transcriptions be destroyed at the end of my analysis. In effect, this is the best form of protection that the IRB can afford my participants. The threat of data acquisition is increasingly a real one for researchers and those who participate in their studies. Take, for example, a recent case at the University of North Carolina–Chapel Hill. There, the Chinese-owned corporation Smithfield Foods subpoenaed Steve Wing, an associate professor of epidemiology, for his data pertaining to fecal pollution and exposure in minority communities, including identifying information. His IRB protocols, like mine, assured participants that their information was confidential. But universities have yet to back that protection with legal counsel, making the destruction of data perhaps the safest way to protect participants in contexts that may attract corporate ire, like industrial agriculture and the nuclear industry.

Destroying data, though, can eliminate the capacity to verify and question, an utmost goal of scientific endeavors. Recently, there has been substantial controversy regarding the ethnographer Alice Goffman's choice to destroy all her research data to protect her participants' identities. Her book *On the Run: Fugitive Life in an American City* (2014) documents illegal activities that could land many of those she writes about in jail. Poaching, too, is illegal, and thus my book raises similar concerns. Since I identify my community of study by name, there is an additional chance to verify the accuracy of what I present here by, for example, attending the churches or examining the parcel data. Even though the interviews have been destroyed, curious researchers can return to Burke County to verify my findings.

My positionality warrants some reflection and scrutiny by readers. Residents regularly asked about my background when trying to understand my purpose. I grew up in the open countryside and attended a single K–12 school building in a town of 550 people in rural Illinois. That school is now closed, and the county I am from is among the four poorest in Illinois. Across racial and class differences, my capacity to understand rural poverty and farming helped me gain some local legitimacy. In speaking to me, people would sometimes implicitly defer to that status, through phrases such as "you know." Relatedly, the skills and knowledge I gained through farmwork and from living in the countryside helped me navigate some of the situations presented in this book. To forge trust across class, race, and gender differences, my rural background proved paramount.

My marriage to a white male immigrant also helped establish local legitimacy through difference and similarity. People regularly asked about my husband, Jason, and it gave them some sense that I adhered to the local moral norms embedded in the church. My bold act of living alone in the country was then afforded some forgiveness. Jason's ethnicity as an Irish immigrant helped open some racial and regional doors. On multiple occasions, those white residents who still harbored palpable resentment against northerners could forgive my status by aligning themselves with my Irish husband. On multiple occasions, white residents equated being Irish with southern, and being English with northern. Accordingly, white northerners were considered the oppressors, and white southerners the oppressed. In such contexts, the Civil War was understood as the War Between the States or the War of Northern Aggression. Being Irish also held currency in the black community. Ireland has a ban on nuclear power, something the black reverends referred to immediately when they first met Jason. Being Irish, to them, denoted being antinuclear. The reverends also knew of Irish oppression, but reversed the white formula, seeing Jason simply as part of an oppressed people, as were black people in the United States. Jason, although white, became distinct from white male American hegemony, an exception that rubbed off on me but was never as fully extended as it was to Jason. In the few times that Jason visited Burke County, he accompanied me to cookouts, church, and the archive building, playing an important role in my local acclimation. As Orne and Bell describe it, these multiple logics of my actions and interactions shaped how I was received and spoken to, and thus the content of this book.

I often include my own questions and responses, and even on some occasions what I was thinking, so that the reader can further reflect on my positionality throughout the book. This would be a different book, with different interviews and observations, if some other researcher had lived in Burke County. That said, the archival and descriptive statistics presented throughout the book offer other data logics, with their own issues—primarily, that numbers do not talk back (and tell only part of the story). Nonetheless, archives, descriptive statistics, and the law are critical facets of my research, and help situate Burke County as a microcosm of national issues. Together, these multiple method logics help validate the claims I make in *For-Profit Democracy: Why the Government Is Losing the Trust of Rural America.*

# APPENDIX 2: A SUMMARY OF PEOPLE AND CONCEPTS

## REACTION

### Chapter 1: Welcome to Burke County

*People*
Jessie Whitehead
Lela Roberts
Vernon Davis
Debbie Davis
John Anderson
Mary Anderson

### Chapter 2: For-Profit Democracy

*People*
Jeff Abbot
Neill Hataway
Dale Fannigan

*Concepts*
Private-public fallacy
For-profit democracy
Profit's tug-of-war
Contradictory state
Corporate-state reaction

## MELTDOWN

### Chapter 3: The Moral Economy of Democracy

*People*
Patty Sutton
Sydney Jackson
Bianca Wethersby
Elijah Bennett
Dean Sawyer
Dave Ray
Beau Turner
Sara Tully

*Concepts*
Interdependence of the democratic state and property rights
Landownership ethic
Moral economy of democracy
For-profit property
Four dimensions of corporate power

Chapter 4: The Rule of Numbers

*People*
Mr. Bailey
Sydney Jackson
Moses Dixon
Jamal Dixon
Veeona Dixon
Raleigh Langston
Vorice Inman
David Hornsby
Patty Sutton

*Concepts*
Rule of numbers
Faulty opposition between private and public rights
Tyranny of the majority
Majority cannibalism
The system
The government
Profit's majority


FALLOUT

Chapter 5: The Rural Rebel

*People*
William Gresham
Ashley Andrews
Landry Axson
Steve Pratt
Tim Dillard
Jamie Gott
Lester Brown

Chester Chanders
Daryl Edmonds

*Concepts*
Rural rebel
In spite of the state
For-profit politics
Environmental honor
Direct justice

## Chapter 6: The Transcendent People

*People*
Reverend Samuel Franklin
Lucie Eagen
Reverend Cole
Reverend George Ellis
Mary Dunn
Jamella Kilgore
Shelby Small
Iris Fewell
Nathaniel Fewell

*Concepts*
Transcendence
A people
The people
Transcendent people

## Chapter 7: Freedom under the Gun

*People*
Bret Mooney
Jimmy Mooney
Cletus Wiley
Bella Laverty
Finn Hunt
Reverend Samuel Franklin
Ula Young
Ms. Rayanna
Leon Lewis
Patty Sutton
Walter Hamilton

Evaline Hamilton
Cora Beth Shaw
Hardy Kessinger
Caroline Kessinger
Thomas Harold
Lacy Harold
Gerald Henry

*Concepts*
Token events
Freedom under the gun
Freedom-from
Freedom-to
Anti body of logic
Pro body of logic
Naturalization of violence

RECOVERY

Chapter 8: The Moral Economy's Freedom

*People*
Sydney Jackson
William Gresham

# NOTES

### Chapter 1. Welcome to Burke County

All quotations in this chapter are taken from field notes.

1. Southern Company is the parent company of major energy and utility companies in the South. These include Alabama Power, Georgia Power, Gulf Power, Mississippi Power, Southern Company Services, Southern LINC Wireless, Southern Nuclear, Southern Company Generation, Southern Power, Southern Telecom, Southern Company Gas, and Power Secure. Southern Company receives the $125 million tax credit if the reactors go online before 2021 and produce 1,000 megawatts yearly of nuclear capacity for the first eight years (Union of Concerned Scientists, "Vogtle Nuclear Plant Expansion: Big Risks and Even Bigger Costs for Georgia's Residents," 2012, accessed March 26, 2015, www.ucsusa .org/sites/default/files/legacy/assets/documents/nuclear_power/Geor gia-nuclear-fact-sheet.pdf). All Fortune and Global 500 figures here and following are from *Fortune* magazine's rankings from 2017. The rankings are based on revenues, profits, balance sheet, employees, earnings per share, total returns to investors, medians, and credits.

2. Hitachi's "About Us" page, accessed April 11, 2017, https://nuclear.ge power.com/company-info/about-ge-hitachi.html.

3. UK Group 4 Securicor, "Nuclear Facility Security," accessed April 11, 2017, www.g4s.us/en-US/Industries/Nuclear.

4. Westinghouse's web page "Why Nuclear," www.westinghousenuclear.com; *Atlanta Journal-Constitution*, "Report: Toshiba Retreating from Nuke Business after Losses on Vogtle," www.ajc.com/business/report-toshiba -retreating-from-nuke-business-after-losses-vogtle/4U87wAh8qnIVX JOVmj4RoK; *New York Times*, "Westinghouse Files for Bankruptcy, in Blow to Nuclear Power," www.nytimes.com/2017/03/29/business/westing house-toshiba-nuclear-bankruptcy.html?_r=0. All articles accessed April 11, 2017.

5. The number of operating nuclear power plants and their locations are as of 2016; see the US Energy Information Administration's "Frequently Asked Questions," accessed April 11, 2017, https://www.eia.gov/tools/faqs

/faq.php?id=207&t=3; for the amount of energy produced in the United States from nuclear power in 2016, see "U.S. Nuclear Power Plants: General U.S. Nuclear Info," accessed April 11, 2017, https://www.nei.org /Knowledge-Center/Nuclear-Statistics/US-Nuclear-Power-Plants.

6. In total, nuclear power plants are owned by sixty-one holding companies. Most of the nuclear power reactors in the United States are owned by private firms traded on the New York Stock Exchange, the largest of which is Exelon Corporation, which owns twenty-four reactors. The rest are owned mostly through cooperatives and related not-for-profit organizations. The Tennessee Valley Authority is the only federally owned corporation, which is what I mean by "public" here. For more, see the Nuclear Energy Institute's "US Nuclear Operators, Owners, and Holding Companies," accessed August 31, 2017, www.nei.org/Knowledge-Center /Nuclear-Statistics/US-Nuclear-Power-Plants/US-Nuclear-Opera tors,-Owners-and-Holding-Companies, and "US Nuclear Power Policy," www.world-nuclear.org/information-library/country-profiles/coun tries-t-z/usa-nuclear-power-policy.aspx.

7. There is a burgeoning literature on the declining line between public and private in American governance and elsewhere in favor of the pursuit of profit. This includes the rich literature on neoliberalism that focuses on privatization. Scholars have documented the transformation of water and land from public goods, or commonage, to commodities sold through the market. Some accounts on the topic include Noel Castree, "Neoliberalising Nature: The Logics of Deregulation and Reregulation," *Environment and Planning A* 40, no. 1 (2008): 131–52; Castree, "Neoliberalising Nature: Processes, Effects, and Evaluations," *Environment and Planning A* 40, no. 1 (2008): 153–73; Karen Cocq and David A. McDonald, "Minding the Undertow: Assessing Water 'Privatization' in Cuba," *Antipode* 42, no. 1 (2010): 6–45; Daniel Jaffee and Soren Newman, "A More Perfect Commodity: Bottled Water, Global Accumulation, and Local Contestation," *Rural Sociology* 78, no. 1 (2013): 1–28. John Campbell and Leon N. Lindberg, in "Property Rights and the Organization of Economic Activity by the State," *American Journal of Sociology* 55, no. 5 (1990): 634–47, point to the changing nature of private property rights, for example, the state's capacity to manipulate them in order to define "the rules that determine the conditions of ownership and control the means of production" (635). Catherine L. Fisk, in her remarkable book *Working Knowledge: Employee Innovation and the Rise of Corporate Intellectual Property, 1800–1930* (Chapel Hill: University of North Carolina

Press, 2009) critiques the growing corporate ownership of intellectual property and the court-imposed favoring of ownership rights that offer to produce a profit. In such trends, she sees rights being stripped from employees and patents being put in the hands of corporations better able to make money. More recently, scholars and lawyers have critiqued the outsourcing of public goods like prisons and road services, which have gone from being publicly funded and operated to being privately operated but publicly funded; see B. C. Burkhardt and B. T. Connor, "Durkheim, Punishment, and Prison Privatization." *Social Currents* 3, no. 1 (2016): 84–99; and Bryan Stevenson, *Just Mercy: A Story of Justice and Redemption* (New York: Spiegel & Grau, 2015). In 2016, the US Justice Department, in the wake of mistreatment and abuse scandals, announced that it would no longer hire private contractors to operate public prisons. Privatization is waning in popularity elsewhere as well; see Amir Hefetz and Mildred E. Warner, "Contracting or Public Delivery? The Importance of Service, Market, and Management Characteristics," *Journal of Public Administration Research and Theory* 22, no. 2 (2011): 289–317, which provides evidence that the privatization of infrastructure services, including waste management and vehicle towing, and of social services such as drug treatment and homeless shelters, is declining in popularity as a result of poor quality and a lack of cost savings.

8. The quotations are from the Final Environmental Statement Related to Proposed Construction of Dresden Nuclear Reactor Units 2 and 3 (1970; 3:70-0293; STN 50–508, 509) on p. 29. There are similar statements in the Final Environmental Statement Related to the Proposed Braidwood Station, Units 1 and 2 (1974; 3:74-0371; STN 50–456, 457) on p. 10-2 (note: this is the numbering system used in the document).

9. Final Environmental Statement Related to the Proposed Alvin W. Vogtle Nuclear Plant Units 1, 2, 3, and 4 (1974; 3:74-2907; STN 50-424, 425, 426, 427) on pp. 3–4.

10. See US Department of Agriculture, Economic Research Service, "Geography of Poverty," accessed April 8, 2016, www.ers.usda.gov/topics/rural-economy-population/rural-poverty-well-being/geography-of-poverty.aspx.

11. US Census Bureau, "Burke County Georgia," accessed March 30, 2015, http://quickfacts.census.gov/qfd/states/13/13033.html.

12. According to W. E. B. Du Bois, the Black Belt is a designation for parts of the South where the black population was especially dense. The term also refers to the fertile black soil. The reason for such a large black pop-

ulation in these regions was the use of slaves to work this profitable land (*The Souls of Black Folk* [New York: Norton, 1895; reprint, 1999]). For his eloquent description, see p. 76.

13. Environment Georgia Research and Policy Center, "10 Million Pounds of Toxic Chemicals Dumped into Georgia's Waterways: Savannah River Ranks 3rd in the Country for Toxic Discharges" (2014), accessed April 8, 2016, http://environmentgeorgia.org/news/gae/10-million-pounds-toxic -chemicals-dumped-georgia%E2%80%99s-waterways.

14. Alexis de Tocqueville, *Democracy in America*, (1835, 1840; abridged ed., trans. George Lawrence, New York: HarperCollins, 2007), 248. Tocqueville, a French aristocrat visiting what he unapologetically called the New World, ostensibly on an inspection tour of its prisons, wrote a famous and long-lasting chronicle of American democracy, one that I cite throughout this book. As citizens gained the right to vote, and as the hereditary and cultural ties of feudalism faded, he warned that people could become individualistic and even egoistic. Therein festered a series of problems, in Tocqueville's view: self-interest, apathy toward government, unchecked bureaucratic control, and majority rule over minority rights. He argued that the act of voting and the thought collectives produced in democracies operate on majority logic, meaning that the minority loses and the majority reigns.

15. See the notes to chapter 7 for details on how the data was compiled from the FBI Crime Database and analyzed.

16. Tocqueville, *Democracy*, 260.

17. James Scott, *The Moral Economy of the Peasant: Rebellion and Subsistence in Southeast Asia* (New Haven, CT: Yale University Press, 1976), 4. Scott leaves the study of revolutionary movements to others, specifically citing the masterly work of Eric Wolf, *Europe and the People without History* (Berkeley: University of California Press, 1982), and Barrington Moore, *Social Origins of Dictatorship and Democracy: Lord and Peasant in the Making of the Modern World* (Boston: Beacon, 1967). Scott focuses instead on acts of resistance and rebellion that occur in conditions of great exploitation yet do not instigate revolution, which he identifies as a much more common end. He is especially interested in understanding the "rage" that can prompt the rebel to risk everything, even in contexts in which revolution does not follow (3).

## Chapter 2. For-Profit Democracy

The epigraph is drawn from the Minnesota Multiphasic Personality Inventory, a psychological test established in 1943. Its popularity has coincided with an increase in bureaucratic oversight and administration. The test is used in a variety of contexts to evaluate mental health in civil and criminal cases, as well as in risky occupations like operating a nuclear power plant or flying an airplane. It was originally designed to test for a potential series of so-called "disorders," including schizophrenia, depression, and masculinity-femininity conformity. More recently, its questions have also been used to measure cynicism and demoralization. Note: Quotations in this chapter from interviews and meetings are taken from audio recordings.

1. US Nuclear Regulatory Commission, "About Us" (2016), accessed April 8, 2016, www.nrc.gov/about-nrc.html.

2. See Jason Kaufman, "Corporate Law and the Sovereignty of States," *American Sociological Review* 73 (2008): 402–25, for a thorough documentation of the role of corporations in the United States during the colonial period. According to Kaufman, Harvard was formed as a college in 1636, but did not become a corporation until 1650 (406). William G. Roy cites the year of charter as 1688 (*Socializing Capital: The Rise of the Large Industrial Corporation in America* [Princeton, NJ: Princeton University Press, 1997], 49). Harvard's website gives the date 1636.

3. In *McCulloch v. Maryland*, 17 U.S. 316 (1819), the Supreme Court upheld the government's right to incorporate banks based on the logic of "incidental power," whereby the corporation was understood as a means to achieve the government's purpose; for more, see Adolf Berle, "Constitutional Limitations on Corporate Activity—Protection of Personal Rights From Invasion Through Economic Power," *University of Pennsylvania Law Review* 100, no. 7 (1952). In the case, Maryland attempted to tax the banknotes of the Second Bank of the United States, because it was not chartered in the state. Against Maryland's charge that the Constitution did not award the government rights of incorporation, Chief Justice Marshall countered: "Among the enumerated powers, we do not find that of establishing a bank or creating a corporation. But there is no phrase in the instrument which, like the Articles of Confederation, excludes incidental or implied powers and which requires that everything granted shall be expressly and minutely described." Corporations may not have been mentioned in the founding documents of the United States, but the court ruled they were simply a creative legal form that achieved the production and regulation of money—a key to economic development. In its carefully worded justification, the Court contended that by electing representatives, the public gave the government the au-

thority to use unique tools like the corporation. The Court thus found in favor of the government's right to charter corporations as incidental to serving public needs.

4. For an excellent review of the seminal role of the railroad in the development of corporations and related law, see Roy, *Socializing Capital*, particularly his chapter "Railroads: The Corporation's Institutional Wellspring."

5. Morton J. Horwitz does a masterly job of explaining the transformation in property rights and just compensation in "Subsidization of Economic Growth through the Legal System," chapter 3 of *The Transformation of American Law, 1780–1860* (Cambridge, MA: Harvard University Press, 1977). Property law was changed in an effort to reduce the costs of economic development, which was hampered by the burden of damage judgments. This issue is still very much alive today. Mildred E. Warner identifies what she calls a "Pandora's Box of compensation" that can "bankrupt the regulatory state or divert financial resources from critical public works" in the case of the North American Free Trade Agreement ("Regulatory Takings and Free Trade Agreements: Implications for Planners," *The Urban Lawyer*, 41, no. 3 [2009]: 427-44). She documents how the notion of private property rights has expanded dramatically since the writing of the Constitution to include things like future profits, market share, and market access. Private investors can claim from the government just compensation if any measure, such as tariff protections, affects their investment negatively. In effect, these impacts make foreign investors "peers" with nation-states (433). The redefinition of property rights to favor profit is a critical element of corporate expansion domestically and abroad.

6. For more on the historical tenets of legal liability, see Merrick Dodd, "The Evolution of Limited Liability in American Industry: Massachusetts," *Harvard Law Review* 61, no. 8 (1948): 1351–79.

7. David Graeber makes the important point, in *The Democracy Project: A History, a Crisis, a Movement* (New York: Spiegel & Grau, 2013), that the Bill of Rights was added to the Constitution to pacify activists at the time who insisted that the Constitution did little to serve democracy. He contrasts a democracy of the republic with a democracy of the people.

8. Horwitz describes how the Court limited just compensation through limited liability to externalize development costs from the government and corporations making use of eminent domain, and to push them onto citizens ("Subsidization of Economic Growth through the Legal System," chap. 3 of *American Law*).

9. For more on the modern and substantial impacts of limited liability, see a discussion of "folding corporations" in Loka Ashwood, Danielle D. Diamond, and Kendall Thu, "Where's the Farmer? Limiting Liability in Midwest Industrial Hog Production" *Rural Sociology* 79, no. 1 (2014): 2–27. In the context of industrial hog production, corporations form and collapse to dodge nuisance suits and pollution liabilities.

10. Horwitz, *American Law*, 70.

11. Roy, *Socializing Capital*.

12. Ibid.

13. In *The Corporate Reconstruction of American Capitalism, 1890–1916: The Market, the Law, and Politics* (Cambridge: Cambridge University Press, 1988), Martin Sklar is careful not to stereotype the corporation as only a tool pushed for by the upper classes against the interests of the poor and the working class. Rather, he points to the broader systems of legitimacy and prevailing norms that promoted global economic dominance through the corporate form as best for most Americans at the time. He documents how the alliances forged between socialists, agrarian populists, and provincial capitalists were not enough to stop the corporate agenda. In the social Darwinist ethos that overtook the country, "it was cooperation that now made firms, economies, and nations fit to survive" (11).

14. Ibid.

15. Based on the tenets of classic liberalism, the corporate form became widely accessible (Roy, *Socializing Capital*). Between 1898 and 1904, industries worth $7 billion, or about one-fifth of the country's gross domestic product at the time, incorporated, with some lingering government regulation of the stock market (Sklar, *Corporate Reconstruction*). The precedence of profit over public increasingly infiltrated the corporate motive. Profit seeking and the corporate form took on an air of inevitability, and its sustenance through the fruit of the state was forgotten.

16. Roy explains that the division between private and public was a product of the corporation (*Socializing Capital*, chap. 3). Corporations in the late 1830s were under attack for serving the corrupt interests of state bureaucrats and businesses barons, which often overlapped. In response to public outrage, corporate business owners successfully reframed the debate according to classic liberalism (although in doing so, they permanently changed its meaning). Under liberal logic, the state's tight rein on corporate charters was identified as the problem, and widespread access to incorporation as the solution. The formation of more corporations

was framed as the solution to corporate corruption. The tactic worked. On a state-by-state basis, legislative debate was removed as a requirement for incorporation.

17. For more on the incredible power of the railroad, see Roy, *Socializing Capital*, and Errol Meidinger, "The 'Public Uses' of Eminent Domain: History and Policy," *Buffalo Legal Studies Research Paper Series* 11 paper no. 1981-002 (1981): 1–66.

18. David Graeber deftly details how democracy came to symbolize the market, and how bureaucracy came to symbolize the government's interference in that market; see *The Utopia of Rules: On Technology, Stupidity, and the Secret Joys of Bureaucracy* (Brooklyn, NY: Melville House, 2011). He captures such processes through his iron law of liberalism: "any market reform, any government initiative intended to reduce red tape and promote market forces will have the ultimate effect of increasing the total number of regulations, the total amount of paperwork, and the total number of bureaucrats the government employs" (9).

19. Meidinger explicitly presses the point that utility development could not have happened without the use of eminent domain (" 'Public Uses' of Eminent Domain"). In the case of railroads and eminent domain, Lawrence Berger writes that "to deny them it would have meant that they could not exist at all" ("The Public Use Requirement in Eminent Domain," *Oregon Law Review* 57 [1977]: 208).

20. Berger helpfully pulls apart the long-lived debate over the meaning of public use in the context of eminent domain ("Public Use Requirement," 209).

21. This is part of a broader critique made by Richard Epstein that later removal of public use from the courts and the placement of it in the hands of the legislature presents a threat to the right to property. Therefore, the power of eminent domain could be used to achieve any end that Congress sought (*Takings: Private Property and the Power of Eminent Domain* [Cambridge, MA: Harvard University Press, 1985], 164).

22. *Fallbrook Irrigation District v. Bradley*, 164 U.S. 112, 168 (1896). Meidinger further contextualizes the impact of this case on state use of eminent domain (" 'Public Uses' of Eminent Domain").

23. *Mt. Vernon-Woodberry Co. v. Alabama Power Co.*, 240 U.S. 30 (1916).

24. The tie between the meaning of "public" and the use of eminent domain points to the central relationship between the corporate form and claims on private property rights. The Supreme Court cases cited in this chapter are, in my view, among the most compelling, but they by no means

cover the diversity of cases leading up to the transformation in the meaning of public use. For more exhaustive accounts, see Epstein, *Takings*; Berger, "Public Use Requirement"; and Meidinger, "'Public Uses' of Eminent Domain." For more recent accounts, see Wendell E. Pritchett, "The 'Public Menace' of Blight: Urban Renewal and the Private Uses of Eminent Domain," *Yale Law and Policy Review* 21 (2003) 1–52; and Daniel Dalton, "A History of Eminent Domain," *State Bar of Michigan Public Corporation Law Quarterly* 3 (2006): 1–5.

25. Final Environmental Statement Related to Proposed Construction of Dresden Nuclear Reactor Units 2 and 3 (1970; 3:70-0293: STN 50-508, 509), A-32.

26. See the American Public Power Association's 2015–2016 Annual Directory and Statistical Report, "U.S. Electric Utility Industry Statistics," accessed April 11, 2017, www.publicpower.org/files/PDFs/USElectricUtility IndustryStatistics.pdf.

27. Nuclear Energy Institute, "US Nuclear Operators, Owners, and Holding Companies."

28. See Georgia Code, Title 22—Eminent Domain, Chapter 1—General Provisions 22–1-1 Definitions, (2010), accessed March 2, 2015, law.justia.com /codes/georgia/2010/title-22/chapter-1/22-1-1.

29. In *The Law of Eminent Domain: Fifty-State Survey 2011/2012* (Chicago: American Bar Association, 2012), William Blake reveals that utility companies continue to be explicitly granted the use of eminent domain in every state in the union, and the book summarizes those statutes.

30. For more on the history of Georgia Power, see details about the owner Henry Atkinson on the company's website, accessed April 11, 2017, https://www.georgiapower.com/docs/about-us/History.pdf. Remarkable transformations in the utility industry over the last forty years have accelerated the privatization of utilities in the United States. For details, see Harland Prechel and George Touche, "The Effects of Organizational Characteristics and State Environmental Policies on Sulfur-Dioxide Pollution in U.S. Electrical Energy Corporations," *Social Science Quarterly* 95, no. 1 (2014): 76–96.

31. The unfortunate outcomes of the corporation's public-private contradiction continue to multiply. Legislation once specific to the economic development of utilities now applies to economic development more broadly. Key is the treatment of profit as synonymous with economic development. When the Supreme Court rendered a verdict favoring a loose conception of public use in 1916, the decision laid the groundwork for a full outsourcing of public goods from the judiciary to the legisla-

ture. In effect, an anything-goes construction of the public triumphed over the judicial defense of individual rights, including the right to property. Charles E. Cohen reports that the Supreme Court ruled in *Berman v. Parker*, 348 U.S. 26 (1954), that department store owners had to give up their property for a private development project because legislative determinants viewed reducing city blights and slums as serving the public good ("Eminent Domain after Kelo v. City of New London: An Argument for Banning Economic Development Takings," *Harvard Journal of Law and Public Policy* 29 [2006]: 491–568). The department store itself was not "blighted" or rundown. Justice Douglas stated, "Subject to specific constitutional limitations, when the legislature has spoken, the public interest has been declared in terms well-nigh conclusive," p. 511. The steady displacement of the right to private property in favor of the greater revenue and tax base generated by corporations culminated in the Supreme Court's decision in *Kelo v. City of New London*, 545 U.S. 469 (2005). Although Susette Kelo valiantly tried to defend her little pink house from condemnation, the Supreme Court agreed with the City of New London that increased tax revenues, revitalization of a so-called depressed area, and construction jobs were in service of the public good and thus outweighed Kelo's right to her property. The private New London Development Corporation had the public right to take her house. In the majority opinion, Justice Stevens rejected "the contention that the mere fact that the State immediately transferred the properties to private individuals upon condemnation somehow diminished the public character of the taking." He went on to cite the *Berman* case: "It is only the taking's purpose, and not its mechanics," that concerns the Court. Legal scholars counter that such an approach to economic development results in the "abuse of existing property owners" and leads to "inordinate private influence" (Cohen, "Eminent Domain after Kelo," 497; Daniel Kelly, "The Public Use Requirement in Eminent Domain Law: A Rationale Based on Secret Purchases and Private Influence," *Cornell Law Review* 92, 1 [2006]: 4). Ironically, the project never moved forward when a key player in the development project, Pfizer, pulled out. Homes, though, had already been demolished, and the land now lies vacant. The ruling, though, left room for state-based restrictions, and in response, forty-three states passed *Kelo* laws that limit the use of eminent domain for economic development and the transfer of private property to another private owner; see Harvey M. Jacobs and Ellen M. Bassett, "After Kelo: Political Rhetoric and Policy Responses," *Land Lines* 22, no. 2 (2010):

14–20. Most of these laws have been labeled symbolic legislation that appeases public outrage, but do little in action; see Timothy Sanefur, "The 'Backlash' So Far: Will Americans Get Meaningful Eminent Domain Reform?," *Michigan State Law Review* (2006): 1–59. Despite *Kelo*'s clearly unfortunate outcome years later, in its immediate wake, some planners viewed the ruling as a victory, particularly because it gave the legislature (viewed as the public) rights to determine what is public use (Harvey M. Jacobs and Kurt Paulsen, "Property Rights: The Neglected Theme of 20th-Century American Planning," *Journal of the American Planning Association* 75, no. 2 [2009]: 134–143). This understanding of democracy, though, overlooks the threat of majority rule by idealizing it. Minority property rights are especially vulnerable to legislative whims, as I document in Burke County.

32. For more on the history of nuclear fission and the private-public collaboration, see Bruno Latour, "Science's Blood Flow: An Example from Joliot's Scientific Intelligence," chapter 3 of *Pandora's Hope: Essays on the Reality of Science Studies* (Cambridge, MA: Harvard University Press, 1999).

33. For a disturbing account of the secrecy surrounding the Manhattan Project, Los Alamos, and experiments conducted as part of the broader nuclear program, see Eileen Welsome, *The Plutonium Files: America's Secret Medical Experiment in the Cold War* (New York: Delacorte, 1999).

34. Part of that prevailing norm was a top-down demand for secrecy; see Louise Kaplan, "Public Participation in Nuclear Facility Decisions," in *Science, Technology and Democracy*, ed. Daniel Lee Kleinman (Albany: State University of New York Press, 2000), 67–83. Communities that housed such lucrative nuclear sites, though, produced a culture of complicity, thanks to the affluence provided by such jobs; see Kate Brown, *Plutopia: Nuclear Families, Atomic Cities, and the Great Soviet and American Plutonium Disasters* (New York: Oxford University Press, 2013).

35. Philip Mirowski and Esther-Mirjam Sent make the point that science has long been influenced by private money, and that neoliberal changes are not as new as they sometime seem; see "The Commercialization of Science and the Response of STS," in *The Handbook of Science and Technology Studies*, ed. Edward J. Hackett, Olga Amsterdamska, Michael Lynch, and Judy Wajcman (Cambridge, MA: MIT Press, 2008), 635–89.

36. Shortly after, congressional rule making supported the transition from public control over nuclear power to private production. For more on the history of nuclear technology, see Joseph G. Morone and Edward J.

Woodhouse, *The Demise of Nuclear Energy? Lessons for Democratic Control of Technology* (New Haven, CT: Yale University Press, 1989).

37. Campbell and Lindberg use the case of nuclear privatization to demonstrate the state's production of property rights. Their definition of private property rights—"the rules that determine the conditions of ownership and control the means of production"—situates nuclear energy producers as the empowered and those unable to harness the energy as less able to participate in the economy ("Property Rights and the Organization of Economic Activity by the State," *American Journal of Sociology* 55, no. 5 [1990]: 635).

38. The Nuclear Energy Institute further details the Price-Anderson Act on its website, accessed January 22, 2018, www.nei.org/Master-Document-Folder /backgrounders/Fact-Sheets/Insurance-Price-Anderson-Act-Provides-Ef fective-Li.

39. For the full speech, see "Military-Industrial Complex Speech, Dwight D. Eisenhower, 1961," accessed August 14, 2017, http://avalon.law.yale.edu /20th_century/eisenhower001.asp.

40. Christopher Dandeker, *Surveillance, Power, and Modernity: Bureaucracy and Discipline from 1700 to the Present Day* (New York: St. Martin's, 1990), 102. Dandeker explains industrial society, Marxism, and Machiavellian theories of surveillance. He interjects his own theory, arguing that warfare and the military lead to bureaucratization. In the process, professional experts come to have an important role in expanding the bureaucracy, as does parliamentary democracy.

41. Ibid. Dandeker points out that geopolitical motives are often rooted in concerns over nuclear bombs, and in the security state necessary to maintain authority over who has access to the technology. He contends that industrial and capital interests also play an important role in the surveillance state.

42. Dandeker further warns: "The advent of nuclear weapons and the partial return to professional systems of organizing the armed services has not entailed a dismantling of the security state. Rather, the security state has continued to flourish and become entrenched as the administrative basis of society permanently ready for war in the nuclear age" (*Surveillance, Power, and Modernity*, 105). Like Dandeker, Rosa Brooks documents how war has expanded beyond the confines of simple violence, and how literacy campaigns and cyberspace "war" have increasingly become part of the battlefield; see *How Everything Became War and the Military Became Everything: Tales from the Pentagon* (New York: Simon and Schuster, 2016).

43. All Vogtle Units are operated by Southern Nuclear Operating Co., a subsidiary of Southern Company. For more details, see http://www.southern company.com/legal/home.cshtml. Ownership in Vogtle Units 3 and 4 is divided as follows: Georgia Power, 45.7 percent, Oglethorpe Power, 30 percent, MEAG Power, 22.7 percent, Dalton Utilities, 1.6 percent. For more details, see http://www.southerncompany.com/what-doing/ energy-innovation/nuclear-energy/pdfs/vogtle-nuclear-brochure.pdf. Ownership in Vogtle Units 1 and 2 has the same breakdown as for Units 3 and 4.

44. Max Weber, "Stages in the Development of Bureaucracy," in *From Max Weber: Essays in Sociology*, ed. H. H. Gerth and C. Wright Mills (New York: Oxford University Press, 1946); first published as chapter 11 of volume 2 of Weber, *Economy and Society*, see p. 235. Max Weber further writes, "The bureaucratization of organized warfare may be carried through in the form of private capitalist enterprise, just like any other business" (222).

45. In *The Nuclear Cage: A Sociology of the Arms Race* (Englewood Cliffs, New Jersey: Prentice Hall, 1988), ed. Lester R. Kurtz. He attributes the escalation of the race for arms in part to bureaucracy. Kurtz identifies as driving forces both an "eye for an eye" human desire for revenge and rituals that smoothly conceal the complexity and dangers of such technology. The book concludes by suggesting that dismantling nationalism can help end the arms race, somewhat coinciding with Dandeker's belief that defense of the democratic nation-state requires surveillance in the age of the nuclear state.

46. In *The Modern Mercenary: Private Armies and What They Mean for World Order* (Oxford: Oxford University Press, 2014), Sean McFate, a former contract worker and paratrooper for the US Army's 82nd Airborne Division, details the rise of the private-contractor military. Conflict entrepreneurs structured as multinational corporations use lethal force and train others to do so. Although these entities account for a minority of the actual forces in combat (12 percent), McFate compellingly documents that they nonetheless do most of the killing and dying: "But size does not matter when it comes to armed contractors. Even though they are fewer in number than their unarmed brethren, their actions resonate disproportionately more loudly, owing to the nature of their work: they kill people" (23).

47. For more, see David Lyon, "9/11, Synopticon, and Scopophilia: Watching and Being Watched," in *The New Politics of Surveillance and Visibility*,

ed. Kevin D. Haggerty and Richard V. Ericson (Toronto: University of Toronto Press, 2006), 35–54.

48. In *No Place to Hide* (New York: Free Press, 2006), Robert O'Harrow reifies Dandeker's notion of the democratization of war. O'Harrow explains that public support in the wake of 9/11 provided the climate for the USA PATRIOT Act to take formerly limited data surveillance technologies and use them widely. He focuses on data collection companies that contract for the government as maintainers and collectors of huge amounts of data. Altogether, he warns that the spreading collection and use of data by private firms bode poorly for civil liberties.

49. Mirowski and Sent, "Commercialization of Science."

50. Christopher Dandeker, "Surveillance and Military Transformation," in Haggerty and Ericson, *New Politics of Surveillance and Visibility.*

51. For more details, see Charles Rabb, "Joined-Up Surveillance: The Challenge to Privacy," in *The Intensification of Surveillance: Crime, Terrorism and Warfare in the Information Age*, ed. K. Ball and F. Webster (London: Pluto, 2003), 42-61.

52. Gary Marx, "Measuring Everything That Moves: The New Surveillance at Work," in *Deviance in the Workplace* (Stanford, CT: IAI Press, 1999). Marx has written extensively on surveillance in America, perhaps most famously in his book *Undercover: Police Surveillance in America* (Berkeley: University of California Press, 1988).

53. Tocqueville, *Democracy in America*, 694.

54. Weber, "The Permanent Character of the Bureaucratic Machine," in Gerth and Mills, *From Max Weber*, 228. Weber's critique of democracy in many senses resonates with Tocqueville's by substituting the idea of rationalization for Tocqueville's equality. Weber argues that mass democracy sweeps away feudal and patrimonial structures, with the intent of also eliminating plutocratic administration. This never quite happens, though, because the demos is an inarticulate mass that elects leaders who direct administrative activities. In action, the democratic mass becomes leveled as the bureaucrats increase their power.

55. Michel Foucault, *Discipline and Punish: The Birth of the Prison* (New York: Vintage, 1995; originally pub. 1977), 168; Foucault, "The Eye of Power," in *Power/Knowledge: Selected Interviews, and Other Writings, 1972–1977*, ed. Colin Gordon (New York: Pantheon, 1980; originally pub. 1977), 155. Foucault explains how he found Jeremy Bentham's book *Panopticon* (1791) to be a turning point in his thinking about the technology of power and surveillance, especially the use of technology to achieve the lowest cost

for the greatest benefit by compelling those who were gazed upon to behave at their own behest. In other words, the self-enactment of utilitarianism for the accumulation of profit.

56. David Graeber's groundbreaking book *The Utopia of Rules* points out that the market and society are equally bureaucratic. Every attempt to remove red tape as part of deregulation to encourage the supposed "free market" actually increases bureaucratic overhead, an effect that he calls the iron law of liberalism. He frames democratic governance as opposed to bureaucratic rule. See p. 18 for quote.

57. In *The Democracy Project: A History, a Crisis, a Movement* (New York: Spiegel & Grau, 2013), David Graeber sees democracy as a consensus, stateless project, which he captures often through the term "direct democracy." He takes little issue with majority voice or majority rule, drawing on his activism in Occupy Wall Street to make his point. Particularly compelling is his documentation of the use of participatory group meetings in which people raise their hands in agreement or disagreement, avoiding as much as possible the act of voting but still defaulting to majority rule as a mechanism to determine authority when consensus stalls. Distinct from Graeber, I explicitly problematize majority rule in democracy and the accounting mechanisms it requires. This critique, further developed in chapter 4, is paramount to my broader concerns related to the democratic state, which draws on Weber's notion of the leveling of the masses or demos.

58. Foucault provides a method to study how the objects of psychopathology, such as madness, speech disorders, and motor disturbances, are identified as components of this particular field of study (*The Archeology of Knowledge and "The Discourse on Language"* [New York: Vintage, 2010; originally pub. 1972], 45). As he writes in "The Eye of Power," the study of madness is largely about facilitating social order and sustaining a centralized apparatus of power.

59. Foucault, *Discipline and Punish*, 191. Here Foucault examines the notion of corrective training through hierarchical observation. He discusses the psychological examination as key to rendering each person a "case" subject to a branch of knowledge and, thus, a branch of power. This turns a person from an indescribable entity to an observation able to become legible through the domination of the state.

60. Ibid., 140, 170. Foucault compellingly documents the reorientation of the human body as a machine subject to mechanics— which makes people more amenable to command and docility. With this reorientation comes a wealth of new descriptions, plans, and data gathered from and

imposed on bodies. A key tenet of Foucault's argument is that this process renders bodies docile from the inside, by self-discipline, and from the outside through mechanisms like examinations. Foucault's mechanisms of control are in line with Dale's experience, but my argument pushes back against the inevitability of docility. Belief in the higher purpose of democracy conflicts with passivity. Dale, Neill, and Jeff are not docile—in great detail they remember and resent infinitesimal methods of domination, precisely because they believe that democracy owes them something more.

61. Graeber, *Utopia of Rules*, 120. Graeber uses *Back to the Future* and *Star Trek* to question why the technological feats once imagined for our time never materialized. In doing so, he argues that the push toward profit has minimized possibilities for dramatic scientific inventions. For more, see the essay "Of Flying Cars and the Declining Rate of Profit" in *Utopia of Rules*.

62. Ann Marie Kyzer, "Sales Tax Not Being Collected on Vogtle Construction," *Waynesboro (GA) True Citizen*, accessed March 18, 2014, www.the truecitizen.com/news/2012-12-12/Front_Page/Sales_tax_not_being_col lected_on_Vogtle_constructi.html.

### Chapter 3. The Moral Economy of Democracy

All quoted material from interviews comes from audio recordings.

1. See "Georgia Power 2016 Annual Report," https://www.georgiapower .com/content/dam/georgia-power/pdfs/call-outs-pdf/gpc-2016-annual report.pdf, accessed February 26, 2018.

2. For more details about these figures, see "Southern Company 2016 Annual Report: The Energy to Lead," http://www.annualreports.com /HostedData/AnnualReports/PDF/NYSE_SO_2016.pdf, Accessed February 26, 2018.

3. Here, I am returning to my earlier reference to Barrington Moore's *Social Origins of Dictatorship and Democracy* and the book's first chapter, "England and the Contributions of Violence to Gradualism," in which Moore identifies yeoman farmers, along with merchants, as key actors in precipitating the English Civil War. Yeomen favored individual variation over the cooperative organization of the feudal system. Small capitalists and individualists wanted a property regime based on individual ownership rather than commonage or landed estates, which Moore identifies as a chief force behind enclosure. Even more alarmingly in a historical

sense, Moore argues that yeoman farmers aimed at producing profit, whereas the goals of the peasant and lord system included sustaining people on the land.

4. In *Private Property: The History of an Idea* (London: George Allen & Unwin, 1973), Richard Schlatter provides a historical review of the idea of private property as a right, and its evolution from ancient Greece up to the nineteenth century. He describes how private ownership has evolved to remain a quintessential component of the Western world for the last millennium. This explanation of Locke is drawn from Epstein, *Takings*.

5. John Locke, *The Works of John Locke In Nine Volumes: The Twelfth Edition. Volume The Fourth* (London: C. Baldwin, 1824; originally pub. 1689), 353–54.

6. Ibid., 364, 359–60.

7. It was a convenient, and inaccurate, view of American Indians for white colonists to hold. Many Indians did cultivate the land, but such nuances proved inconvenient to those bent on the forceful acquisition of Indian lands and the extermination of the tribes.

8. John Bartram, "Diary of a Journey through the Carolinas, Georgia, and Florida from July 1, 1765, to April 10, 1766," *Transactions of the American Philosophical Society*, n.s., 33 (Dec. 1942): 25. It was another seventy years before someone took formal notice of the prehistoric oyster shell formation.

9. Quoted in Timothy S. Arthur and William H. Carpenter, *History of Georgia* (Philadelphia: Lippincott, 1861), 35–36.

10. Ibid.

11. Walter Clark, in *A Lost Arcadia: Or, The Story of My Old Community* (Augusta, GA: Chronicle Job Print, 1909). Clark's account is informed by his service in the Confederacy. He explains that he wrote the book "to please my friends. . . . to please myself," p. v. The first chapter is titled "The Red Man's Rule." Despite its open racism, the book contains specific documentation of the tribes that once existed in Burke County, biographical nuances, and local descriptions valuable to understanding Burke County at the time.

12. George R. Gilmer, *Sketches of Some of the First Settlers of Upper Georgia, of the Cherokees, and the Author* (London: D. Appleton and Company, 1854), 53. Gilmer, a former governor of Georgia, recorded the tale of a Mr. Hughes who was visiting his Uncle Patrick Hughes in Burke County, known to be "a frolicking, card-playing Irishman." Young

Mr. Hughes fell into the habits of his uncle and became a gambler. While riding through a dense forest with some of his companions, a shot rang out. Governor Gilmer reported: "Those before, hearing the report of a pistol, looked back and saw young Hughs falling from his horse, covered with his blood and brains."

13. In *Poor White Trash: The 400-Year Untold History of Class in America* (New York: Penguin, 2016), Nancy Isenberg brings attention to the overlooked history of the landless white poor. See p. 14.

14. Isenberg takes Locke to task in her chapter "John Locke's Lubberland" (*Poor White Trash*).

15. Ibid., 58.

16. Arthur and Carpenter, *History of Georgia*, 49.

17. See Robert Scott Davis, *Georgians in the Revolution: At Kettle Creek (Wilkes Co.) and Burke County* (Easley, SC: Southern Historical Press, 1986), 81. Isenberg dates crackers back to British official records from the 1760s, which identify white settlers as a "lawless set of rascals on the frontiers of Virginia, Maryland, and the Carolinas and Georgia, who often change their places of abode" (*Poor White Trash*, 109–10). She too documents that such poor whites were often framed as "worse than Indians" (110).

18. Steven Hahn's *The Roots of Southern Populism: Yeoman Farmers and the Transformation of the Georgia Upcountry, 1850–1890*, (Oxford: Oxford University Press, 2006) is rich in detail, including that pertaining to American Indians, p. 18. Most valuable for the presentation of yeoman and planter relations in my review of Burke County is Hahn's transformative message that southern yeoman farmers, against their will, were forced to work with southern planters and serve their markets. Such farmers favored Locke's labor-centric notions of labor over the industrial-scale mentality predominant among planters and slave owners.

19. Louis Hartz, *The Liberal Tradition in America* (New York: Harcourt, Brace and Company, 1955), 76. Hartz treats the existence of slavery as an anomaly in a society that otherwise flourished on Lockean idealism. At heart, he argues, was citizens' belief in propertied liberalism, which stood against the ancien régime. Individualism in conjunction with property rights defined America, in his view. I challenge this approach to liberalism in the next chapter.

20. Davis, *Georgians in the Revolution*.

21. Ibid., 91.

22. Quoted in ibid., 92.

23. Albert M. Hillhouse, *A History of Burke County, Georgia, 1777–1950*, (Spartanburg, SC: Reprint Co., 1985; originally pub. 1950), documents much of this time period. Ten years after the Revolutionary War, lawlessness lingered, but the formation of courts and local militias restored some order. Grand jurors in the Burke County Superior Court proposed laws to punish arsonists who set fire to woods and property of fellow citizens, to moderate adultery, and to bar the illegal sale of liquor.

24. Tocqueville, *Democracy in America*, 261.

25. See Matthew Mariola, "Losing Ground: Farmland Preservation, Economic Utilitarianism, and the Erosion of the Agrarian Ideal," *Agriculture and Human Values* 22, no. 2 (2005): 209–23. Also see Nancy Naples, "Contradictions in Agrarian Ideology: Restructuring Gender, Race-Ethnicity, and Class," *Rural Sociology* 59, no. 1: 110–35. In this ethnographic study of Iowa, Naples provides a helpful review of agrarianism.

26. David B. Danbom, *Born in the Country: A History of Rural America*. Second edition (Baltimore: Johns Hopkins University Press, 2006), 67. Danbom provides a basic explanation of agricultural and rural history, interweaving the vitality of the rural with the vitality of agriculture.

27. Tocqueville, *Democracy in America*, 638–39.

28. Donald Last, "Private Property Rights with Responsibilities: What Would Thomas Jefferson Say about the 'Wise Use' Movement?," in *Who Owns America? Social Conflict over Property Rights*, ed. Harvey M. Jacobs (Madison: University of Wisconsin Press, 1998), 45–53. See p. 47.

29. See Schlatter, *Private Property*.

30. Ibid.

31. These figures come from Hillhouse, *History of Burke County*, pp. 20–21 and 64.

32. Emily Burke, *Pleasure and Pain: Reminiscences of Georgia in the 1840's* (Savannah, GA: Beehive, 1978; originally pub. 1850), 220. Burke described antebellum Burke County in a journal she wrote on a visit from the North. She concluded: "But slavery in its best form is nothing more nor less than a cruel bondage of which any country ought to be ashamed, much more one that makes such loud boasts of freedom as ours is always ready to trumpet far and wide."

33. The invention of the cotton gin by Eli Whitney around 1793 marked a further expansion of plantation culture. The production of cotton was formerly limited by the intensive labor necessary to pick and clean upland cotton. A slave would spend a day cleaning a pound of cotton, and a slave family would work from dawn until dusk picking ten pounds. The

cotton gin mechanized the laborious step of cleaning the cotton. Bales of cotton came flowing out of Georgia, and cotton became the major cash crop of Burke County. For more details, see Lawton Evan, *A History of Georgia: For Use in Schools* (New York: University Publishing Company, 1898).

34. See US Department of Commerce, Bureau of the Census, "Negroes in the United States: 1920–32" (Washington, DC: Government Printing Office, 1935), p. 632.

35. The slave population numbered 12,052, and the white population had declined to 5,013 (Hillhouse, *History of Burke County*), p. 105.

36. See C. Van Woodward, *Origins of the New South, 1877–1913* (Baton Rouge: Louisiana State University Press, 1971).

37. Ibid.

38. Quoted in Hahn, *Roots of Southern Populism*, 89.

39. Quoted in David Williams, *Bitterly Divided: The South's Inner Civil War* (New York: Norton, 2010), 109.

40. Ibid.

41. David Williams, Teresa C. Williams, and R. David Carlson, *Plain Folk in a Rich Man's War: Class and Dissent in Confederate Georgia* (Gainesville: University Press of Florida, 2002), 72.

42. For more on the derogatory labels applied to whites who stood against white wealth, see Matt Wray, *Not Quite White: White Trash and the Boundaries of Whiteness* (Durham, NC: Duke University Press, 2006).

43. Hahn, *Roots of Southern Populism*.

44. Alan Conway, *The Reconstruction of Georgia* (Minneapolis: University of Minnesota Press, 1966), p. 12.

45. Hahn, *Roots of Southern Populism*, p. 153.

46. Woodward, *Origins of the New South*.

47. See Conway, *Reconstruction of Georgia*, 81, for whipping details. See Hillhouse for contract details, 142.

48. Quoted in Hahn, *Roots of Southern Populism*, 205.

49. For further details, see "Department of Commerce, Bureau of the Census, Negro Population, 1790–1915" (Washington, DC: Government Printing Office, 1918), 646. Also see p. 710, "Table 73." These figures compare owners (free, mortgaged and part) to tenants (cash share, and share-cash). At the time, Georgia had the most black residents of any state in the country. Burke County had the second highest number of black residents of any Georgia county.

50. Bureau of the Census, "Negroes in the United States: 1920–32," 6.

51. US Department of Commerce, "Sixteenth Census of the United States:

1940, Agriculture, Volume 3, General Report" (Washington, DC: Government Printing Office, 1940).

52. Burke County, the acreage owned by black and white farmers, the number of farmers who owned their own ground, and the total acreage under cultivation all reached their high points for the twentieth century. Two hundred twenty-nine black farmers owned 34,461 acres, and 287 white farmers owned 304,729 acres. Before and after this point, the absolute acreage owned by farmers, and the number of farmers who operated their own farms, declined in Burke County. Today, there are only 81 black operators in Burke County. These figures are based on statistics compiled from the following Census Bureau reports: "Thirteenth Census of the United States Taken in the Year 1910, Volume 6: Agriculture: 1909 and 1910, Alabama-Montana" (1913); "Negro Population, 1790–1915" (1918); "Fourteenth Census of the United States: 1930, Agriculture, Volume 2, Part 2—The Southern States" (1932); "Negroes in the United States: 1920–32" (1935); "Fifteenth Census of the United States: 1940, Agriculture, Volume 3, General Report" (1942); "Fifteenth Census of the United States: 1940, Agriculture, Volume 2, Third Series, State Reports, Part 2: Statistics for Counties" (1942); "United States Census of Agriculture, 1945, Volume 1: Part 17, Georgia, Statistics for Counties" (1946); "United States Census of Agriculture, 1950, Volume 1: Part 17, Georgia, Counties and State Economic Areas" (1952); "United States Census of Agriculture, 1954, Volume 1: Counties and State Economic Areas, Part 17, Georgia, Counties and State Economic Areas" (1956); "United States Census of Agriculture, 1959, Final Report, Volume 1, Part 28, Counties, Georgia" (1961); "United States Census of Agriculture, 1964, Volume 1, Part 28, Georgia" (1967); US Department of Agriculture, "Census of Agriculture, Historical Census Publications," 1978–2007, www.agcensus.usda.gov /Publications/Historical_Publications; US Department of Agriculture, "Census of Agriculture, 2012 Census, Volume 1, Chapter 2: County Level Data, Table 54: White Operators," www.agcensus.usda.gov/Publications /2012/Full_Report/Volume_1,_Chapter_2_County_Level/Georgia/ st13_2_054_054.pdf; US Department of Agriculture, "Census of Agriculture, 2012b, 2012 Census, Volume 1, Chapter 2: County Level Data, Table 52, Black or African American Operators," www.agcensus.usda.gov /Publications/2012/Full_Report/Volume_1,_Chapter_2_County_Level /Georgia/st13_2_052_053.pdf.

53. In 1930, there were forty-four white managers and ten black. By 1959, there were only five white managers and one black manager in the county.

54. For more on the important work done by rural sociologists on responses to land taking for hydraulic fracturing, see Stephanie Mailin and Kathy Teigen DeMaster, "A Devil's Bargain: Rural Environmental Injustices and Hydraulic Fracturing on Pennsylvania's Farms," *Journal of Rural Studies* 47A (2016): 278–90; Kai A. Schafft, Yetkin Borlu, and Leland Glenna, "The Relationship between Marcellus Shale Gas Development in Pennsylvania and Local Perceptions of Risk and Opportunity," *Rural Sociology* 78, no. 2 (2013): 143–66; and Coulter Ellis, Gene L. Theodori, Peggy Petrzelka, Douglas Jackson-Smith, and A. E. Luloff, "Unconventional Risks: The Experience of Acute Energy Development in the Eagle Ford Shale," *Energy Research and Social Science* 20 (2016): 91–98.

55. For more, see Thomas Mitchell, "From Reconstruction to Deconstruction: Undermining Black Landownership, Political Independence, and Community through Partition Sales of Tenancies in Common," *Northwestern University Law Review* 95 no. 2 (2000): 505–80. Mitchell more recently provided a way to counter these deleterious consequences in "Restoring Hope for Heirs Property Owners: The Uniform Partition of Heirs Property Act," *Legal Studies Research Paper Series No. 17-04. State & Local Law News*, 40, no. 1 (2016): 5–15. See also Jess Gilbert, Gwen Sharp, and M. Sindy Felin, "The Loss and Persistence of Black-Owned Farms and Farmland: A Review of the Research Literature and Its Implications," *Southern Rural Sociology* 18, no. 2 (2002): 1–30; Janice F. Dryer, Conner Bailey, and Nhuong Van Tran, "Ownership Characteristics of Heir Property in a Black Belt County: A Quantitative Approach," *Southern Rural Sociology* 24, no. 2 (2009): 192–217.

56. For his introduction of this idea, see p. 79 in E. P. Thompson, "The Moral Economy of the English Crowd in the Eighteenth Century," *Past and Present* 50 (1971): 76–136; and Thompson, *The Making of the English Working Class* (New York: Pantheon, 1963).

57. See the extensive discussion of this by Thomas Merrill and Henry Smith in "The Morality of Property," *William and Mary Law Review* 48, no. 5 (2007): 1849–95. They assert that "the moral right to property is not qualitatively different from those moral rights we describe as human or civil rights" (1894).

58. See Milton Friedman, "Economic Freedom behind the Scenes," in *Economic Freedom of the World: 2002 Annual Report*, ed. James Gwartney and Robert Lawson (Vancouver, BC: Fraser Institute, 2002), xvii–xxi.

59. Hernando de Soto, for example, makes the case in *The Mystery of Capital: Why Capitalism Triumphs in the West and Fails Everywhere Else* (New York:

Basic Books, 2000), that live capital belongs only to property codified by the state. Otherwise, it stays in a dead form, existing on black markets and under mattresses, outside the penetrating grasp of capitalism. For capital to compile, he argues, states (especially developing ones) must have a strong property rights regime that allows economic activity to be made legible. This contention is critical to mainstream economists, who widely recognize private property regimes and the states that uphold them as crucial for the operations of markets.

60. Scott, *Moral Economy of the Peasant*, 3. Scott's book concerns itself with peasants, and thus my argument diverges here by applying moral economy to the context of the democratic state. Since the work by Scott and Thompson, the use of moral economy has spread widely into other circles; for the moral economy of fair trade, see Michael K. Goodman, "Reading Fair Trade: Political Ecological Imaginary and the Moral Economy of Fair Trade Foods," *Political Geography* 23, no. 7 (2004): 891–915; for the moral economy of grades and standards, see Lawrence Busch, "The Moral Economy of Grades and Standards," *Journal of Rural Studies* 16, no. 3 (2000): 273–83; for the moral economy of science, see Lorraine Daston, "The Moral Economy of Science," *Constructing Knowledge in the History of Science* 10 (1995): 2–24. The similarities between Scott's moral economy in the peasant context and the moral economy I document in the rural context become more apparent in my discussion of poaching, faith, and guns as outlets for justice. Scott argues that the moral economy can help us develop an understanding of why rebels are willing to "risk everything" to stand up against the wealthy and powerful. Overall, he sees such rebellion as often existing in the context of exploitation and misery facilitated by ecological, price-system, and monoculture vulnerability. The notion of the moral economy speaks well to democracy by pointing to expanding police and coercive power as straws that can break the back of rural allegiance (see Scott's discussion in *Moral Economy of the Peasant*, 230). Scott further argues that "only a close study of folk culture can define the major points of friction and correspondence" in rural contexts (239).

61. Karl Polanyi, *The Great Transformation: The Political and Economic Origins of Our Time* (Boston: Beacon, 1957; originally pub. 1944), particularly the discussion on 66–70, compellingly establishes the heavy-handed role of the state in creating markets and regulating their perpetual crises that result from the rendering of the lifeblood of society into fictitious commodities. I, though, diverge from Polanyi by seeing the double movement as more than action through the state, but often action outside it. Confining the

double movement to the walls of formal governance assumes that the state apparatus is the solution to a problem that is much of its own making.

62. Ibid., 71.

63. Friedman, "Economic Freedom behind the Scenes."

64. Polanyi, *Great Transformation*, 71–72.

65. Thompson "Moral Economy of the English Crowd," 78. The violation of rights and customs by different types of development is not always clear in the present moment. Take, for example, the issue of property rights in the context of concentrated animal feeding operations (CAFOs), often called factory farms. These facilities often "trespass" on private property rights by polluting air and water, hampering owners' capacity to enjoy their property. While these takings agitate some rural community members —see, for example, Lisa Pruitt and Linda Sobczynski, "Protecting People, Protecting Places: What Environmental Litigation Conceals and Reveals about Rurality," *Journal of Rural Studies* 47A (2016): 326–36— these facilities simultaneously use the rhetoric of "right to farm" and "feed the world" to pit rural residents against one another. In part, the difference in residents' reception of CAFOs and the nuclear power plant in Burke County can be explained because of the longevity of the plants, which were first proposed in the late 1960s. At that time, they seemed like a better idea and enjoyed more support, like CAFOs that initially were more welcomed, and then with time proved to be a burden.

66. In a rare sociological study of eminent domain, Debbie Becher makes important inroads in the cultural meanings of private property; see Becher, "The Rights behind Eminent Domain Fights: A Little Property and a Lot of Home," in *Property Rights and Neoliberalism: Cultural Demands and Legal Actions*, ed. Wayne V. McIntosh and Laura J. Hatcher (Burlington, VT: Ashgate, 2010), 75–93; and also Becher, *Private and Public Power: Eminent Domain in Philadelphia* (Oxford: Oxford University Press, 2014).

67. For a compelling discussion of the role of memories in shaping attachment to place, see Michael M. Bell, "The Ghosts of Place," *Theory and Society* 26 (1997): 813–36.

68. Page 173 in Morton J. Horwitz, "Santa Clara Revisited: The Development of Corporate Theory," *West Virginia Law Review* 88 (1985): 173–224.

69. *Santa Clara County v. Southern Pacific Railroad Co.*, 118 U.S. 394 (1886), built on *Louisiana's Slaughterhouse Cases*, 83 U.S. 36 (1873), in which the Supreme Court ruled that application of the Equal Protection Clause of the Fourteenth Amendment was limited to national rights of citizenship

(which were few) and did not apply to state rights of citizenship (which were numerous). The dissenters, including Justice Stephen Field, argued for a more expansive definition of the Fourteenth Amendment to create a federal charter of constitutional rights.

70. I focus on key rulings here to point to the accumulation of legal rights in corporate hands. That said, there was ample protest against the corporate domination of capitalism and democracy. The corporation, what Horwitz calls "the most powerful and prominent example of the emergence of non-individualistic or, if you will, collectivist legal institutions," engendered a crisis of legitimacy for liberalism at the time ("Santa Clara Revisited," 181). The pro-corporate movement used liberal ideology to support its own agenda by developing a language of public versus private, as discussed in chapter 2. Those who theoretically and practically viewed individualism as "under attack" lost the political battle as the debate took to the courts, where the idea of economic development began to prevail in favor of corporate rights.

71. *Hale v. Henkel*, 201 U.S. 43 (1906). The decision is available at https://supreme.justia.com/cases/federal/us/201/43/case.html.

72. *Ludwig v. Western Union Telegraph Co.*, 216 U.S. 146 (1910). For more details on the corporate claim of personhood and its associated rights, see Gerard Carl Henderson, *The Position of Foreign Corporations in American Constitutional Law: A Contribution to the History and Theory of Juristic Persons in Anglo-American Law* (Cambridge, MA: Harvard University Press, 1918).

73. The ruling in *Ludwig* is available at https://supreme.justia.com/cases/federal/us/216/146/case.html.

74. *Burwell v. Hobby Lobby*, 573 U.S. (2014), available at https://supreme.justia.com/cases/federal/us/573/13-354.

75. *Citizens United v. Federal Election Commission*, 558 U.S. 310 (2010), available at https://supreme.justia.com/cases/federal/us/558/08-205.

## Chapter 4. The Rule of Numbers

All quoted material from interviews (except for the opening scene) comes from audio recordings.

1. Accusations of "NIMBYism" often come in the form of insults accusing owners of simply practicing "resistance to change"; see p. 268 in Robyn Bartel and Nicole Graham, "Property and Place Attachment: A Legal Geographical Analysis of Biodiversity Law Reform in New South Wales," *Geographical Research* 54, no. 3 (2016): 267–84.

2. For more, see C. B. Macpherson, *The Political Theory of Possessive Individ-*

*ualism* (London: Oxford University Press, 1962). I refer specifically to the section "Hobbes: The Political Obligation of the Market," subsections 2, "Human Nature and the State of Nature," and (ii), "The State of Nature."

3. Thomas Hobbes, *Leviathan*, ed. Richard Turk (Cambridge: Cambridge Press, 1996; originally pub. 1651).

4. Macpherson, *Possessive Individualism*, 29.

5. Ibid., 39.

6. Jeremy Bentham, *An Introduction to the Principles of Morals and Legislation* (Oxford: Clarendon Press, 1789), 3.

7. See Polanyi's discussion of Bentham (*Great Transformation*, 106, 110).

8. John Stuart Mill, *Utilitarianism*, ed. Colin Heydt (Peterborough, ON: Broadview, 2001; originally pub. 1863), 15. It is important to note that in the case of majority rule, Mill clarified that those doing the judging should have experienced the pain that they require of someone else. Mill does not recognize it himself, but his argument points to a structural problem with representative democracy. Elected officials can hardly experience the numerous and extensive sacrifices regularly and historically demanded from the minority. Thus, those doing the demanding are not feeling the pain.

9. This line of logic is a key reason why progressive planners see the Supreme Court's ruling in *Kelo v. City of New London* as a great success. Since the public gained authority over private property rights, the outcome appears to them to be a good one. Even though the main plaintiff was trying to save her home against an economic development corporation building a shopping-research-business center—something that clearly serves profit—the private-public binary around property prevented a larger discussion of private property motives. As a result, private property rights in such progressive circles often remain synonymous with selfish pursuits and money making, as opposed to ends that serve the noble public. For more, see Ezra Rosser, "The Ambition and Transformative Potential of Progressive Property," *California Law Review* (2013): 107–72.

10. For a thorough treatment on the role of republicanism in shaping US democracy, see Gordon S. Wood, "Republicanism," in *The Creation of the American Republic, 1776–1787* (Chapel Hill: University of North Carolina Press, 1969), 46–83.

11. J. G. A. Pocock, "The Americanization of Virtue," in *The Machiavellian Moment: Florentine Political Thought and the Atlantic Republican Tradition* (Princeton, NJ: Princeton University Press, 1975), 506–52.

12. Wood, *Creation of the American Republic*, 58.

13. Quoted in Angela Cobb, *Roster of the Confederate Soldiers of Burke County, Georgia, 1861–1865* (Baltimore: Gateway, 1998), 28.

14. In a sense, it seems a great irony to use a white aristocratic property-owning man to make an argument about inequality in democracy. For example, in one passage characteristic of attitudes at the time, Tocqueville states that African Americans and American Indians are "naturally distinct" and "below" white men (*Democracy in America*, 317). Further, women are hardly mentioned except in subservient roles. What is helpful about Tocqueville's argument about inequality is his recognition of the delinking of the chain of community through voting. The act of voting turned people into individual links as part of the equality of conditions, which could give rise to a series of problems: self-interest, apathy toward government, unchecked bureaucratic control, and majority rule over minority rights. Tocqueville failed to give attention to state inclusion or economic inequality, which can result in a multitude of oversights with regard to class, racism, xenophobia, and patriarchy. But he did provide a framework for understanding domination and oppression within democratic institutions through the tyranny of the majority, a concept that remains an understudied and underused tool. His writings help clarify how the democratic state's rendering of people into numbers can give rise to inequality. For a fuller explication of this argument, see Loka Ashwood and Katherine MacTavish, "Tyranny of the Majority and Rural Environmental Injustice," *Journal of Rural Studies* 47(A): 271–77.

15. Tocqueville, *Democracy in America*, 255.

16. See Phil McMichael, *Development and Social Change: A Global Perspective*, 6th ed. (Thousand Oaks, CA: Sage, 2016), especially chapter 2, "Instituting the Development Project," and chapter 3, "The Development Project."

17. Cheryl Harris, "Whiteness as Property," *Harvard Law Review* 106, no. 8 (1993): 1707–91. The article begins with a vignette about her grandmother's capacity to pass as white and work at a department store in order to provide economic security for her family. Every day, her grandmother would take the bus from her black neighborhood to the white-serving department store, keeping her background as a black woman hidden. Harris goes on to establish how whiteness pervades the property rights regime, and thus helps determine who has a particular economic status.

18. Meg Collins and I photographed a hard copy of the 1966 tax digest for Burke County, Georgia. I converted the photographs into a PDF and

then ran text-recognition software to identify the text. I worked with James Patterson and Hunter Hall to type the data for Militia Districts 66 and 68 into an Excel spreadsheet. These two militia districts include some portion of the Vogtle evacuation zone and land that was later purchased by the company or the State of Georgia. For example, Sydney's land rests in Militia District 66. The parcel data for this militia district separated "colored" owners from white owners; 1966 was the last year that data was sorted by race. We found that 32,448 total acres were taxed in the district. Of that total, 8,586 acres belonged to black families, and 23,880 acres belonged to white families. This acreage was claimed by fifty black owners of more than one acre, and seventy-one white owners of more than one acre. The market value of black-owned land was $278,798, and $477,144 for white-owned land. I determined the 39 percent difference by comparing the land's valuation with the amount actually owned. Militia District 66 does not include an incorporated town. The soil in this region includes clay and sand, and although there is some space for difference in tax assessment accordingly, from what I was told from black and white locals, the poorest of the poor land primarily belonged to black families. Altogether, these findings suggest race as a distinguishing factor in why black families paid higher taxes.

19. Page 26 in Elijah Anderson, Duke W. Austin, Craig Lapriece Holloway, and Vani S. Kulkarni "The Legacy of Racial Caste: An Exploratory Ethnography," *Annals of the American Academy of Political and Social Science* 642 (2012): 25–42.

20. Page 467 in Eduardo Bonilla-Silva, "Rethinking Racism: Toward a Structural Interpretation," *American Sociological Review* 62, no. 3 (1997): 465–80.

21. C. Eric Lincoln, *Race, Religion, and the Continuing American Dilemma* (New York: Hill and Wang, 1984), 230. The section "Looking from the Outside," in the final chapter, "Moral Resources for Resolution," aptly captures the deleterious consequences of the majority's judgmental perceptions of the black minority.

22. For an excellent summary of racism as hegemonic in and endemic to US democracy, see Angela Harris, "Critical Race Theory," in *International Encyclopedia of the Social and Behavioral Sciences* (Oxford: Elsevier, 2001), 12:2976–80; available at https://works.bepress.com/angela_harris. See also Richard Delgado and Jean Stefancic, *Critical Race Theory: An Introduction* (New York: NYU Press, 2012); R. Delgado, "Biographic Essay: Critical Race Theory," *SAGE Race Relations Abstracts* 19 (1994), 3–28; Haney Lopez, *Racism on Trial: The Chicago Fight for Justice* (Cambridge, MA: Har-

vard University Press, 2003); Michelle Alexander, *The New Jim Crow: Mass Incarceration in the Age of Colorblindness* (New York: New Press, 2012).

23. *Waynesboro (GA) True Citizen*, "Vogtle Pays $19 Million in Property Taxes," accessed April 4, 2015, www.thetruecitizen.com/news/2013-02-06 /News/Vogtle_pays_19_million_in_property_taxes.html.

24. These figures were determined by comparing the surnames from Militia District 66 and District 68 in data from 1966 and 2014. These militia districts include portions of the Vogtle evacuation zone (for example, Raleigh lives in 68 and Sydney lives in 66). The names of owners from 1966 were then compared with those in current tax parcel data (see chapter 3). Rozalynn Klaas at the University of Wisconsin–Madison's Applied Population Laboratory layered the old militia district maps onto current geocoded data to impose militia district boundaries, since current data is no longer organized this way. We then compared the names of current and historical owners from 1966 and 2014 according to surname. If we were uncertain whether identical surnames belonged to the same family, I drew on my local knowledge of the area. When I was not familiar with the families, I used Facebook and online obituaries to double-check family ties. For cases in which we were not certain whether the land belonged to the same family, we excluded it from the total. Altogether, 15,671 acres maintained intergenerational ownership between 1966 and 2014. It should be noted that this method does not capture those pieces of property transferred within a family to a person with a different surname. The figure of 13 percent was determined by dividing the total number of intergenerational black- and white-owned acreage (15,671) by the total acreage in the districts (32,448 acres in 66 and 88,955 in 68). The tax parcel data I acquired for Militia Districts 66 and 68 list only human, no corporate or state, owners in 1966.

25. These figures were determined by comparing ownership in 1966 and 2014 for the families that maintained intergenerational landowners. White intergenerational owners had 15,118 acres in 1966, and 6,311 acres in 2014. Black intergenerational owners had 7,799 acres in 1966 and 9,360 in 2014.

26. Anderson et al., "Legacy of Racial Caste," p. 39.

27. This is an enormously popular way to study the efficacy of social movements that aim for reform through existing democratic channels. See Robert Benford and David Snow, "Framing Processes and Social Movements: An Overview and Assessment," *Annual Review of Sociology* 26 (2000): 611–39. While Benford and Snow's paper rests somewhat outside

my argument because I am not talking about inner-state protest, I find notions of shared framings and collectivity valuable. Within the broader context of for-profit democracy, acting through the state is irrelevant because it is seen as a corrupt player. Since my argument is based on the shared moral economy and the landownership ethic, it is helpful to recognize how majority rule in democracy fosters dissent and difficulties for locals trying to build on their shared moral standards rather than their differences.

28. Douglas Schrock, Daphne Holden, and Lori Reed, "Creating Emotional Resonance: Interpersonal Emotion Work and Motivational Framing in a Transgender Community," *Social Problems* 51, no. 1 (2004):61–81. Their paper discusses framing as informed by shared resonance over an issue.

29. See Kimberlé Crenshaw, "Mapping the Margins: Intersectionality, Identity Politics, and Violence against Women of Color," *Stanford Law Review* 42 (1991): 1241–99, specifically subsection 2, "Race and the domestic violence lobby."

30. Page 4 in Patricia Hill Collins, "Intersectionality's Definitional Dilemmas," *Annual Review of Sociology* 41 (2015): 1–20.

31. On a more positive note, and continuing the metaphor, a land stripped of its resources can be left fallow, possibly allowing it to rejuvenate when the exploiters are gone. This is the beauty of the moral economy of democracy, but also a tragedy of market society. There is needless waste and suffering at the hand of profit's rule.

32. Isenberg, *Poor White Trash*.

33. Hartz largely writes off the majority as a problem for democracy, in part because he pays very little attention to race, treating it as a problem that was solved with the abolition of slavery. For more, see *The Liberal Tradition in America*, chapter 5, "The American Democrat: Hercules and Hamlet," section 3, "Individualist Fear: The Problem of the Majority," 129.

34. These numbers come from p. 271 in Gene Wunderlich, "The U.S.A.'s Land Data Legacy from the 19th Century: A Message from the Henry George–Francis A. Walker Controversy over Farm Land Distribution," *American Journal of Economics and Sociology*, 41, no. 3 (1982): 269–280.

35. These figures come from table 1, "Urban and Rural Population: 1900 to 1990," US Census Bureau, October 1995, https://www.census.gov/population/censusdata/urpop0090.txt.

36. According to US Census data for 2010, the states with a population that is more than 50 percent rural are Maine, 61.45 percent; Mississippi, 50.65

percent; Vermont, 60.1 percent; and West Virginia, 51.28 percent; see https://www.census.gov/geo/reference/ua/urban-rural-2010.html.

37. For a copy of the report, see www.ejnet.org/ej/cerrell.pdf; see also Giovanna Di Chiro, "Environmental Justice from the Grassroots: Reflections of History, Gender, and Expertise," in *The Struggle for Ecological Democracy: Environmental Justice Movements in the United States*, ed. Daníel J. Faber (New York: Guilford, 1998), 104–35.

38. Robert Bullard said as much in some of his foundational writing; see "Anatomy of Environmental Racism and the Environmental Justice Movement," in *Confronting Environmental Racism: Voices from the Grassroots*, ed. Robert D. Bullard (Cambridge, MA: South End, 1993), 15–39.

39. See the *Code of Federal Regulations*, "Title 10. Part 50-Domestic Licensing of Production and Utilization Facilities," accessed February 26, 2018 https://www.nrc.gov/reading-rm/doc-collections/cfr/.

40. My thanks to Michael M. Bell for spearheading the compilation of these figures in our textbook *An Invitation to Environmental Sociology* (Thousand Oaks, CA: Pine Forge, 2016); see in particular chapter 1, "Environmental Problems and Society."

41. Tocqueville, *Democracy in America*, 248.

## Chapter 5. The Rural Rebel

The quoted material on pp. 111–15 (excluding Ashley and Steve), bottom of p. 126, and pp. 136–55 are from field notes. The rest comes from audio recordings.

1. To read more about my interviews with Savannah River Site workers, their radiation exposure, and their deep-seated distrust of the government and corporate contractors, see Loka Ashwood and Steve Wing, "Exposure and Compensation for Nuclear Weapons Workers," *New Solutions* 26, no. 1 (2016): 55–71.

2. E. J. Hobsbawm, *Primitive Rebels* (New York: Norton, 1959), 13. Hobsbawm's two formative books on rebels—the other is *Bandits* (London: Weidenfeld and Nicolson, 2000; originally pub. 1969)—greatly inform my discussion of modern rural rebellion. My findings sometimes diverge from and sometimes symmetrically align with his, which contain a historical breadth and richness that inspired much of my analysis here.

3. Al Gedick, *Resource Rebels: Native Challenges to Mining and Oil Corporations* (Cambridge, MA: South End, 2001), captures the modern challenge to corporate profit pursuits. While I use the term "rebel" similarly to talk about protest outside state boundaries against profit motives, Gedick

captures extreme contexts of exploitation, in particular the genocidal and ethnocidal assault on native peoples worldwide. The movements he documents are collective ones to try to regain native rights for land and culture, whereas I focus on more individualistic ones.

4. In *Bandits*, Hobsbawm deftly captures the dominion of the state: "The central state apparatus reaches down directly to every single person on the national territory and, in democracies at least, every adult citizen, having the right to vote, reaches up directly to the national government by electing it. Its powers are immense—far greater, even in liberal democracies, than those of the greatest and most despotic empires before the eighteenth century" (14).

5. Benford and Snow, "Framing Processes and Social Movements."

6. Hobsbawm, *Bandits*, 40.

7. Ibid., 44.

8. In *Born Fighting: How the Scots-Irish Shaped America* (New York: Broadway, 2005), Jim Webb explores his Scots-Irish roots and finds parallels with the Iraqi people as another fighting culture. He notes the arrogance in the idea that American will can be imposed on another people.

9. In *Deer Hunting with Jesus: Dispatches from America's Class War* (New York: Three Rivers Press, 2007), Joe Bageant explains rural conservative voting patterns in part by describing the rural as stupid and dumb.

10. I draw this brief summary from Anthony Harkins, *Hillbilly: A Cultural History of an American Icon* (Oxford: Oxford University Press, 2004).

11. Isenberg, *Poor White Trash*, 1; see also her chapter 5, "Andrew Jackson's Cracker Country."

12. *Duck Dynasty* is a case in point, an A&E reality TV show that has broken records for its popularity, attracting as many as 11.8 million viewers. The show features a family that became wealthy through marketing the Duck Commander, a special duck-calling tool for duck hunters. While the family certainly does not live in the country, nor is it hard pressed for money, it projects a particular image of the rural lifestyle. Similarly, *Swamp People* (History Channel, 2010–) chronicles alligator hunters. The National Geographic Channel's *Life Below Zero* (2013–) follows hunters trying to maintain a subsistence lifestyle through the Alaskan winter (although their clothes and tools appear fresh and new). The Discovery Channel's *Deadliest Catch*, which follows fishermen in Alaska, has run for eleven seasons. These latest infatuations were preceded by countless historical representations and derogatory exaggerations of rural poverty: television shows like *The Beverly Hillbillies*, and films like *Deliverance*

(1972) and, from a generation earlier, *I Am a Fugitive from a Chain Gang* (1932).

13. Karl Marx and Friedrich Engels, "Manifesto of the Communist Party" (1848), in *The Marx-Engels Reader*, edited by R. C. Tucker (New York: Norton, 1972), 331–62. Marx writes of rural idiocy and peasants as a sack of potatoes. Further, Marx argues that industrialization is the solution to a plethora of rural "problems," namely, people who refused the centralized authority of a progressive, communist state. This approach is now endemic in notions of modernization and industrialization, which leave rural people to be understood as secondary, peripheral, and unsuccessful. Arlie Russell Hochschild's *Strangers in Their Own Land: Anger and Mourning on the American Right* (New York: New Press, 2016) is a beautifully written text that aims at reaching across the aisles of left and right politics in the United States today. She captures the emotive responses of conservatives, one of which is the rebel that blames the state for the problems in the first place, similar to what I describe here. In her conclusion, she writes what she imagines to be helpful letters trying to share from a left and right perspective how each can speak to the other. Even amid this well-meaning attempt, there remains an assumption that what is conservative is merely raw horsepower and what is liberal is talent (see 233). In "The Geography of the Class Culture Wars," *Seattle University Law Review* 34 (2011): 767–814, Lisa Pruitt pushes back against such stereotypes in the academy, arguing that "social progressives reserve their greatest contempt—and increasingly also their ire—for whites in rural America, the vast majority of whom are working class" (769).

14. J. D. Vance's *Hillbilly Elegy* (New York: Harper Collins, 2016) is such an example. In chapter 4, he explicitly talks about the laziness of his neighbors —Vance grew up in Appalachia—and what "saved" him (60). He refers to rural Appalachian people as "pessimistic" (4), "socially isolated" (4), and, in his own case, wedded to "resentment" (173). He places the blame for white poverty on the situation at home (245). The optimism he finds came from getting out, going to school, and, in the end, not coming back.

15. Hobsbawm, *Primitive Rebels*, 2–3.

16. John Gaventa, in his masterpiece *Power and Powerlessness: Quiescence and Rebellion in an Appalachian Valley* (Urbana: University of Illinois Press, 1980), parallels in many senses what I document here. Indeed, the land grabbing, the oppression by absentee landlords, the sense of hopelessness, and the disengagement in Appalachia that he documents echo similar experiences in rural Georgia. But there are distinctions that call for

a theoretical framework in my text different from Gaventa's: the grievance of land loss is clearly articulated across racial and class boundaries (it isn't only poor blacks and poor whites who are losing their land); I explicitly recognize land grabbers as both corporate and governmental; and participation does happen, just not through formal politics. This last point is perhaps the most important one to delve into. Gaventa proposes three dimensions of power, centered on the idea of the powerful and the powerless, with the intention of learning why some people did, and other people did not, participate. He notes that relative independence from established powers facilitated much greater participation in community development corporations deemed to be separate from the government or the union. He favors collectivization as a means to confront power, as when a local case plagued with problems can be redeemed by the power of just law and governance. My approach views exploitation as incestuous with, and endemic to, the democratic state, and not limited to a specific case. Relatedly, I take the consistent exploitation of rural America as a case in point for critiquing the broader dynamics of the state. Gaventa concludes that "rebellion, to be successful, must both confront power and overcome the accumulated effects of powerlessness" (258). While that is certainly true, I see the state not simply as a venue for overcoming the problem (of capitalism), but as part of the problem (of for-profit rule).

17. Revelation 21:21: "And the twelve gates were twelve pearls; and every several gate was of one pearl: and the street of the city was pure gold, as it were transparent glass" (King James Version).

18. Hobsbawm, *Bandits*, 10.

19. Aldo Leopold, *A Sand County Almanac, with Essays on Conservation from Round River* (New York: Sierra Club/Ballantine, 1966; originally pub. 1949), 34.

20. See "Augusta Mill," accessed April 2, 2015, www.internationalpaper.com/US/EN/Company/Facilities/Augusta.html, and Ben Werner, "What's Left in 'the Bag'?," *Savannah Morning News*, April 28, 2002, accessed April 2, 2015, http://savannahnow.com/stories/042802/LOCIPmainstory .shtml.

21. Hobsbawm, *Primitive Rebels*, 4.

22. With the recent consequences of global warming, such a gendered view hopefully is in decline.

23. For more on gender and environmental dominance, see Joni Seager, *Earth Follies: Feminism, Politics, and the Environment* (London: Earthscan,

1993); and Vandana Shiva, *Staying Alive: Women, Ecology, and Development* (London: Zed, 1988).

24. In *Our Roots Run Deep as Ironwood* (Champaign: University of Illinois Press, 2013), Shannon Bell gives a rich firsthand account of protest constraints and possibilities through the stories of female activists. In "Community Economic Identity: The Coal Industry and Ideology Construction in West Virginia," *Rural Sociology* 75, no. 1 (2010): 111–143, Shannon Bell and Richard York document the gendered nature of protest against mountaintop removal. Also see Rebecca Scott, "The Gendered Politics of Pro-Mountaintop Removal Discourse," chap. 3 of *Removing Mountains: Extracting Nature and Identity in the Appalachian Coalfields* (Minneapolis: University of Minnesota Press, 2010).

25. The USDA describes its Conservation Reserve Program as "a voluntary program available to agricultural producers to help them safeguard environmentally sensitive land" (1). See "Fact Sheet: Conservation Reserve Program Sign-up 26, Environmental Benefits Index" (May 2003), accessed August 23, 2017, https://www.fsa.usda.gov/Internet/FSA_File /crpebi03.pdf. This Farm Service Agency document includes the cultivation of southern pines as a cover practice promoting conservation.

26. Hobsbawm, *Bandits*, 31.

27. Ibid., 36.

28. Ibid., 41.

29. See "About the Savannah River Site," accessed April 12, 2017, www.savan nahrivernuclearsolutions.com/about/about_srs.htm.

30. For more, see Karl Jacoby, *Crimes against Nature: Squatters, Poachers, Thieves, and the Hidden History of American Conservation* (Berkeley: University of California Press, 2001).

31. Mary Grigsby, *Noodlers in Missouri: Fishing for Identity in a Rural Subculture* (Kirksville, MO: Truman State University Press, 2012) records this persistent yet illegal form of fishing. In "Everyone Knows the Game: Legal Consciousness in the Hawaiian Cockfight," *Law and Society Review* 48, no. 3 (2014): 499–530, Kathryne M. Young documents another such illegal subculture related to animals, and suggests that such rituals serve as a conscious affront to the legitimacy of the law.

32. For more on the distinction between violence and political radicalism in rural contexts, see Catherine McNicol Stock, *Rural Radicals: Righteous Rage in the American Grain* (Ithaca, NY: Cornell University Press, 1996), and Thomas Kiffmeyer, *Reformers to Radicals: The Appalachian Volunteers and the War on Poverty* (Lexington: University Press of Kentucky, 2008).

Stock is concerned with neo-Nazi white supremacist radicals who capitalize on racial terror to achieve their ends. Such radicalism, she argues, combines frontier culture with class, race, gender, and Christianity to push forward "radical" and often violent ends. Kiffmeyer uses the word "radical" a bit more liberally, trying to capture those who use direct forms of education to challenge the industrial and centralized message of formal institutions of higher education. This approach—in which "radical" refers to direct local engagement against institutions of profit—resonates with my conception of the rural rebel.

33. See Hobsbawm, *Bandits*, for a description of the rebel (20) and on rural versus urban (8).

34. In *The Democracy Project*, David Graeber gives a vivid description of such action in New York City, which he identifies as a bastion of radical thinkers. He identifies anarchists as the key leaders behind the Occupy Wall Street movement. Anarchist motives can be mischaracterized as only urban, and divisively so for rural people who may share anarchist ideals. Arguably, the sometimes unfavorable representation by the media coverage of the Occupy Wall Street protests, which Graeber writes about, points to ways in which the divide between the antistatist tendencies in rural and urban areas are exacerbated.

35. Katherine Cramer Walsh, "Putting Inequality in Its Place: Rural Consciousness and the Power of Perspective," *American Political Science Review* 106, no. 3 (2012): 517–32. Walsh follows up this article with a rich account of the growing "us" versus "them" divide between the urban and the rural in *The Politics of Resentment: Rural Consciousness and the Rise of Scott Walker* (Chicago: University of Chicago Press, 2016).

36. Hobsbawm, *Primitive Rebels*.

37. Hobsbawm, *Bandits*, 8.

38. Hobsbawm, *Primitive Rebels*, 16.

39. Ross Harrison, *Democracy* (London: Routledge, 1993), 31.

40. Foucault, "On Popular Justice: A Discussion with Maoists," in *Power/Knowledge*, 8–9.

### Chapter 6. The Transcendent People

The tour of Lela's neighborhood, the meeting interactions, and the Bible study with Reverend Ellis are ethnographic observations. All other quoted material, including that from the revival, is from audio recordings.

1. Robert Putnam makes this argument in *Bowling Alone: The Collapse and Revival of American Community* (New York: Simon & Schuster, 2000).

He worries that a decline in participation signals a decline in democracy. A wealth of sociological literature is explicitly devoted to social movements premised on this point—that collective protest pushes the state to continually best serve democratic society.

2. This discussion draws heavily on C. Eric Lincoln and Lawrence H. Mamiya, *The Black Church in the African American Experience* (Durham NC: Duke University Press, 1990). This particular detail comes from chapter 2, "The Black Baptists: The First Black Churches in America." For the first quote, see p. 92.

3. Ibid., 201.

4. Ibid., particularly the section titled "Baptist Policy and Ministry" in chap. 2.

5. Aldon D. Morris, *The Origins of the Civil Rights Movement: Black Communities Organizing for Change* (New York: Free Press: 1984), p. 4.

6. This brief summary of the important services provided by the black church is drawn from Mary Pattillo-McCoy, "Church Culture as a Strategy of Action in the Black Community," *American Sociological Review* 63, no. 6 (1998): 767–84, and Aldon D. Morris, "Reflections on Social Movement Theory: Criticisms and Proposals," *Contemporary Sociology* 29, no. 3 (2000): 445–454.

7. Lincoln and Mamiya, *The Black Church*, 213.

8. Lincoln, *Race, Religion, and the Continuing American Dilemma*, xxiii.

9. Morris, *Civil Rights Movement*.

10. James H. Cone, *The Cross and the Lynching Tree* (Maryknoll, NY: Orbis, 2011) discusses the horrifying history of lynching in the United States, with particular attention to women in chapter 5. The book presses the point that black people are like Christ figures—suffering without choice. Jesus is an emblem of that suffering, and Cone concludes that "if America has the courage to confront the great sin and ongoing legacy of white supremacy with repentance and reparation there is hope 'beyond tragedy'" (166).

11. Thanks to Michael M. Bell for helping me articulate transcendence as an escape from the political to the apolitical.

12. Michael M. Bell and I talk about the joy of transcendence in Loka Ashwood and Michael M. Bell, "Affect and Taste: Bourdieu, Traditional Music, and the Performance of Possibilities," *Sociologia Ruralis* 57, no. S1 (2017). We push back against Pierre Bourdieu's argument that class is an infallible predictor of taste. We counter through the case of traditional music, where crossing class can happen through the shared joy of music

and the rural place. Moral virtues, like the experience of joy, challenge the structured rule of numbers by class and state.

13. Du Bois, *Souls of Black Folk*, 81. On a related note, Aldon Morris makes a compelling case for Du Bois's foundational role in sociology in *The Scholar Denied: W. E. B. Du Bois and the Birth of Modern Sociology* (Chicago: University of Chicago Press, 2015).

14. Thanks to Wylin Wilson for helping me think through the significance of a people, in the church and the literature. She lays out her thinking further in *Economic Ethics and the Black Church* (Springer, 2017).

15. In *Sidewalk* (New York: Farrar, Straus and Giroux, 1999), Mitch Dunier encounters a similar dynamic when he first begins studying poor black men who make a living by selling goods on the sidewalks of New York City. Writing as a white Jewish man, he acknowledges, "I felt unwelcome in ways I had not felt during previous studies that had brought me into contact with African Americans. This was because many of the conversations I heard were about so-called black books and because the people participating in them seemed to be defining themselves as a people" (20). The street vendors that Dunier studied sold used books from tables set up on sidewalks, and some specialized in books by black authors ("black books").

16. These approaches to black spirituality and deliverance can be found in the writing of Lawrence Levine, *Black Culture and Black Consciousness: Afro-American Folk Thought from Slavery to Freedom* (Oxford: Oxford University Press, 1977), and Cornel West, *Prophecy Deliverance! An Afro-American Revolutionary Christianity* (Philadelphia: Westminster, 1982).

17. My direct exposure to Botsford Baptist Church was limited—I went there for services once. But I regularly visited with and interviewed people who went there faithfully, and the people referred to who went there were consistently white.

18. Michael O. Emerson and Christian Smith, *Divided by Faith: Evangelical Religion and the Problem of Race and America* (New York: Oxford University Press, 2000), draws on a wealth of survey and interview data regarding white evangelical Americans and their attempts to overcome racism interpersonally but not structurally.

19. Howard Thurman, *Jesus and the Disinherited* (Boston: Beacon Press, 1976; originally pub. 1949).

20. Crenshaw, "Mapping the Margins," 1297.

21. Thurman, *Jesus and the Disinherited*, 26. The book offers a beautiful tribute to the place of Jesus in black survival and reform. An editor notes: "We realize that inclusive language is noticeably absent in Howard

Thurman's writings. As gifted and prophetic as he was, Howard Thurman was also a product of his times, and inclusive language was not a part of the social consciousness." Indeed, Thurman slips into a language of symbolic violence, in some places limiting his message. Still, his key message remains profoundly important today: the minority status of Jesus is a centerpiece of black Christian faith.

22. Du Bois, *Souls of Black Folk*, 50.

23. I do not specifically identify this group in an attempt to protect the identities of Lela and Mary.

24. See, for example, CNN's report on Plant Vogtle, available on the Georgia Women's Action for New Directions website, http://gawand.org/2011/03/13/cnn-story-on-shell-bluff-community-around-plant-vogtle; see also *On the LAKE Front* (blog), "CNN Report on Cancer in Shell Bluff, GA: Near Nuclear Plant Vogtle," accessed August 23, 2017, www.l-a-k-e.org/blog/2012/07/cnn-report-on-cancer-in-shell-bluff-ga-near-nuclear-plant-vogtle.html.

25. For more on the central role of racism in inspiring the environmental justice movement, see Luke Cole and Sheila R. Foster, *From the Ground Up: Environmental Racism and the Rise of the Environmental Justice Movement* (New York: New York University Press, 2001); Daniel Faber, ed., *The Struggle for Ecological Democracy: Environmental Justice Movements in the United States* (New York: Guilford, 1998); and Joni Adamson, Mei Mei Evans, and Rachel Stein, eds., *The Environmental Justice Reader: Politics, Poetics, and Pedagogy* (Tucson: University of Arizona Press, 2002).

26. For more on the central role of the black church in the environmental justice movement, see Henry Bullard's, introduction to *Unequal Protection: Environmental Justice and Communities of Color* (San Francisco: Sierra Club Books, 1993). Also, Melissa Checker carefully documents the central role of the black church and faith in countering environmental injustice in *Polluted Promises: Environmental Racism and the Search for Justice in a Southern Town* (New York: New York University Press, 2005), chap. 2. Her book plays out in a town on the edge of Augusta, Georgia, less than an hour's drive from the Vogtle Nuclear Reactors.

27. Laura Pulido, "A Critical Review of the Methodology of Environmental Racism Research," *Antipode* 28, no. 2 (1996): 142–59, remains a classic in the field, and formative for my thinking about race in this chapter. Pulido turns the question of race or class in environmental justice research on its head. She argues that racism is not simply purposeful—for example, what was there first, the people or the toxin—but also an interrelation

between ideologies and practices. In short, the system permeates the existence of environmental injustices, in which race informs class as well as ideologies and institutional practices.

28. See p. 597, in David Pellow, "Environmental Inequality Formation: Toward a Theory of Environmental Injustice," *American Behavioral Scientist* 43, no. 4 (2000): 581–601, builds on Pulido, stressing that environmental inequality involves many groups with contradictory and shifting interests. It isn't simply a perpetrator-and-victim scenario. To better understand environmental injustices, he calls for attention to be paid to process, history, and life cycles, with particular attention to historical context. Rebecca Scott explicitly critiques environmental racism as sometimes "reductive" by treating "whites" as a monolithic category in *Removing Mountains* (Minneapolis: University of Minnesota Press, 2010), 19.

29. Thurman, *Jesus and the Disinherited*, 11, 13.

30. P. 137 in Michael M. Bell, *City of the Good: Nature, Religion, and the Ancient Search for What Is Right* (Princeton, NJ: Princeton University Press, 2018), chap. 5.

31. For more on Botsford Church, see Georgia's Virtual Library, http://georgiainfo.galileo.usg.edu/topics/historical_markers/county/burke/botsford-church-1773.

32. Gayraud S. Wilmore, *Black Religion and Black Radicalism* (Garden City, NY: Doubleday, 1972), 25.

33. Cone explains that faith and the imagery of Jesus on the cross serve as a survival mechanism and reminder of the horrifying violence practiced against black people (*The Cross and the Lynching Tree*).

34. Reza Aslan, *Zealot: The Life and Times of Jesus of Nazareth* (New York: Random House, 2013).

35. Cone, *The Cross and the Lynching Tree*, 155.

36. For more on straddling the balance between universalism and difference, and overcoming the fear that can fester between religious distinctions, see Johnathan Sacks, *The Dignity of Difference: How to Avoid the Clash of Civilizations* (London: Bloomsbury Academic, 2003).

*Chapter 7. Freedom under the Gun*

Excluding the opening vignette from Bret Mooney, and my conversation with Thomas and Lacy Harold, all the quoted material presented in this chapter comes from audio recordings.

1. Thurman, *Jesus and the Disinherited*, 36.

2. I computed Burke County crime rates in two ways. I extracted Georgia crime data from the Uniform Crime Reporting Program's Master File, which for 2009, 2010, and 2011 included reported data from the towns of Waynesboro, Midville, Keysville, and Blythe as well as Burke County. These numbers are the most comprehensive in capturing overall crime in the county and the state. Thus, any comparisons in this time period to the rest of Georgia also include all the crime statistics from town, city, and county jurisdictions. From 2012 to 2014, the Master Files do not include data from the town of Keysville, potentially making the crime data incomplete in Burke County, especially when compared with the rest of the state. For these years, I instead used table 10 data from the Uniform Crime Reporting program, which is all data reported from counties across the state of Georgia. This data does not include towns within the counties. I used these two methods to try to make the best estimate possible comparison between crime rates in Burke County and the rest of Georgia. Still, the crime numbers are lower from 2012–14, and I think this discrepancy could in part be explained by the exclusion of Keysville. To compute the rates of crime, I divided the number of crimes by the overall population in the county as reported by the FBI in table 10 or in the Master File. No year contains complete records of all counties, and all data are subject to jurisdictional limitations on who reports, for example, municipal versus county law enforcement. Some locals were skeptical about the rankings of some neighboring counties that appeared to have lower violent crime rates than they expected. When looking at the data I compiled in detail, these locals believed that full countywide data was not being reported from 2012 on, which is understandable, since Keysville numbers appear to be missing. It is important to note that the Uniform Crime Reporting Program warns against trying to establish rankings like the one I made here for this very reason: the data is flawed, and a county that simply does better reporting can appear to have more crime. In response, I triangulated this data with interviews and other supporting archival materials in this chapter.

3. I determined this specific crime rate by dividing incident of crimes by population and then multiplying it by 1,000. The precise figure for Burke County is 7.7890.

4. For the national average, see "Crime in the United States, 2011," https://ucr.fbi.gov/crime-in-the-u.s/2011/crime-in-the-u.s.-2011/violent-crime/aggravated-assault, accessed September 6, 2017.

5. These figures pertain to violent crime rates known to law enforcement,

the same FBI figures that I used to determine the Burke County statistics. These figures are compiled in the 2015 National Center for Victims of Crime Resource Guide, available at http://victimsofcrime.org/docs /default-source/ncvrw2015/2015ncvrw_stats_urbanrural.pdf?sfvrsn=2.

6. See Kieran Bonner, *A Great Place to Raise Kids: Interpretation, Science, and the Rural-Urban Debate* (Montreal: McGill-Queen's University Press, 1997).

7. For more, see Jennifer Sherman, *Those Who Work, Those Who Don't: Poverty, Morality, and Family in Rural America* (Minneapolis: University of Minnesota Press, 2009), an analysis of the work ethic as a moral pivoting point for the rural poor.

8. Michael M. Bell, *Childerley: Nature and Morality in a Country Village* (Chicago: University of Chicago Press, 1994), explores the experience of nature in its social and moral context, or more simply, how people in the Western world think about nature and use it in their everyday lives. Bell finds that the natural conscience is particularly salient in the rural village he studies, and he sees it as a moral thinking based on truths considered to be above and free from the polluting interests of social life.

9. See Wendell Berry, "Land, People, and Community," in *Art of the Commonplace: The Agrarian Essays of Wendell Berry* (Berkeley, CA: Counterpoint, 2002).

10. Researchers have found evidence of a relationship between hunting and sportsmanship and patterns of gun ownership; see Alan Lizotte and David Bordua, "Firearms Ownership for Sport and Protection: Two Divergent Models," *American Sociological Review* 45, no. 2 (1980): 229–44; and Alan J. Lizotte, David J. Bordua, and Carolyn S. White, "Firearms Ownership for Sport and Protection: Two Not So Divergent Models," *American Sociological Review* 46, no. 4 (1981): 499–503.

11. Tom W. Smith kindly put these figures together for me on request. For more on his work at NORC, see Tom W. Smith and Jaesok Son, "General Social Survey Final Report: Trends in Gun Ownership in the United States, 1972–2014" (March 2015), accessed October 22, 2016, http://www .norc.org/PDFs/GSS%20Reports/GSS_Trends%20in%20Gun%20 Ownership_US_1972-2014.pdf.

12. I sometimes asked about gun ownership explicitly. Usually, I saw guns or asked about them indirectly through discussions about hunting and safety.

13. For details on the murder, see Elizabeth Billips, "In Murder of Pregnant Mother, Investigators Determined to Find Killer," *Waynesboro (GA) True Citizen*, March 4, 2012, www.thetruecitizen.com/news/2012-03-14

/Front_Page/In_murder_of_pregnant_mother.html. The murder remains unsolved; see Elizabeth Billips, "New Details Released in BFE Murder," March 3, 2015, www.thetruecitizen.com/news/2015-03-04/Front_Page /New_details_released_in_BFE_murder.html.

14. On the BFE murder, see Billips, "New Details Released."

15. René D. Flores, "Taking the Law into Their Own Hands: Do Local Anti-Immigrant Ordinances Increase Gun Sales?," *Social Problems* 62, no. 3 (2015): 363–90, shows the correlation between a rise in gun ownership and the prospect of anti-immigration laws. Just the idea of violent minorities, with no empirical backing, can become a perceived threat that motivates people to buy guns.

16. Dana Cloud, "Hegemony or Concordance? The Rhetoric of Tokenism in 'Oprah' Oprah Rags-to-Riches Biography," *Critical Studies in Mass Communication* 13, no. 2 (1996): 115–37; and Matt Desmond and Mustafa Emirbayer, *Racial Domination and Racial Progress* (New York: Mc-Graw-Hill Humanities, 2010).

17. For more on how perceptions often diverge from crime rates, see Robert J. Sampson and Stephen W. Raudenbush, "Systematic Social Observation of Public Spaces: A New Look at Disorder in Urban Neighborhoods," *American Journal of Sociology* 105, no. 3 (1999): 603–51; and Sampson and Raudenbush, "Seeing Disorder: Neighborhood Stigma and the Social Construction of 'Broken Windows,'" *Social Psychology Quarterly* 67, no. 4 (2004): 319–42.

18. Again, Tom Smith, senior fellow at NORC, was kind enough to provide data drawn from the General Social Survey.

19. For more, see Isaiah Berlin, "Two Concepts of Liberty," in *Four Essays on Liberty* (Oxford: Oxford University Press, 1969).

20. I use the terms "freedom-to" and "freedom-from" distinctly from the way they are used in chapter 4 of Arlie Russell Hochschild's *Strangers in Their Own Land*. She describes freedoms-to, such as the right to drive a car or carry a gun, as motivating conservative values. She argues that those she spoke with were little concerned about freedoms-from, like protection from violent crime or toxic pollution. Our distinct approaches to the state reflect our different uses of these terms. Hochschild ultimately sees the state as serving the needs of rural people, and I instead argue that it often is explicitly oriented toward their exploitation. Consequently, I see locals seeking freedom from the state through the use of their guns, since they are denied freedom to securities that they believe it ought to ensure.

21. Jack Katz describes violence in painstaking and vivid detail, in part attributing it to "respectability's last stand," in *Seductions of Crime: A Chilling Exploration of the Criminal Mind; From Juvenile Delinquency to Cold-Blooded Murder* (New York: Basic Books, 1988). See p. 9.

22. Freedom under the gun makes sense of places where crime is higher, especially in rural places strapped for resources. Rural areas often have fewer resources to deal with and mitigate crime, in effect making freedom-to less possible; see Ralph Weisheit and Joseph Donnermeyer, "Change and Continuity in Crime in Rural America," *Criminal Justice* 1, no. 1 (2000): 309–57.

23. For example, a white woman was arrested in 2012 on suspicion of shooting and killing her husband; see WDRW-TV, "Update: Burke Co. Woman Arrested, Considered Suspect in Husband's Death," June 20, 2012, accessed April 11, 2017, www.wrdw.com/home/headlines/Burke_Co_woman_arrested_considered_suspect_in_husbands_death_159612645.html. A seven-months-pregnant woman shot her husband and left his body to decay on the living room floor in 2006; see Anne Marie Kyzer, "Guilty Amy Walden to Be Sentenced for Killing Her Husband, Clint," *Waynesboro (GA) True Citizen*, April 19, 2006, accessed April 11, 2017, www.thetruecitizen.com/news/2006-04-19/Front_page/001.html.

24. Lauren J. Krivo and Ruth D. Peterson, "Extremely Disadvantaged Neighborhoods and Urban Crime," *Social Forces* 75, no. 2 (1996): 619–48; Ruth D. Peterson and Lauren J. Krivo, "Racial Segregation and Black Urban Homicide," *Social Forces* 71, no. 4 (1993): 1001–26; Alyssa W. Chamberlain and John R. Hipp, "It's All Relative: Concentrated Disadvantage within and across Neighborhoods and Communities, and the Consequences for Neighborhood Crime," *Journal of Criminal Justice* 42, no. 6 (2015): 431–43.

25. Demographics for the Edmund Burke Academy are not available publicly. The figure presented here for Burke County schools comes from the Georgia Department of Education.

26. For more, see the figures provided by the Georgia Department of Education on CRCT statewide test scores; see "CRCT Statewide Scores," on the Georgia Department of Education's website, accessed April 11, 2017, https://www.gadoe.org/Curriculum-Instruction-and-Assessment/Assessment/Pages/CRCT-Statewide-Scores.aspx. There are no scores or graduation rate details available for the Edmund Burke Academy.

27. Cynthia Duncan, *Worlds Apart: Poverty and Politics in Rural America*, 2nd ed. (New Haven, CT: Yale University Press, 2014).

28. Annette Lareau, *Unequal Childhoods: Class, Race, and Family Life* (Berkeley: University of California Press, 2011; originally pub. 2003) remains a classic in the field. Through interviews and detailed observations in homes, she demonstrates that class-based distinctions leave "have" children often feeling entitled, while those from poorer households feel constrained. Her findings exemplify a freedom-to logic interaction with freedom-from. Freedom-to for middle-class children is predicated upon a belief that those of lesser means really do deserve less.

29. Thurman, *Jesus and the Disinherited*, 79.

30. Ibid., 86.

### Chapter 8. The Moral Economy's Freedom

Sydney is quoted from an audio recording, and William from field notes.

### Appendix 1.

1. To work back and forth between observations and theory, I used the method given in Jason Orne and Michael M. Bell, *An Invitation to Qualitative Methods* (New York: Routledge, 2015). This is thus dialogic, rather than simply extended, as suggested by Michael Burawoy, "The Extended Case Method," *Sociological Theory* 16, no. 1 (1988): 4–33.

# ILLUSTRATION CAPTIONS AND CREDITS

Page xvi: Plant Vogtle transmission tower. Megan Collins.

Page 6: Road sign in Shell Bluff. Megan Collins.

Page 13: Ashwood's borrowed Smith & Wesson handgun. Loka Ashwood.

Page 21: "No Trespassing" sign by River Road approaching Plant Vogtle. Megan Collins.

Page 32: Plant Vogtle entrance sign. Loka Ashwood.

Page 44: Plant Vogtle transmission tower. Megan Collins.

Page 48: Transmission towers cut through fields as they move power from Plant Vogtle to the national grid. Megan Collins.

Page 61: Sydney, holding his hat. Megan Collins.

Page 91: The lane leading to Sydney's home. Megan Collins.

Page 105: The front yard of a local residence. Loka Ashwood.

Page 108: Plant Vogtle transmission tower. Megan Collins.

Page 117: Savannah River Site warning signs along SC 125, also known as Atomic Road. Loka Ashwood.

Page 129: A field near Shell Bluff. Loka Ashwood.

Page 144: Plant Vogtle cooling towers viewed from the Savannah River. Loka Ashwood.

Page 155: William hunting in the woods. Loka Ashwood.

Page 163: Protesters gathered to commemorate the Fukushima Daiichi nuclear disaster. Loka Ashwood.

Page 168: Gravestones at the Botsford Baptist Church cemetery. Loka Ashwood.

Page 180: Ebenezer Baptist Church asking passersby to "Come Witness God's Word." Loka Ashwood.

Page 189: A dead alligator in the pond behind the trailer rented by Ashwood. Loka Ashwood.

Page 196: A graveyard in Girard, one of the Burke County towns nearest the reactors. Loka Ashwood.

Page 220: Plant Vogtle transmission tower. Megan Collins.

Page 229: Shell Bluff pinecone. Megan Collins.

# INDEX

Illustrations are indicated by italicized page numbers; maps are indicated by "m" following the page number.
See Appendix 2 for a summary of people and concepts.

**DATE DUE**

This item is Due on
or before Date shown.

JUN - - 2018